The American Adam

Innocence
Tragedy and Tradition
in the Nineteenth Century

By

R. W. B. Lewis

Phoenix Books

THE UNIVERSITY OF CHICAGO PRESS

CHICAGO AND LONDON

This book is also available in a clothbound edition from
THE UNIVERSITY OF CHICAGO PRESS

FOR MY FATHER

Leicester Crosby Lewis
1887–1949

THE UNIVERSITY OF CHICAGO PRESS, CHICAGO & LONDON
The University of Toronto Press, Toronto 5, Canada

Acknowledgments

AN EARLIER version of this book was completed under the auspices of the Committee on Social Thought of the University of Chicago. It is a pleasure to record my appreciation of that committee —in particular, of Daniel J. Boorstin and John U. Nef—for considerable guidance and encouragement and for an enlightened program of graduate studies.

Many persons have read all or parts of the manuscript. I remember with special gratitude the generous assistance of Daniel Aaron, Newton Arvin, Elizabeth Drew, Joseph Frank, Stanley Edgar Hyman, Alfred Kazin, and Murray Kempton. My former students at Smith College, Bennington College, and the Salzburg Seminar in American Studies have contributed more than they may have imagined.

My debt to F. O. Matthiessen's *American Renaissance* will be evident on many pages; more important and less evident is a debt to the man himself, to a wise and dedicated teacher and an unforgettable friend.

Other contributions are harder to define, though one is conscious of them in a dozen places. The chapter on Melville, for example, profited belatedly from conversations with Howard Nemerov; and reflected in my treatment of Parkman are several talks with Howard Doughty, whose own book on Parkman is the one many of us are waiting for.

In the closing phases of the book I was lucky to have the invaluable help of Mrs. Margaret Kelton Lindau. I shall not try to say what I owe to my wife: it is of too long standing, and runs too deep.

Parts of some of the chapters have appeared in *Yale Review, Hudson Review,* and *American Literature* and are reprinted with the permission of those periodicals. Permission to quote from T. S. Eliot's *Four Quartets* has been granted by Harcourt, Brace and Company, and from James Joyce's *Finnegans Wake* by the Viking Press.

R. W. B. Lewis

PRINCETON, NEW JERSEY
July 1955

Table of Contents

Here's for the plain old Adam, the simple genuine self against the whole world.

R. W. EMERSON, *Journals*

That is the true myth of America. She starts old, old, wrinkled and writhing in an old skin. And there is a gradual sloughing off of the old skin, towards a new youth. It is the myth of America.

D. H. LAWRENCE, *Studies in Classical American Literature*

This is the use of memory:
For liberation—not less of love, but expanding
Of love beyond desire, and so liberation
From the future as well as the past.

T. S. ELIOT, *Little Gidding*

Prologue
The Myth and the Dialogue

THIS book has to do with the beginnings and the first tentative outlines of a native American mythology. The period I cover runs from about 1820 to 1860; the scene, for the most part, is New England and the Atlantic seaboard. The cast of characters is large, and would be a great deal larger if every person were included who, by act or utterance, contributed to the formation of the American myth. But I am not concerned with matters of anthropology and sociology, or with folklore and legend; nor am I primarily concerned with the psychology of myth, any more than with the facts of economic geography and political history. I am interested rather in the history of ideas and, especially, in the representative imagery and anecdote that crystallized whole clusters of ideas; my interest is therefore limited to articulate thinkers and conscious artists. A century ago, the image contrived to embody the most fruitful contemporary ideas was that of the authentic American as a figure of heroic innocence and vast potentialities, poised at the start of a new history. This image is the title of the book.

It was an image crowded with illusion, and the moral posture it seemed to indorse was vulnerable in the extreme. But however vulnerable or illusory, this image had about it always an air of adventurousness, a sense of promise and possibility—of a sort no longer very evident in our national expression. Its very openness to challenge, its susceptibility to controversy, made possible a series of original inquiries and discoveries about human nature, art, and history. I shall have many an occasion to comment on the present relevance of the Adamic myth. But here I should introduce the terminology and method I shall employ.

I want, first, to suggest an analogy between the history of a culture —or of its thought and literature—and the unfolding course of a dialogue: a dialogue more or less philosophic in nature and, like Plato's, containing a number of voices. Every culture seems, as it advances toward maturity, to produce its own determining debate over the ideas that preoccupy it: salvation, the order of nature, money, power, sex, the machine, and the like. The debate, indeed, may be said to *be* the culture, at least on its loftiest levels; for a culture achieves identity not so much through the ascendancy of one particular set of convictions as through the emergence of its peculiar and distinctive dialogue. (Similarly, a culture is on the decline when it submits to intellectual martial law, and fresh understanding is denied in a denial of further controversy.) Intellectual history, properly conducted, exposes not only the dominant ideas of a period, or of a nation, but more important, the dominant clashes over ideas. Or to put it more austerely: the historian looks not only for the major terms of discourse, but also for major pairs of opposed terms which, by their very opposition, carry discourse forward. The historian looks, too, for the coloration or discoloration of ideas received from the sometimes bruising contact of opposites.

As he does so and as he examines the personalities and biases of the men engaged in debate at any given historical moment, the historian is likely to discover that the development of the culture in question resembles a protracted and broadly ranging conversation: at best a dialogue—a dialogue which at times moves very close to drama.[1]

In America, during the second quarter of the nineteenth century, the chief intellectual spokesmen—novelists and poets, as well as essayists, critics, historians, and preachers—appear to have entered into just such a lively and creative dialogue. The subject, stimulated by the invigorating feeling that a new culture was in the making, touched on the moral, intellectual, and artistic resources of man in the new society. Whatever else they may have been talking about, all interested persons seem invariably to have been talking about that. And in the perspective of history, they give the impression of talking to and about one another—within separate fields of activity and across them. Historians, telling of the past, at the same time illuminated or contradicted the imagery of contemporary novelists; novelists enacted or challenged, in their stories, the patterns of experience proposed by theologians, the focus in all these cases being the peculiar capacities of the inhabitant of the new world. Among the terms and ideas that turned up most frequently in the debate were: innocence, novelty, experience, sin, time, evil, hope, the present, memory, the past, tradition. Almost any one of them can be found, in the docu-

1. An excellent example of intellectual history seizing upon the dialectical and dramatic qualities of its subject has been the volumes on the New England mind by Perry Miller.

ments of the day, paired off with or against almost any other; and there were consequently many changes of coloration and many unexpected conclusions. The shifting weight of emphasis and import is too rapid for accurate analysis; but these are some of the main ideas with which this book is concerned. It is one of my aims to account for the dialogue that emerged as those ideas were invoked by American writers and speakers, from 1820 onward, in their contentious effort to define the American character and the life worth living.

But the purpose of a cultural conversation, to judge from our American example, is not, after all, simply to settle the terms of discussion. It goes beyond that to provide materials for the creative imagination. The intellectual historian should accordingly look beyond the terms of discussion for something else. He should, in fact, look for the images and the "story" that animate the ideas and are their imaginative and usually more compelling equivalent. For what is articulated during the years of debate is a comprehensive view of life, in an ideal extension of its present possibilities. And while the vision may be formulated in the orderly language of rational thought, it also finds its form in a recurring pattern of images—ways of seeing and sensing experience—and in a certain habitual story, an assumed dramatic design for the representative life. (The Passion of Christ, for example, is the story behind most Christian argumentation.) The imagery and the story give direction and impetus to the intellectual debate itself; and they may sometimes be detected, hidden within the argument, charging the rational terms with unaccustomed energy. But the debate in turn can contribute to the shaping of the story; and when the results of rational inquiry are transformed into conscious and coherent narrative by the best-attuned artists of the time, the culture has finally yielded up its own special and identifying "myth."

The relation between idea and story is considered further, in the practical illustrations offered in this book. This much can be said in advance: the narrative art inevitably and by nature invests its inherited intellectual content with a quickening duplicity; it stains ideas with restless ambiguity. For the *experience* of the aims and values of an epoch is apt to be more complex and even more painful than the simple statement of them; and narrative deals with experiences, not with propositions. The narrative art, moreover, dramatizes as human conflict what is elsewhere a thoughtful exchange of ideas; and art projects—in a single packed dramatic image—conflicting principles which the discursive mind must contemplate separately and consecutively.

Perhaps the rather narrow context in which I am using words like "myth" and "mythology" can be explained by citing an instance from classical culture. The Roman myth received its final magnificent and persuasive form in the *Aeneid* of Virgil. The *Aeneid*, however, was unmistakably a dramatization on a vast scale of the humanistic ideas set forth and debated in the philosophical dialogues of Cicero, two or three decades earlier. Cicero, in his turn, had only brought together the conflicting opinions of the contemporary schools of thought; and these opinions reflected an earlier imaginative feeling about the limits and aims of human experience. Cicero discovered *the* dialogue of his generation. It became the matter for the myth consciously created by Virgil: an essentially political myth, the myth of "the city" or "the republic"; a vision of life as shaped and bounded by the *polis*, with all other human concerns (love, for example, or scientific investigation) subordinated to the political and moral. And what Virgil was able to do in his mythical narrative of the origins of the city was, as one historian has observed, to provide the "dynamic [which] was needed in order to impart to Ciceronianism the vitality which it lacked."[2] But "the tears of things" so prevalent in the *Aeneid* reflect Virgil's poetic ambivalence toward the Roman ideals that his poem nonetheless affirmed.

My intention, then, is to disentangle from the writings and pronouncements of the day the emergent American myth and the dialogue in which it was formed. The American myth, unlike the Roman, was not fashioned ultimately by a single man of genius. It was and it has remained a collective affair; it must be pieced together out of an assortment of essays, orations, poems, stories, histories, and sermons. We have not yet produced a Virgil, not even Walt Whitman being adequate to that function.[3] *Leaves of Grass* (1855) did indeed set to a music of remarkable and original quality many attitudes that had been current for several decades—as I indicate in my first two chapters. But *Leaves of Grass* is scarcely more than a bundle of lyrics which

2. Charles N. Cochrane, *Christianity and Classical Culture* (Oxford, 1946).

3. It is worth noting that the one poem which set out quite deliberately to provide America with its definitive myth—Hart Crane's *The Bridge* (1930)—was inspired at once by Whitman and Virgil. The Whitman strain is, of course, very evident throughout *The Bridge*; but Crane remarked in letters and conversations that his ambition was to do for his own age what Virgil had done for his, and that the *Aeneid* was the exemplary poem.

Prologue

gives us only one phase of the story imbedded in the American response to life; to round it out, other writings had to follow.[4]

Unlike the Roman myth, too—which envisaged life within a long, dense corridor of meaningful history—the American myth saw life and history as just beginning. It described the world as starting up again under fresh initiative, in a divinely granted second chance for the human race, after the first chance had been so disastrously fumbled in the darkening Old World. It introduced a new kind of hero, the heroic embodiment of a new set of ideal human attributes. America, it was said insistently from the 1820's onward, was not the end-product of a long historical process (like the Augustan Rome celebrated in the *Aeneid*); it was something entirely new. "Our national birth," declaimed the *Democratic Review* in 1839, "was the beginning of a new history . . . which separates us from the past and connects us with the future only." "American glory begins at the dawn," announced Noah Webster in 1825. Edward Everett found an acceptable prescription for national health in the simple italicized phrase, *separation from Europe* —separation from its history and its habits.

The new habits to be engendered on the new American scene were suggested by the image of a radically new personality, the hero of the new adventure: an individual emancipated from history, happily bereft of ancestry, untouched and undefiled by the usual inheritances of family and race; an individual standing alone, self-reliant and self-propelling, ready to confront whatever awaited him with the aid of his own unique and inherent resources. It was not surprising, in a Bible-reading generation, that the new hero (in praise or disapproval) was most easily identified with Adam before the Fall. Adam was the first, the archetypal, man. His moral position was prior to experience, and in his very newness he was fundamentally innocent. The world and history lay all before him. And he was the type of creator, the poet par excellence, creating language itself by naming the elements of the scene about him. All this and more were contained in the image of the American as Adam.[5]

4. More than one critic of Henry James has suggested that James's last three novels —*The Ambassadors, The Wings of the Dove,* and *The Golden Bowl,* all published in the very early 1900's—may be taken as a trilogy comprehending the totality of the distinctively American vision of experience.

5. Here, and occasionally later, I must distinguish between the notion of progress toward perfection and the notion of primitive Adamic perfection. Both ideas were current, and they overlapped and intertwined. On the whole, however, we may settle for the paradox that the more intense the belief in progress toward perfection, the more it stimulated a belief in a present primal perfection (see pp. 44 and 163).

The American Adam

Such were the first impulses which begot the myth. Such were the first fertile illusions. The changes they suffered and the further insights they elicited, as they were challenged, transcended, and dramatized over the years, are precisely the burden of this study. But it is worth remarking that while the Adamic image was invoked often and explicitly in the later stages of our history, during earlier stages it remained somewhat submerged, making itself felt as an atmospheric presence, a motivating idea. It was the concealed cause of an ethical polemic, and it lurked behind the formal structure of works of fiction. The image was slow to work its way to the surface of American expression; and the reader will notice that it tends to appear toward the end of sections or discussions in this book. The significant fact is that the literal use of the story of Adam and the Fall of Man—as a model for narrative—occurred in the final works of American novelists, the works in which they sought to summarize the whole of their experience of America. *The Marble Faun* and *Billy Budd*, where the Adamic imagery is altogether central and controlling, were the last finished writings of Hawthorne and Melville. And it was in *The Golden Bowl* of Henry James that the protagonist's name was Adam. Those novels were perhaps as close as American culture ever came to the full and conscious realization of the myth it had so long secreted.

It is also worth remarking that the ideal of newborn innocence was both rejoiced in and deplored. The opposed reactions set the dialogue in motion that later constituted the energizing conflict in narrative fiction. Emerson, recoiling from the sense of antique pressures in Europe, might voice the epochal remark: "Here's for the plain old Adam, the simple genuine self against the whole world." But Henry James the elder, that formidable and explosive man, came back (in 1857) with the contention that "nothing could be more remote . . . from distinctively *human* attributes . . . than this sleek and comely Adamic condition." This was not, in fact, an effort simply to repudiate the current mythology. James wanted rather to enrich it, by educating his listeners in the fact and the value of tragedy, for, as he said, "Life flowers and fructifies out of the profoundest tragic depths." And just as the more optimistic moral principles were challenged and converted in the course of the dialogue, so the narrative figure of Adam—introduced as the hero of a new semidivine comedy—was converted into the hero of a new kind of tragedy, and grew thereby to a larger stature. It was the tragedy inherent in his innocence and newness, and it established the pattern for American fiction.

6

Prologue

This brings me to a final word about the several "voices" in our dialogue and the names I will give them. We might begin by noticing that Emerson saw no dialogue at all, but only a "schism," a split in culture between two polarized parties: "the party of the Past and the party of the Future," as he sometimes called them, or the parties "of Memory and Hope, of the Understanding and the Reason." The schism began, according to Emerson's retrospective meditation of 1867, in about 1820. But Emerson subscribed too readily perhaps to a two-party system in intellectual affairs; and he was always puzzled by the attitude of a man like Hawthorne, who seemed skeptically sympathetic toward both parties and managed to be confined by neither.

Historians after Emerson have either gone along with his dichotomies and have talked about the "dualism" of American culture; or they have selected one of Emerson's two parties as constituting *the* American tradition, rejecting the other as a bleak foreign hangover or as immature native foolishness. But if we attend to the realities of American intellectual history, we must distinguish in it at least *three* voices (sometimes more). American culture has traditionally consisted of the productive and lively interplay of all three.

In the chapters which follow, I adopt one of Emerson's pairs of terms to identify the two parties he himself recognized: the party of Hope and the party of Memory. For the third party, there is no proper name: unless we call it the party of Irony.

As an index to the "hopeful" stand on national morality, I cite the editorial (of 1839) which hailed the birth in America of "a clear conscience unsullied by the past." The national and hence the individual conscience was clear just because it was unsullied by the past—America, in the hopeful creed, had no past, but only a present and a future. The key term in the moral vocabulary of Emerson, Thoreau, Whitman, and their followers and imitators consequently was "innocence." To the "nostalgic"—that is, to the party devoted to Memory—the sinfulness of man seemed never so patent as currently in America. As the hopeful expressed their mounting contempt for the doctrine of inherited sin, the nostalgic intoned on Sundays the fixed legacy of corruption in ever more emphatic accents; and centers of orthodox Calvinism, like Andover and Princeton, became citadels of the old and increasingly cheerless theology. But the ironic temperament—as represented, say, by the elder Henry James—was characterized by a tragic optimism: by a sense of the tragic collisions to which innocence was liable (something unthinkable among the hopeful), and equally

7

by an awareness of the heightened perception and humanity which suffering made possible (something unthinkable among the nostalgic).

The debate over morality echoed the general debate over time: the connecting links, or the lack of them, between the present and the past. And in this respect the parties of Hope and of Memory virtually created each other. The human mind seems by nature to be "contrary," as by nurture it becomes dialectical. This was demonstrated afresh in early nineteenth-century America, when a denial of the past generated, by compensation, a new nostalgia, a new veneration for the past in its pastness. As the present and the future became objects of worship and inquiry, historical research began greatly to increase and the past to be discovered; there had been no need to discover it previously, for it had never been lost. But now statistical guesses about the material growth of the new society were countered by the efforts of a Prescott to re-create the historical reality of the old societies. The prescription of Edward Everett (*separation from Europe*) cut both ways. It was steadily more difficult to decide which of the two continents had been isolated; separation from Europe resulted in the first American expatriates.

Although Emerson listened with pleasure to "the clangor and jangle of contrary tendencies," there were those—and I collect them under my third heading—who found that constant discord unsatisfying. This group inspected the opposed tendencies and then arrived at a fresh understanding of the nature of tradition and America's practical involvement with the past. Their conclusion was a curious, ambivalent, off-beat kind of traditionalism. It expressed itself in many forms, but it was particularly striking in the field of fiction. For here it affected both form and content: an organic relation between past experience and the living moment became a factor in narrative—a recurring theme *of* narrative; and at the same time—most notably in the novels of Hawthorne and Melville—the narrative revealed its design through an original use of discredited traditional materials. And beyond fiction the resources of tradition, dispensed with by one sort of theologian in the name of religious freedom, were re-established by another as the essential means of human redemption.

There may be no such thing as "American experience"; it is probably better not to insist that there is. But there has been experience in America, and the account of it has had its own specific form. That form has been clearest and most rewarding when it has been most dialectical. Only recently has the dialogue tended to die away. For only recently has the old conviction of the new historical beginning seemed to vanish altogether, and with it the enlivening sense of possibility, of intellectual and artistic elbow-room, of new creations and fresh initiatives. Our culture will at the very least be a great deal drearier without it.

The dangers, both to life and to letters, of the Adamic ideal were acknowledged at once and have been repeated endlessly. The helplessness of mere innocence has been a primary theme of novelists in almost every decade, and a source of bewilderment to our political and diplomatic historians. The dismissal of the past has been only too effective: America, since the age of Emerson, has been persistently a one-generation culture. Successive generations have given rise to a series of staccato intellectual and literary movements with ever slighter trajectories. The temper which despised memory not unnaturally fostered a habit of forgetfulness, and writers who even forgot that there was anything to remember have found themselves remote alike from their predecessors and their contemporaries. The unluckiest consequence, however, has not been incoherence, but the sheer dulness of unconscious repetition. We regularly return, decade after decade and with the same pain and amazement, to all the old conflicts, programs, and discoveries. We consume our powers in hoisting ourselves back to the plane of understanding reached a century ago and at intervals since.

The vision of innocence and the claim of newness were almost perilously misleading. But they managed nonetheless to provide occasions for reflection and invention, for a testing of moral and artistic possibilities. The illusion of freedom from the past led to a more real relation to the continuing tradition. The vision of innocence stimulated a positive and original sense of tragedy. Without the illusion, we are conscious, no longer of tradition, but simply and coldly of the burden of history. And without the vision, we are left, not with a mature tragic spirit, but merely with a sterile awareness of evil uninvigorated by a sense of loss. For the notion of original sin draws its compelling strength from the prior notion of original innocence. Recent literature has applauded itself for passing beyond the childlike cheerfulness of Emerson and Whitman; but, in doing so, it has lost the profound tragic understanding—paradoxically bred out of cheerfulness—of a Hawthorne or a Melville.

A century ago, the challenge to debate was an expressed belief in achieved human perfection, a return to the primal perfection. Today the challenge comes rather from the expressed belief in achieved hopelessness. We stand in need of more stirring impulses, of greater perspectives and more penetrating controversies. Perhaps a review of that earlier debate can help us on our way. We can hardly expect to be persuaded any longer by the historic dream of the new Adam. But it can pose anew, in the classic way of illumination as it did in the American nineteenth century, the picture of what might be against the knowledge of what is, and become once more a stimulus to enterprise and a resource for literature.

I

The Danger of Innocence

Prince, subject, father, son are things forgot
For every man alone thinks he has got
To be a Phoenix, and that then can be
None of that kind, of which he is, but he.

JOHN DONNE, *First Anniversary*

O foenix culprit! ex nickylow malo comes micklemassed
bonum.

JAMES JOYCE, *Finnegans Wake*

1

The Case against the Past

Democracy . . . is revolutionary, not formative. It is
born of denial. It comes into existence in the way of deny-
ing established institutions. Its office is rather to destroy
the old world, than fully to reveal the new.

HENRY JAMES, SR., "Democracy and Its Issues" (1853)

IN THE decade following the end of the War of 1812, an air of
hopefulness became apparent in American life and letters. It expressed the sense of enormous possibility that Americans were beginning to share about the future of their new country; but hopefulness at the outset was combined with feelings of impatience and
hostility. For believers in the future could not fail to notice, dotted
across the American scene, many signs of the continuing power of the
past: institutions, social practices, literary forms, and religious doctrines—carry-overs from an earlier age and a far country and irrelevant obstructions (as it seemed) to the fresh creative task at hand.
Emerson, tracing the haphazard movement for social reform in New
England, remembered the "noise of denial and protest" which was the
first symptom of the reformist spirit; "much was to be resisted," he
said, "much was to be got rid of by those who were reared in the old,
before they could begin to affirm and to construct." More vehement
patriots even regretted that Americans were forced to communicate
with one another in an old, inherited language. Indeed, the urge
to root out vestiges of the culture and society of the Old World became so intense over the years that a commentator like the elder
Henry James was led to identify democracy itself with a program of
denial and destruction.

Nothing was to be spared. Thus it was, according to one story, that
a huge crowd of people gathered together on some broad western
prairie to build an immense bonfire: a cosmic bonfire, upon which was
piled all the world's "outworn trumpery." The heraldry of ancient

aristocratic families fed the flames, to the crowd's mounting enthusiasm; after that came the robes and scepters of royalty; the scaffold and other symbols of repressive institutions; and finally the total body of European literature and philosophy. "Now," declared the chief celebrant, "we shall get rid of the weight of dead men's thoughts."

The story is a fantasy, to be sure—a fantasy composed by Nathaniel Hawthorne in 1844 and called "Earth's Holocaust." But it was close enough to history, and, like every good story, it was truer than history. Its theme may have been suggested by the historic activities of a religious group known as the "Millerites," though the Millerites were only among the more extreme and disappointed of the age's millennialists. But Hawthorne, as usual, enlarged upon his historical materials; and, in doing so, he managed very accurately to catch in a fable the prevailing impulse to escape from every existing mode of organizing and explaining experience, in order to confront life in entirely original terms. And at the same time, in the divided attitude that gives his story its vital tension, Hawthorne managed to convey the deep reservations that certain Americans felt about the contemporary passion to destroy. A genuine sympathy informs the irony and melancholy of "Earth's Holocaust"; but though one can tell from Hawthorne's notebooks that he too would have set fire to many symbols of injustice, he makes it clear at the end of his story that the true source of oppression—the human heart—has remained untouched by the conflagration: a conclusion Melville was to find at once profound and appalling.

The drama of "Earth's Holocaust" has a ritual quality, and much of its dialogue is incantatory in tone. Behind the story, one sees such ritualistic historic events as the burning of the Bastille, and, beyond that, the recurring human instinct to purge by fire. Hawthorne had articulated the need he detected in the atmosphere of the day for a purgatorial action—preceding, as it were, the life of the new Adam in the new earthly paradise. Thoreau, alert to the ritual aspects of human behavior and the primitive energy of words, gave voice to the same instinctive need while he was reflecting on "the essential facts of life" at Walden Pond. He made semantic fun of a deacon whose dreary effects had been sold at auction: "Instead of a *bonfire*, or purifying destruction of them, there was an *auction*, or increasing of them." This private little joke led Thoreau to wonder whether the tribal customs of "some savage nations" might not be usefully instituted in America —the ceremony of the "busk," for example, which he found described in William Bartram's eighteenth-century travel-book: "When a town celebrates the busk . . . they have previously provided themselves with new clothes, new pots, pans, and other household utensils and furniture, they collect all their worn out clothes and other despicable things, sweep and cleanse their houses, squares and the whole town, of their filth, which with all the remaining grain and other old provisions they cast together into one common heap and consume it with fire." The whole of *Walden*, according to one reading, is a metaphoric expansion of Bartram's busk—the busk of the human spirit, when clothes and pots and pans are discarded as symbols of ambitions and interests.

But the rite of purification was more than a poetic invention. The need for it, in fact, had long been expressed in a series of concrete political and economic proposals, all of them voicing a belief in the need for periodic and radical change in the very structure of American society.

II

The American argument against institutional continuity drew its force and its fervor from the native conviction about the rights of man. For the principle of the rights of *man* led to a restriction on the rights of *men*. In order to insure the freedoms of future men, those of the present (the argument ran) must have only temporary validity; and rights, consequently, were given a time limit. The constant in the argument was "the present generation," and the principle of judgment was the sovereignty of the living.[1] The principle had been formulated and flaunted in the writings of Jefferson and Paine; it helped to ease the painful break with the past that the political situation demanded. "The Creator," Jefferson pronounced, no doubt consciously echoing St. Matthew, "has made the earth for the living, not the dead. Rights and powers can only belong to persons, not to things, not to mere matter, unendowed with will. The dead are not even things." These are metaphysical statements: rights are attributed to that which can be said to be real; and the question of reality turns upon a dialectic of dead and living which is essentially biological. The author of that extraordinary contribution to natural history, *Notes on Virginia*, was among the first to make natural history the queen of the sciences, the new metaphysic, and to turn the inquiry of reality into an investiga-

1. See the study by Daniel J. Boorstin, *The Lost World of Thomas Jefferson* (New York, 1948), especially the chapter entitled "The Sovereignty of the Present Generation."

tion of natural processes. In the generation of hope, his logical successor was Oliver Wendell Holmes.

Although we currently all too often employ a pious phrase about our heritage when we mention Thomas Jefferson, he himself was opposed to several kinds of inheritance, finding them, in the name of the sovereign present, mere forms of slavery. He posed the general problem in a letter written to Madison from Paris, in 1789: "The question, whether one generation of men has a right to bind another, seems never to have started on this or our side of the water. Yet it is a question of such consequence as not only to merit decision, but place, also, among the fundamental principles of government. . . . I set out on this ground which I suppose to be self-evident, *'that the earth belongs in usufruct to the living'*; that the dead have neither power nor rights over it." Jefferson was even willing to calculate the approximate life-expectancy of any single generation: it amounted to about nineteen years. The arithmetic was applied. The devices by which society orders itself must be introduced and consented to by the living; hence legislation may not endure longer than the estimated life of the consenting generation, and a complete review of all laws should be made every nineteen years. Such a policy would, of course, have meant periodic administrative chaos, and the proposal was not acted upon; though there was administrative chaos enough, as Tocqueville discovered. It was, however, administrative fear that operated against the proposal; an older argument against change in law, which considered the effect of change on the stability of moral habits, scarcely entered the discussion; habit was already a term of abuse.

Jefferson could not have foreseen, nor would he have approved, all the consequences of the principle of the sovereign present. He was attempting to make the practical controls of life dependent upon the voluntary agreement of the living. He did not mean to reject the whole scheme of values of the past, or to assert that each generation in turn should do so. And yet this is what was proposed, stage by stage, over the first half of the nineteenth century. In 1829 the *economic* authority of the living was affirmed with some violence in a book called *The Rights of Man to Property, Being a Proposition To Make It Equal among the Adults of the Present Generation*. The author was one Thomas Skidmore, a leader in the Workingmen's movement in New York and Philadelphia and for a time a follower of Fanny Wright and the progressive laborites. The reforms urged by Skidmore seemed extreme even to his associates; but his manner of reasoning was symptomatic of a deepening sense of the disjunction between generations. Skidmore reflected the contemporary awareness, on which the first tentative efforts toward a labor movement were based, that, without equality of economic opportunity, the great phrases of the Declaration of Independence rang somewhat hollowly. In developing his thesis, Skidmore managed to attack the whole concept of inheritance. "If property is to descend to particular individuals from the previous generations, and if the many are born, having neither parents nor any one else, to give them property, equal in amount to that which the sons of the rich receive, from their fathers or other testators, how is it established that they are created equal?" Transmission in any kind from one generation to another was a fiction: "One generation cannot sell, give or convey, even if it had the right, to another. The reason is, that the one is dead; the other living. The one is present; the other absent. They do not and cannot *meet*, to come to a treaty, to make delivery; to give or receive." The terms "testator" and "heir" should be dispensed with, Skidmore went on; and the question to be answered was simply: "*How long* does a man own property?" Skidmore's general principles were shared far beyond the bounds of the labor movement, and they continued to be enunciated. From the main contention, that denied commerce between generations, the argument could easily be extended beyond the political and economic areas.

To an acute foreign observer, visiting this country a few years after the appearance of Skidmore's polemic, such an extension of principle seemed already to be operative. Alexis de Tocqueville had probably the handsomest talent in the century for sensing the significant drift of contemporary social and intellectual history; and his experience and wisdom told him that the disjunction between generations was inevitably becoming a striking aspect of democracy as such: "for among democratic nations each generation is a new people." The insight followed from Tocqueville's analysis of the intellectual character of democracy in America, in the second volume of his great study (published in translation here in 1840); but it gained additional force from his survey of institutions in the preceding volume (1837).

He had observed there, in a section called "Instability of the Administration in the United States," that "no one cares for what occurred before his time. . . . In America, society seems to live from hand to mouth, like an army in the field. Nevertheless, the art of administration is undoubtedly a science, and no sciences can be improved if the discoveries and observations of successive generations are not connected together in the order in which they occur." On the evidence, Tocqueville could infer that "democracy, pushed to its furthest limits, is . . . prejudicial to the art of government," something the Jeffersonians might cheerfully have confirmed. Tocqueville noticed a similar brevity of life in philosophic theories or literary conventions. Democratic literature, he thought, was not only shorn of received conventions, it was inherently almost incapable of generating its own; "if it should happen that the men of some one period were agreed upon any such rules, that would prove nothing for the following period." That circumstance was to comprise an important part of the artist's dilemma in America.

As the principle of the sovereign present thrust upward from its political and economic roots, it managed to affect not only literature, but educational beliefs, too, and religious doctrines (fifty years before John Dewey elaborated it into a coherent philosophic statement). In the forties, those who favored territorial expansion in the direction of Oregon but who found activity hampered by long-standing laws were able to reiterate Jefferson's suggestions about change in laws with considerably larger confidence.[2] By 1850, when Hawthorne was writing *The House of the Seven Gables*, he could draw a plausible portrait of a young reformer who wanted to apply the idea of the sovereign present to every imaginable phase of life:

Shall we never, never get rid of this Past? It lies upon the present like a giant's dead body! In fact, the case is just as if a young giant were compelled to waste all his strength in carrying about the corpse of the old giant his grandfather, who died a long while ago, and only needs to be decently buried. Just think a moment, and it will startle you to see what slaves we are to bygone times,—to Death, if we give the matter the right word! . . . For example, a dead man, if he happen to have made a will, disposes of wealth no longer his own; or, if he died intestate, it is distributed in accordance with the notions of men much longer dead than he. A dead man sits on all our judgment-seats; and living judges do but search out and report his decisions. We read in dead men's books! We laugh at dead men's jokes, and cry at dead men's pathos! We are sick of dead men's diseases, physical and moral, and die of the same remedies with which dead doctors killed their patients! We worship the living Deity according to dead men's forms and creeds. Whatever we do of our own free motion, a dead man's icy hand obstructs us. . . . And we must be dead ourselves before we can begin to have our proper influence on our own world, which will then be no longer our world, but the world of another generation, with which we shall have no shadow of right to interfere.

The profession of the speaker, Holgrave, adds to the content of the speech, for this young ex-Fourierite and earnest member of the party of Hope ("How you hate everything old!" his audience, Phoebe

2. Cf. *Manifest Destiny*, by Albert K. Weinberg (New York, 1935), chap. v, especially.

Pyncheon, tells him) is not only an artist; he is a practitioner of the peculiarly appropriate new art of photography. The instrument of Daguerre could achieve in art what the hopeful sought for in life: the careful and complete differentiation of the individual in time and space, the image of the single person in all his rugged singularity. Dead forms and conventions of art are implicit in the catalogue of the oppressive past, to be destroyed at set intervals, in the proposition Holgrave brings forward a moment later:

> If each generation were allowed and expected to build its own houses, that single change, comparatively unimportant in itself, would imply almost every reform which society is now suffering for. I doubt whether even our public edifices—our capitols, statehouses, courthouses, city-halls and churches—ought to be built of such permanent materials as stone or brick. It were better that they should crumble to ruin once in twenty years or thereabouts, as a hint to people to examine and reform the institutions which they symbolise.

The estimated time-span for the life of institutions is close to Jefferson's; but both of Holgrave's speeches, as their references move forward from money and laws to moral principles and religious doctrines, indicate the expanded application since 1789 of the notion of periodic "purification." According to the opposition party, the real trouble was that the suggestions of the Holgraves had long been put into practice. The immediate had triumphed, someone said in the alert New York weekly, the *Literary World*, in the same year (1850); education was sacrificed to "the immediately practical"; houses were built "which fall into tombs and monuments upon the passer-by; . . . anybody makes a new religion nowadays, a patent Christianity. The old," the article concluded, "was better."

But the physical environment had changed enormously since 1789, and these changes were the warrant urged for the changes in attitude and expression suggested by Holgrave. For example, in a sequence in the *Democratic Review*, there was an article on material progress since 1789 in one issue (October, 1839), and an editorial on the need for new ideas in the next. In the former, a German political refugee named Francis Lieber drew up a memorandum for Congress on the statistics of progress over the half-century beginning in 1789, with a now familiar reverence for arithmetic. Lieber found that the territory of the country had tripled and that the population had quadrupled; at the same rate of increase, he went on, the American people would, after one hundred more years, be equal in numbers to all of Europe. He calculated that exports of domestic origin had increased from less than 20,000,000 to nearly 100,000,000 products annually, and tonnage from half a million to three times that much. Miles of post road had multiplied from 1,300 to 134,818, and post offices from 75 to 12,000. Six hundred steamboats had been constructed in thirty years ("The immediate builds steamboats of tinder, and roasts passengers alive," the *Literary World* was to mutter); and 1,000 miles of railroad track had been laid down. It was in the following issue of the *Democratic Review* that there appeared the editorial mentioned in the Prologue: a manifesto of liberation from the past, followed by the demand for an independent literature to communicate the novelty of experience in the New World.

III

"We have the Saint Vitus dance." This was Thoreau's view of the diversion of energies to material expansion and of the enthusiastic arithmetic by which expansion was constantly being measured. Miles of post roads and millions of tons of domestic export did not convince Thoreau that first principles ought to be overhauled; but a close interest in these matters did convince him that first principles had been abandoned. Probably nobody of his generation had a richer sense of the potentiality for a fresh, free, and uncluttered existence; certainly no one projected the need for the ritual burning of the past in more varied and captivating metaphors. This is what *Walden* is about; it is the most searching contemporary account of the desire for a new kind of life. But Thoreau's announcement of a spiritual molting season (one of his favorite images) did not arise from a belief that the building of railroads was proof of the irrelevance of too-well-remembered doctrines. Long before Whitman, himself a devotee of the dazzling sum, attacked the extremes of commercialism in *Democratic Vistas*, Thoreau was insisting that the obsession with railroads did not demonstrate the hope for humanity, but tended to smother it. "Men think it is essential that the *Nation* have commerce, and export ice, and talk through a telegraph and ride thirty miles an hour, without a doubt, whether *they* do or not; but whether we should live like baboons or men is a little uncertain."

Watching the local railroad train as it passed near Walden Pond on the recently laid track between Fitchburg and Boston, Thoreau noticed that while the narrow little cars moved eastward along the ground, the engine smoke drifted skyward, broadening out as it rose. The picture (it occurs in the chapter called "Sounds") provided him with a meaningful glimpse of that wholeness, of interrelated doubleness, which was for Thoreau the required shape of the life that was genuinely lived. The trouble with railroads—he said it, in fancy, to the scores of workmen he saw starting up in protest against him—was that so few persons who rode on them were heading in any definite direction or were aware of a better direction than Boston; quite a few persons were simply run over, while the building of railroads crushed the heart and life out of the builders. The trouble, in general, with expending one's strength on "internal improvements" was that the achievement, like the aim, was partial: there was nothing internal about them. The opportunity that Thoreau looked out upon from his hut at Walden was for no such superficial accomplishment, but for a wholeness of spirit realized in a direct experience of the whole of nature. The words "nature" and "wholeness" have been overworked and devitalized (Thoreau and Emerson are partly to blame), and now they are suspect; but they glow with health in the imaginatively ordered prose of Henry Thoreau.

The narrator of *Walden* is a witness to a truly new world which the speaker alone has visited, from which he has just returned, and which he is sure every individual ought to visit at least once—not the visible world around Walden Pond, but an inner world which the Walden experience allowed him to explore. Thoreau liked to pretend that his book was a purely personal act of private communion. But that was part of his rhetoric, and *Walden* is a profoundly rhetorical book, emerging unmistakably from the long New England preaching tradition; though here the trumpet call announces the best imaginable news rather than apocalyptic warnings. Thoreau, in *Walden*, is a man who has come back down into the cave to tell the residents there that they are really in chains, suffering fantastic punishments they have imposed on themselves, seeing by a light that is reflected and derivative. A major test of the visionary hero must always be the way he can put his experience to work for the benefit of mankind; he demonstrates his freedom in the liberation of others. Thoreau prescribes the following cure: the total renunciation of the traditional, the conventional, the socially acceptable, the well-worn paths of conduct, and the total immersion in nature.

Everything associated with the past should be burned away. The past should be cast off like dead skin. Thoreau remembered with sympathetic humor the pitiful efforts of one John Field, an Irishman living at near-by Baker Farm, to catch perch with shiners: "thinking to live by some derivative old-country mode in this primitive new country." "I look on England today," he wrote, "as an old gentleman who is travelling with a great deal of baggage, trumpery which has accumulated from long housekeeping, which he has not the courage to burn." Thoreau recorded with approval and some envy a Mexican purification rite practiced every fifty-two years; and he added, "I have scarcely heard of a truer sacrament." These periodic symbolic acts of refreshment, which whole societies ought to perform in each generation ("One generation abandons the enterprises of another like stranded vessels"), were valid exactly because they were images of fundamental reality itself. Individuals and groups should enact the rhythmic death and rebirth reflected in the change of season from winter to spring, in the sequence of night and day. "The phenomena of the year take place every day in a pond on a small scale." These were some of the essential facts discovered by Thoreau when he fronted them at Walden; and the experience to which he was to become a witness took its shape, in act and in description, from a desire to live in accordance with these facts. So it was that he refused the offer of a door-mat, lest he should form the habit of shaking it every morning; and, instead, every morning "I got up early and bathed in the pond; that was a religious exercise, and one of the best things which I did."

The language tells us everything, as Thoreau meant it to. He had his own sacramental system, his own rite of baptism. But his use of the word "nature" indicates that the function of sacraments was to expose the individual again to the currents flowing through nature, rather than to the grace flowing down from supernature. The ritual of purification was no less for Thoreau than for St. Paul a dying into life; but Thoreau marched to the music he heard; it was the music of the age; and he marched in a direction *opposite* to St. Paul. His familiar witticism, "One world at a time" (made on his deathbed to an eager abolitionist named Pillsbury, who looked for some illumination of the future life from the dying seer) was a fair summary of his position: with this addition, that poetry traditionally taken as hints about what could be seen through a glass darkly about the next world was taken by Thoreau as what had been seen by genius, face to face with this one. He was among the first to see Christian literature as only the purest and most inspiring of the fables about the relation of man to nature and about the infinite capacities of the unaided human spirit. The Bible (Thoreau referred to it simply as "an old book") was the finest poem which had ever been written; it was the same in substance as Homeric or Hindu mythology, but it was richer in metaphor. The Bible spoke more sharply to the human condition. This was why Thoreau, like Whitman, could employ the most traditional of religious phrases and invest them with an unexpected and dynamic new life.

It is not surprising that transcendentalism was Puritanism turned upside down, as a number of critics have pointed out; historically, it could hardly have been anything else. Transcendentalism drew on the vocabularies of European romanticism and Oriental mysticism; but the only available local vocabulary was the one that the hopeful were so anxious to escape from, and a very effective way to discredit its inherited meaning was to serve it up in an unfamiliar context. There was something gratifyingly shocking in such a use of words: "What demon possessed me that I behaved so well?" Thoreau spoke as frequently as he could, therefore, about a *sacrament*, a sacred mystery, such as baptism: in order to define the cleansing, not of St. Paul's natural man, but of the conventional or traditional man; in order, precisely, to bring into being the natural man. For the new tensions out of which insights were drawn and moral choices provoked were no longer the relation of nature and grace, of man and God, but of the natural and the artificial, the new and the old, the individual and the social or conventional. Thoreau had, as he remarked in his other deathbed witticism, no quarrel with God; his concern was simply other.

His concern was with the strangulation of nature by convention. The trouble with conventions and traditions in the New World was that they had come first; they had come from abroad and from a very long way back; and they had been superimposed upon nature. They had to be washed away, like sin, so that the natural could reveal itself again and could be permitted to create its own organic conventions. They had to be renounced, as the first phase of the ritual; and if renunciation was, as Emily Dickinson thought, a piercing virtue, it was not because it made possible an experience of God in an infusion of grace, but because it made possible an experience of self in a bath of nature.

Thoreau had, of course, learned a good deal from Emerson, whose early energy was largely directed toward constructing "an original relation with the universe" and who reverted time and again to the same theme: "beware of tradition"; "forget historical Christianity"; "lop off all superfluity and tradition, and fall back on the nature of things." And what was this nature of things which men were enjoined to fall back on? Lowell understood some of it, in one of the better sentences of his querulous and uneven essay on Thoreau (1865): "There is only one thing better than tradition, and that is the original and eternal life out of which all tradition takes its rise. It was this life which the reformers demanded, with more or less clearness of consciousness and expression, life in politics, life in literature, life in religion." But even in this moment of qualified approval, Lowell makes it sound too pallid, soft, and ethereal. Nature was not merely the mountains and the prairie, any more than it was merely the bees and the flowers; but it was all of those things too, and it must always include them. If nature was partly represented by "Higher Laws," as the title of one chapter in *Walden* tells us, it was represented also by "Brute Neighbors," "Winter Animals," and a "Bean-Field," as we know from the titles of other chapters. Thoreau's nature is bounded by an irony which applies the phrase "Higher Laws" to a chapter that, for all its idealism, talks at some length about fried rats.

Irony too—the doubleness of things—Thoreau could learn from Emerson, as each of them had learned from Coleridge and Plato. "All the universe over," Emerson wrote in his journal (1842), "there is just one thing, this old double." The old double, the ideal and the actual, the higher law and the fried rat, required a double consciousness and found expression in a double criticism; nature could be satisfied with nothing else. Emerson tramped in mud puddles, and Thoreau, more adventurously, swam in Walden Pond; the puddle and the pond were instances of unimpeded nature; but both men searched, in their separate ways, for the spiritual analogues which completed the doubleness of nature. Their ability to address themselves with very nearly equal fluency to both dimensions of consciousness gave later comfort to idealists and nominalists alike, though neither group understood the Emersonian principle that only the whole truth could be true at all. Bronson Alcott was the most high-minded of the contemporary idealists, but Emerson chided him for neglecting the value of the many in his rapture for the one, and thought he had genius but no talent. "The philosophers of Fruitlands," Emerson said in 1843, naming Alcott's experimental community, "have such an image of virtue before their eyes, that the poetry of man and nature they never see; the poetry that is man's life, the poorest pastoral clownish life; the light that shines on a man's hat, in a child's spoon." He was harder, of course, on those who saw only the hat and the spoon: the materialists and the tradesmen whom he excoriated in many essays, and writers who stuck too obstinately to the ordinary (Emerson would say, the "vulgar") aspects of the visible world.

Thoreau's personal purification rite began with the renunciation of old hats and old spoons and went forward to the moment—as he describes himself in the opening paragraph of "Higher Laws"—when the initiate stood fully alive in the midst of nature, eating a woodchuck with his fingers, and supremely aware, at the same instant, of the higher law of virtue. "I love the wild not less than the good," Thoreau admitted, announcing duplicity in his own peculiar accent. The structure of *Walden* has a similar beginning and a similar motion forward. The book starts amid the punishing conventions of Concord, departs from them to the pond and the forest, explores the natural surroundings, and exposes the natural myth of the yearly cycle, to conclude with the arrival of spring, the full possession of life, and a representative anecdote about the sudden bursting into life of a winged insect long buried in an old table of apple-tree wood.[3]

Individual chapters are sometimes carried along to the same rhythm. "Sounds," for example, starts with conventional signs and then looks to nature for more authentic ones; it picks up the cycle of the day, as Thoreau listens to sounds around the clock; and it concludes with a total surrender to the vitalizing power of unbounded nature. Thoreau had been talking about his reading in the previous chapter; now he reminds us: "While we are confined to books . . . we are in danger of forgetting the language which all things and events speak without metaphor." Sounds are elements of this natural language: the sound of the trains passing in the morning; the church bells from Lincoln, Bedford, or Concord; the lowing of cows in the evening; "regularly at half-past seven," the vesper chant of the whip-poor-wills; the "maniacal hooting of owls," which "represent the stark twilight and unsatisfied thoughts which all have"; "late in the evening . . . the distant rumbling of wagons over bridges,—a sound heard farther than almost any other at night,—the baying of dogs . . . the trump of bullfrogs"; and then at dawn the morning song of the cockerel, the lusty call to awaken of the chanticleer which Thoreau offered on the title-page as the symbol of the book. "To walk in a winter morning, in a wood where these birds abounded . . . think of it! It would put nations on the alert." Finally, in a morning mood, Thoreau closes his chapter rejoicing that his hut has no yard, no fence, but is part of unfenced nature itself.

It was with the ultimate aim of making such an experience possible —a life determined by nature and enriched by a total awareness— that Thoreau insisted so eloquently upon the baptismal or rebirth

3. I am indebted here to the analysis of *Walden* as a rebirth ritual by Stanley Hyman, "Henry Thoreau in Our Time," *Atlantic Monthly*, CLXXVIII (November, 1946), 137–46. Mr. Hyman acknowledges his own debt, which I share, to F. O. Matthiessen's treatment of Thoreau in *American Renaissance* (New York, 1941).

rite. What he was demanding was that individuals start life all over again, and that in the new world a fresh start was literally and immediately possible to anyone wide enough awake to attempt it. It was in this way that the experience could also appear as a return to childhood, to the scenes and the wonder of that time. In a particularly revealing moment, Thoreau reflected, while adrift on the lake in the moonlight and playing the flute for the fishes, on a boyhood adventure at that very place. "But now," he said, "I made my home by the shore." Thoreau reflected the curious but logical reverence of his age for children: "Children, who play life, discern its true law and relations more clearly than men, who fail to live it worthily." Children seemed for Thoreau to possess some secret which had been lost in the deadening process of growing up, some intimation (like Wordsworth's child) which had faded under the routine pressure of everyday life. Emerson found the new attitude of adults toward children the appropriate symbol with which to introduce his retrospective summary of the times (1867): "Children had been repressed and kept in the background; now they were considered, cosseted and pampered." Thoreau thought he knew why: because "every child begins the world again"; every child managed to achieve without conscious effort what the adult could achieve only by the strenuous, periodic act of refreshment. In this sense, the renewal of life was a kind of homecoming; the busks and the burnings were preparatory to recapturing the outlook of children.

Psychologists who have followed Jung's poetic elaboration and doctrinaire schematizing of the guarded suggestions of Freud could make a good deal of the impulse. They might describe it as an impulse to return to the womb; and some support could doubtless be found in the image-clusters of Walden: water, caves, shipwrecks, and the like. This approach might persuasively maintain that the end of the experience narrated by Thoreau was the reintegration of the personality. And since, according to Jung, "the lake in the valley is the unconscious," it is possible to hold that *Walden* enacts and urges the escape from the convention-ridden conscious and the release of the spontaneous energies of personality lying beneath the surface, toward a reuniting of the psychic "old double." An analysis of this sort can be helpful and even illuminating, and it could be applied to the entire program of the party of Hope, substituting terms associated with the unconscious for all the terms associated with Emerson's "Reason." A certain warrant for the psychological interpretation can be found in the novels of Dr. Holmes, and the methodological issue arises more sharply in that discussion. But we may also remind ourselves that the psychological vocabulary simply manipulates a set of metaphors other than those we normally use. Probably we do not need to go so far afield to grasp what Thoreau was seeking to explain; we may even suspect that he meant what he said. And what he said was that he went to the woods in order to live deliberately, "to front only the essential facts of life"; because human life and human expression were so burdened with unexamined habits, the voice of experience so muffled by an uninvestigated inheritance, that only by a total rejection of those habits and that inheritance and by a recovery of a childlike wonder and directness could anyone find out whether life were worth living at all.

Thoreau, like most other members of the hopeful party, understood dawn and birth better than he did night and death. He responded at once to the cockerel in the morning; the screech owls at night made him bookish and sentimental. And though their wailing spoke to him about "the low spirits and melancholy forebodings of fallen souls," the whole dark side of the world was no more than another guaranty of the inexhaustible variety of nature.[4] Thoreau knew not evil; his American busk would have fallen short, like the bonfire in Hawthorne's fantasy, of the profounder need for the purification of the human heart. He would have burned away the past as the accumulation of artifice, in the name of the natural and the essential. But if the natural looked to him so much more wholesome and so much more dependable than others have since thought it, his account of the recovery of nature was never less than noble: the noblest expression, in fact and in language, of the first great aspiration of the age.

4. Thoreau goes on to say that the hooting of owls "is a sound admirably suited to swamps and twilight woods which no day illustrates, suggesting a vast and undeveloped nature which men have not yet recognized." The figurative language here is suggestive and may be surprising to anyone who supposes Thoreau unaware of the very existence of the cloacal regions of mind and nature.

2

The New Adam: Holmes
and Whitman

"And now," observes Adam, "we must again try to discover what sort of world this is, and why, we have been sent hither."

HAWTHORNE, "The New Adam and Eve"

THE fullest portrayal of the new world's representative man as a new, American Adam was given by Walt Whitman in *Leaves of Grass*—in the liberated, innocent, solitary, forward-thrusting personality that animates the whole of that long poem. *Leaves of Grass* tells us what life was made of, what it felt like, what it included, and what it lacked for the individual who began at that moment, so to speak, where the rebirth ritual of *Walden* leaves off. With the past discarded and largely forgotten, with conventions shed and the molting season concluded, what kind of personality would thereupon emerge? What would be the quality of the experience which lay in store for it?

Leaves of Grass was not only an exemplary celebration of novelty in America: it also, and perhaps more importantly, brought to its climax the many-sided discussion by which—over a generation—innocence replaced sinfulness as the first attribute of the American character. Such a replacement was indispensable to Whitman's vision of innocence, though, of course, it did not account for his poetic genius. But the fact was that, of all the inherited notions and practices which the party of Hope studied to reject, by far the most offensive was the Calvinist doctrine of inherited guilt: the imputation to the living individual of the disempowering effects of a sin "originally" committed by the first man in the first hours of the race's history. In New England, where the argument was most intense, the traditional view of human character was that of orthodox Calvinism. And Calvinism, according to the hopeful, not only maintained doctrines of ancient and obscure origin; it even argued in one of them that an ancient and obscure misdemeanor could have a positive effect upon the living man. Traditionally, an inherited taint was postulated coldly in an inherited dogma. It was time to renounce both the taint and the dogma.

The Unitarians—and among them, especially, the Unitarian wit and healer, Dr. Oliver Wendell Holmes—mounted the strongest attack against the doctrine of inherited guilt; and their efforts are to be noted before coming to Whitman. But the Unitarian attitude is not easily disentangled from the general epidemic of confidence in human nature which seemed to be spreading everywhere and which even infected the party of Memory. Indeed, the nostalgic had been watching the new cheerfulness with increasing agitation for a number of years, and thought they could spot it within their own citadels. One of them put the case as follows: "For a considerable time past, it has been unhesitatingly maintained that all mankind . . . are born free from sin and have no moral corruption of nature or propensity of evil—that they are perfectly innocent—that they . . . come into existence in the same state in which Adam was before the fall." One might think that this polemic was directed against Emerson, who was known to believe that "the entertainment of the proposition of depravity is the last profligacy and profanation," and who smiled his acknowledgment of "each man's innocence"; or perhaps against Thoreau, who found that "the impression made on a wise man is that of universal innocence"; or else against Walt Whitman, the self-styled "chanter of Adamic songs." In fact, its target lay inside its own party; it was a reaction as early as 1828 to the whispers of extremely modified hope which could be heard at Calvinist Yale in the gentle voices of men like Nathaniel Taylor.

It is not easy to imagine that anyone who held, as Taylor did, that "the entire moral depravity of mankind is by nature," that sin is a real and universal thing to be "truly and properly ascribed to *nature* and *not* to circumstances," and that men sin "as soon as they become moral agents . . . *as soon as they can*," was considered a dangerous radical. But Taylor was regarded as such, and so even was Moses Stuart, professor of theology at relentlessly orthodox Andover. For these men seemed to be retreating some small distance at least from the sound principles of Jonathan Edwards. They seemed to be saying and teaching that, although human beings did observably disobey the commandments of God, they did so on their own, by an assertion of their own nature, and not because of a total corruption transmitted at the instant of their conception from a diseased ancestry originally and fatally infected by Adam. They seemed to be embracing the false doctrine which had given rise to all the grievous dissensions of New England Protestantism; they seemed, almost, as bad as the Unitarians.[1]

But there was no stopping the force of the new optimism. Everybody professed a little of it, and everybody complained that his neighbor was professing too much. The march of heresy was punctuated by the blows visited by one combatant upon the head of him next on the left. While Moses Stuart was being chided for yielding an inch on total depravity, he himself was busy replying to the larger yieldings indicated by the sermons and essays of Unitarians Channing and Andrews Norton; and the dismay of Norton at being, as he said, so badly misconstrued by Moses Stuart exploded in the rage and fear aroused by Emerson's sublimely confident address to the Harvard Divinity School in 1836. Theodore Parker, in turn, after valiantly reinforcing Channing's hopeful Unitarian gospel, was almost hustled out of the American Unitarian Association, since, as Lowell put it, "from their orthodox kind of dissent, he dissented." The human stock, one might say, tracing the development chronologically, was rising steadily, until it achieved its highest value in the figure of Adam. The status of Jesus declined proportionately, or, at least, it continued to until Emerson, who deified everybody, also deified Jesus once more—thereby, in a characteristic Emersonian paradox, demonstrating the fulness of Jesus' humanity.

The Unitarians, consequently, stood at approximately the middle point in the controversy—between someone like Moses Stuart, on the one hand, and Emerson, on the other. They took their name from their rejection of the Trinity in favor of Unity; but if they could get along without two of three persons of the Trinity, it was because of a prior conviction about the nature of man.

As the Unitarian minister and historian of the movement, George A. Ellis, wrote in 1857, looking back on *A Half-Century of the Unitarian Controversy*, "The doctrine, that God visited the guilt of Adam's personal sin upon the unborn millions of his posterity . . . was infi-

---

1. Cf. Sidney Earl Mead, *Nathaniel William Taylor* (Chicago, 1942), p. 215: the orthodox attitude suggested that "the Unitarians will just send out a boat and tow [Taylor] in." In his *Autobiography* (New York, 1869), p. 157, Lyman Beecher recalled the utter dismay with which he heard a colleague express doubt about the depravity of infants: "The moment I heard that, I saw the end. I never felt so bad." Cf. also "Backgrounds of Unitarian Opposition to Transcendentalism," by Clarence A. Faust, *Modern Philology*, February, 1938; and Joseph Haroutinian, *Piety versus Moralism* (New York, 1932).

nitely more objectionable to some liberal Christians than the Trinitarian theory." To the Unitarians, the Calvinist picture of man sounded like this:

> A corrupted nature is conveyed by ordinary generation, to all of Adam's posterity, in consequence of his personal sin. . . . If this Orthodox doctrine is not a most shameful trifling with solemnities, as well as with language, it asserts that, by the constitution and appointment of God, the one man Adam had like power to communicate a vitiated nature, like a hereditary disease, not merely to the bodies, but to the souls of all human beings. . . . This doctrine either contradicts truth and reason, in affirming that any one can be partaker in sin committed before his birth, or it contradicts justice and righteousness, by subjecting us to punishment for the offence of another.

That was the issue, as the Unitarians read it, on the whole correctly, in the contemporary discussion. If all the force and meaning of the old idea of original sin had disappeared from the religious consciousness of the day, it was largely the fault of orthodoxy, the religious element in the party of Memory. For that party, too, argued the case in almost exclusively historical terms, affirming the enslavement of the present by the past as heatedly as the hopeful insisted on its freedom. But the orthodox showed little awareness of the organic vitality of history, of the way in which the past can enliven the present: the past was simply the place where the issues had been decided, and the decision was all that mattered. The orthodox habit of presenting the end-product of religious belief drained of the spiritual impulses which had gone into the historical shaping of it led to a frozen but fragile structure, and one not likely to hold very long against the assaults of the opposition. The energetic hostility of the hopeful to the influence of the past, to the transmission of anything—be it laws, property, or ideas —gathered against the doctrine of transmitted guilt—and overwhelmed it.

The stand on the Trinity followed. For if the individual started on his spiritual career with an unsullied conscience, there was no need for expiation; there was no need, as the Unitarians were willing to say quite explicitly, of a propitiation for our sins. The sacrifice of the god satisfied a human yearning for a redemption possible only by a divine action; but the yearning vanished along with the sense of sin. The reason for the divinity of Jesus evaporated; and he became, like Paul, one of the most admirable of the characters in ancient history. The third member of the Trinity was no less rapidly defunctionalized by the hopeful attitude; for in a view which rested upon a freedom from history, upon a lack of communion between one generation and the next, there was no function for a continuing presence in time and history, for a guaranty of the unity of all ages.

The Unitarian *controversy* can be dated, as George Ellis dated it, from about 1805, when the Unitarian theories about man and God were introduced at Harvard by Henry Ware and given some sanction by his position as Hollis Professor of Divinity. Unitarianism itself, of course, went back much farther. Most of its doctrine had been preached by such disciples of Enlightenment and such anti-Edwardseans as Charles Chauncy and Jonathan Mayhew (who died in 1766). The natural goodness of man, the unlikelihood of hell, the benevolence and probable singularity of God were none of them novel propositions. They had made their appearance with the birth of Christianity; and the various heresies about the nature of Jesus, with their shifting corollaries about the nature of man, had been meticulously outlawed one by one in the great church councils of the first Christian centuries. They have recurred since at such regular intervals that their appearance can never be adequately explained in terms of immediate intellectual "background." Perhaps social psychology would be more helpful: what governs the rise and fall of man's evaluation of himself?

II

"If for the Fall of man, science comes to substitute the Rise of man, sir, it means the utter disintegration of all the spiritual pessimisms which have been like a spasm in the heart and a cramp in the intellect of man for so many centuries." The operative word in that utterance of Oliver Wendell Holmes, with its Johnsonian stance and its thoroughly Holmesian metaphor, is "science." For Holmes was not merely echoing the current Unitarian resentment against orthodoxy's picture of fallen nature: he was advocating a new picture of man and indicating the sources of his evidence.

"Science" meant many things, but in the ethical discussion it meant primarily the pre-Darwinian evolutionary hypothesis of Lamarck, a hypothesis about the steady development of the human species which happily coincided with and could be taken as a kind of proof of the contemporary high estimate of human nature. Holmes took the Lamarckian theory as the basis for his best-known (though not at all his most attractive) poem, "The Chambered Nautilus" (1858), in which the soul is compared to the shellfish and enjoined, like it, to build itself ever more stately mansions, "each new temple nobler than the last."

What science was replacing, according to Holmes, was a view of life ordered by the moralism of a desiccated Calvinist theology. He saw orthodoxy as embodying a set of beliefs and precepts inherited from a remote Asiatic epoch: tradition in its most paralyzing form. "Our dwellings are built on shell-heaps," he said; "the kitchen-midden of the age of stone. Inherited beliefs, as obscure in their origin as the parentage of the cave-dwellers, are stronger with many minds than the evidence of the senses and the simplest deductions of the intelligence." Holmes bent his energies to removing ancient ideas from the head and an ancient anxiety from the heart of living man. His motivation was that of his fellow-Unitarians; but his special weapon was empirical science: the evidence of the senses.

Holmes is an instructive guide for us, as we leave the wastelands of orthodoxy and approach the new Eden of Walt Whitman, for he himself made almost the entire journey. He went to school at orthodox Andover, where a whipping he received evidently produced a sort of traumatic experience. He came on to Harvard, in 1825, when Unitarianism was in the ascendancy, and became its wittiest exponent. He moved on to be one of America's leading men of science. In fact, Oliver Wendell Holmes, whose long life (1809–94) spanned the century, ought to have been a most arresting figure, perhaps the representative man of his age; it is not easy to say why he so often disappoints us. Perhaps it is because he was at the center of so many tendencies and managed to occupy the middle only by achieving a consistent mediocrity.

Holmes stood midway between the vanishing virility of his father's Calvinism and the emerging vitality of his son's militant humanism; what seems to have been available to him from either direction was frequently only the secondary or illusory. The suspicions which clouded his kindly view of human nature lacked the terrible strength which his father, Abiel Holmes, brought to his Calvinist ministry, while his enlightened repudiation of the divine elect took him only as far as the socially eligible, and his replacement of the visible saints by the Boston quality had little of the astringent social philosophy of his son, the Justice. Holmes stood at the heart of his own time. He was, of course, a Harvard man forever, and the class poet par excellence; he was also a respected colleague and friend of the Swiss zoölogist, Louis Agassiz. Holmes could listen attentively to the Swedenborgian mystifyings by which the elder James mapped the way of regeneration; he could equally grasp and expound the therapeutic methods by which clinical psychology hoped to accomplish the same thing. He led the attack on the old theology; but he was a competent critic and a great lover of the old literature. His interests were rich and varied; yet what

The American Adam

we are apt to find in him is less a synthesis of these interests than a good-humored shrewdness about them all, a solid common sense not deep enough for skepticism, not large enough for faith.

At the same time, it is probably misleading to say of him, in the phrase which has clung, that he was an "authentic Brahmin"—unless Brahminism is a more complex state of mind than is commonly allowed. For Holmes, like his partially autobiographical character Byles Gridley in *The Guardian Angel*, was "a strange union of trampling radicalism in some directions and high-stepping conservatism in others." The traditionalist side is better known and remembered; it included familiar traits of the party of Memory, and it has helped to associate him with that party far more than Holmes would have wanted. He was old-fashioned with respect to manners: he remained, that is, a stickler for common courtesy. He talked a good deal, no doubt too much, about the virtues of breeding, with an eyebrow cocked at the "large, uncombed youth" who outdid his betters at study. He was cautious on the issue of slavery, not because, like Hawthorne, he could see beyond it to its source in the darker corners of the heart, but because he found the uproar a trifle vulgar. He was bored by strident nationalism in literature, or in anything else; and he thought that the dead hand of the past need not always (as Holgrave felt) choke the life out of us, but that it could be used according to the old medical superstition to cure our swellings: "to take down our tumid egotism and lead us into the solemn flow of our race." Holmes's views on these matters were relaxed; they were points in the world about him which he was inclined to accept without the exertion of dispassionate analysis. When he began to talk about the nature and function of science, he had something new to say and a resonant vocabulary in which to say it: "The attitude of modern science is erect, her aspect serene, her determination inflexible, her onward movement unflinching; because she believes herself, in the order of providence, the true successor of the men of old who brought down the light of heaven to men."

Almost all of the Holmes that interests us here is in that sentence. The qualities that Holmes attributes to science could be attributed with the same buoyant confidence to the individual in America. As the profile of the new Adam emerges, we can notice that he too is erect, serene, inflexible, unflinching: and, according to Dr. Holmes, exactly because "modern science" had liberated him, explained him to himself, and imparted to him science's own stalwart nature. For science would provide the new religion and the new prophets and mediators;

science would write the new testament and invent the new metaphors. If Dr. Holmes, as one of the first champions of science, did very well at this game, it was largely because he understood to a remarkable extent what the game was about. Perhaps the most succinct statement of Holmes's achievement was that he recast traditional religious concepts in scientific and humanistic terms, that he extracted what he saw as the *facts* of the human situation from the metaphors of myth and posited them anew in the language of psychology and anthropology.

Holmes's artful and sometimes even compelling transpositions are illustrated best in two of his scientific or "medicated" novels, *Elsie Venner* and *The Guardian Angel.* The very genre to which Holmes ascribed these books was a sign of his enterprise; for while Emerson and Whitman were trying their best to convert medical facts into inspirational poetry, Holmes was converting a literary form into a vehicle for a medical case history. Each of the books also enacts the crucial shift in the long arguments between minister and doctor, with the doctor getting the final word in every discussion. Holmes's "novels" are suggestive if, out of fairness to their author, we do not ask of them any questions prompted by a literary bias.

In *Elsie Venner* (1861), Holmes tested the dreary theories which George Ellis and his Unitarian associates imputed to orthodoxy: that a living individual could be "a partaker in a sin committed before his birth"; that he can consequently suffer punishment "for the offence of another." Holmes said in the Introduction that he had attempted "to illustrate the doctrine of inherited moral responsibility for other people's misbehavior." This way of formulating or loading the question indicates the extent to which Holmes conceived of his work as an exercise in scientific history. Holmes took Hawthorne's *The Marble Faun* (written later than *Elsie Venner,* but published a year before) as giving the same answer to the same question: though Hawthorne was testing innocence rather than its opposite, and the similarity of the two novels is essentially the similarity of ethics to medicine. For Holmes, that similarity was close: how close, he demonstrated in his narrative of the hapless Elsie, whose case emerged as an analogy to what Holmes took to be the doctrine of original sin.

As the mother of the human race, Eve, was corrupted by the serpent, with calamitous results for her children, so the mother of this child was bitten by a rattlesnake, with horrid consequences for the still unborn Elsie. As a baby, Elsie exhibits features and bodily motions reminiscent of the *Crotalus,* and as she grows up her behavior shows a certain repellent snakelike quality. The essence of Holmes's novel is the gradual revelation to a cluster of stock characters in a stock New England village of the source and cause of Elsie's disposition, her odd facial contortions, and her tendency to hiss; and the whole direction of the argument is toward liberating Elsie from responsibility. The point the author takes some five hundred pages to make is carried in this characteristic colloquial speech of an old Negro governess: "It a'n't her fault! It a'n't her fault! If they knew all that I know they would'n' blame that poor child." Elsie, the narrative says, was not morally present at the moment of the prenatal accident; she participated in it by no act of will; hence she must not be held responsible for the actions which flowed from it. The inherited traits were dismal facts, medically established; what could not be inherited, Holmes maintained, was culpability. The analogy between Mrs. Venner's child and the children of Eve was drawn in the Introduction, "Wherein lies the difference between her position at the bar of judgment human or divine, and that of the unfortunate victim who received a moral poison from a remote ancestor before he drew his first breath?"

Within the novel, the only persons who might at least have carried that question further are the local clergy; and their theology is remarkably insecure. The case for the defense is vivaciously argued by two members of the medical profession: the Professor, who follows the story of Elsie's life and early death and who comments from afar, in Boston; and the country doctor, who tries to enlighten the spokesmen of the various sects. The relatively easy victory of Dr. Kittredge is due partly to his ability to transfer the question from the field of religion, where his interlocutors might have been more at home, to the scientific laboratory. Through the conversations by which Dr. Kittredge manages to convert the Calvinist minister, we catch an early glimpse of the transition from the confessor, with his concern about souls, to the physician, with his interest in nervous disorders. From the medical point of view, Dr. Kittredge argues, a sin and a headache can be subjected to an identical diagnosis. "Our notions of bodily and moral disease, or sin, are apt to go together. We used to be as hard on sickness as you were on sin. We know better now. . . . We know that disease has something back of it, which the body isn't to blame for, at least in most cases; and which very often it is trying to get rid of. Just so with sin."

The character of the treatment is determined by the character of the diagnosis, as we learn from the Professor: "Treat bad men exactly as if they were insane. They are in-sane, out of health morally." This is the hypothesis of the book; for the Professor is the seer, the magician, in Holmes's medical myth; he is, literally, the medicine man.

Holmes never pretended that there was nothing wrong with the world or with individual human beings; he was not innocent, he was merely kind. The defense of Elsie Venner sprang from Holmes's awareness of and his compassion for human failings, and it communicated his warming belief that to understand is to forgive. But he was sure that theology, or at least the only theology he knew much about, would not help anyone to understand. That was to be the function of science. Science could teach a man to search for the origins and causes of bad actions; and if it discovered them to lie in "external influences," in "bad ancestors, abuse in childhood, bad company," science was prepared to argue that the actions themselves were not in any moral sense bad after all.

What he wanted, in short, was a renovation of the moral vocabulary. In order to get it, Holmes felt the necessity of rejecting the entire traditional scheme of thought, replacing it with those studies by which his friend President Eliot was simultaneously revamping the Harvard curriculum: "The truth is," wrote Holmes in an essay on Jonathan Edwards, "that the whole system of beliefs which came in with the story of the 'fall of man,' the curse of the father conveyed by natural descent to his posterity . . . is gently fading out of enlightened intelligence. . . . Astronomy, Geology, Ethnology, and a comparative study of Oriental religions have opened the way; and now Anthropology has taken hold of the matter."

Holmes's own renovated vocabulary—his chosen symbols for describing renovated human nature—consisted of a series of medical metaphors. "Like a spasm in the heart and a cramp in the intellect"; "our tumid egotism"; "treat bad men as if they were insane": these are examples of Holmes's favorite device, and one which he managed with uncommon dexterity. He shared the prevalent belief in the doctrine of correspondences, or likeness in the elements of the physical and the spiritual world, but in his own peculiar way. For while Emerson, Thoreau, and Melville found gleams of spiritual meaning in the physical scene, a dim outline of the ideal in the actual, Holmes pointed to the operation in the ideal realm of actual or physical functions. Emerson thought that science (as he said in *Nature* and in other essays) should be completed and validated by his own brand of metaphysics; Holmes thought that the realm of spirit could be overhauled by going about it in a scientific manner. "For what we want in the religious and political organisms," he wrote, "is just that kind of vital change which takes place in our bodies,—interstitial disintegration and reintegration."

If the bad habits of Elsie Venner were pardoned because they sprang from a bad ancestry, the self-destructive instinct of Myrtle Hazard, the heroine of Holmes's second medicated novel, *The Guardian Angel* (1867), was overcome by the gracious influence of a good ancestor. The books are not at all contradictory in theme; indeed, they serve to resolve the apparent contradictions in their author; and the second novel is a valuable complement to the volume published six years earlier. *The Guardian Angel* tells of the escape of a young girl from the New England household of her tight-lipped Aunt Silence and from a ménage further aggravated by the unwelcome attentions of the local Calvinist minister. It tells of her attempt at suicide by drowning and of her rescue from the river. It describes her convalescence under the affectionate care of a doctor and his friends, and concludes with her emotional and physical fulfilment in marriage and a new life. It hints, all along, at a shadowy "power"—Myrtle's "guardian angel"— who walks beside her pointing the way or speaks from the depths within her.

In Myrtle's departure from the orthodox environment and her regeneration in the doctor's home, there is a symbolism, almost stiffening into allegory, of the succession by science of the dried-up moralism of "religion." But in *The Guardian Angel* Holmes is less interested in continuing the battle against a moldering theology than in describing the anatomy of the mental personality and in exposing the scientific bases of the rebirth ritual.[2] The experience of Myrtle's immersion in water, for example, though projected with slight dramatic effectiveness (much less, say, than the comparable experience of the young hero at the end of Melville's *White-Jacket* [1850]), is handled with an acute consciousness of its psychic significance. Holmes is careful to introduce images of her dimly remembered mother into the girl's disturbed imagination, just before she makes the plunge—which is explicitly intended to be what later psychologists would call a return to the womb. Holmes knew what he was about, to the extent that it scarcely measures his awareness to say only that he "anticipated" some of the insights of Freud and Jung. On this ground, Holmes may be admired in his own right. He centered his story on a genuine mental

2. Holmes as a philosophical psychologist is the subject of an interesting book by Dr. Clarence P. Oberndorf, *The Psychiatric Novels of Oliver Wendell Holmes* (New York, 1943).

illness, revealed its causes in austerity and repression, and suggested a therapy which much later practice would not seriously dispute. We may recognize in the domination of the young heroine by Aunt Silence what Freud would call the repression of the ego by the superego. An excessive control by the superego—the repository of conventional moral attitudes—results, according to Freud, in a melancholy which can lead toward self-destruction; and that was precisely the effect of Aunt Silence. Perhaps more striking yet was Holmes's exposure, in a pre-Jungian manner, of the presence within the recesses of the mind of personality types filtered down from the past. The theme of *The Guardian Angel* and its title are derived from this notion, as Holmes explains in the opening pages: "There is recorded an experience of one of the living persons mentioned in this narrative which tends to show that some, at least, who have long been dead, may enjoy a kind of secondary and imperfect, yet self-conscious life in these bodily tenements which we are in the habit of considering exclusively our own." And Myrtle Hazard's habit, during moments of stress, of revealing in her features the welling-up of ancestral influence permits Dr. Hurlbut, the Tiresias of this novel, to utter the book's message: "Live folks are just dead folks warmed over." The theme is more persuasively stated than it is dramatized; but Holmes's awkward technique for showing in action what he meant in theory was a failure of narrative art (to which he hardly aspired) rather than of psychological insight.

Holmes did succeed, moreover, in distinguishing between those remote influences, treating them, the way Jung would do, as dramatis personae encountered on the psychic journey. Among them, in Myrtle's case, we find an Indian forebear, who appears in the girl's occasional gestures of violence; and the guardian angel, the "guide" who shepherds Myrtle through a variety of perils, an ancestor named Anne Holyoake, a sixteenth-century Puritan martyr. It is her image that Myrtle confuses with that of her mother. Holmes's story thus follows the symbolic pattern later proposed by Jung as the myth of psychic reintegration: the escape, the plunge, the journey, the dangerous and the saving encounters, the magical guidance to the journey's end, and the final healing of the personality.

The Guardian Angel, though without merit as literature, is a telling contribution toward resolving the tensions between Memory and Hope. Ancestry was the point of intersection for Holmes. Both of his novels and most of his essays make it plain that he sought, with the hopeful, to rid the living of the oppressive misdirection of "bad ancestors," and to stand the present on its own feet. But Holmes had a

Brahmin's respect for family and good breeding; and he was able to see how the past might nourish as well as stifle. The conservatism in him was peculiarly reinforced by his advanced psychiatric understanding of the value of the past as directive. The example of Oliver Wendell Holmes might support a contention that the renewed persuasion about the necessity of tradition could best emerge not in theological but in psychological terms: by demonstrating the powerful stabilizing and energizing effect which the past may have upon the isolated personality.

The pathos of such isolation was felt and expressed even by that archetypal man of good hope, Emerson, who captured the sense of confusion and aimlessness which afflicted his more sensitive contemporaries with the words: "Here we drift. . . . To what port are we bound? Who knows!" Those wistful questions illustrated the point which, a century later, Thomas Mann would discover from the psychology of Freud and Jung: the point that the individual "would be confused, helpless, unstable" if his career "consisted merely in the unique and the present." Mann would argue that experience took on meaning and purpose only when it was regarded as typical, not unique —the re-enactment of the past, not the pure event in the present. Holmes hinted at much the same thing, as he set about answering those Emersonian questions by turning to psychotherapy. The question for him was, How had the lost child—Myrtle Hazard, for example —arrived at her condition? And the cure required an adjustment in the working relations between the present and the past.

But the genuinely hopeful were not really interested in either Holmes's analysis or his proposals. Emerson, with total assurance, referred his own questions for answer to the Oversoul; and a moment later could rejoice in the very adventurousness of the uncharted journey. Every tendency in the age which Holmes himself most admired was pushing toward a total neglect of the past rather than a last-minute attempt to restore some of its value. The dominant emotion was exhilaration, not wistfulness. "The expansive future is our arena," declaimed that hopeful organ, the *Democratic Review*. "We are entering on its untrodden ways . . . with a clear conscience unsullied by the past." The excitement of life, for the hopeful, lay exactly in its present uniqueness; the burden of doubt and guilt had been disposed of when the whole range of European experience had been repudiated, for the burden was the chief product of that experience. The individual moral course was thus to be plotted—not in terms of readjustment or of identification with any portion of the past, and much less in terms of redemption—but simply in terms of the healthy cultivation of natural, unimpaired faculties.

The American was to be acknowledged in his complete emancipation from the history of mankind. He was to be recognized now for what he was—a new Adam, miraculously free of family and race, untouched by those dismal conditions which prior tragedies and entanglements monotonously prepared for the newborn European. Nathaniel Hawthorne, in his sympathetic and ironic way, had already furnished the working metaphor for this phase in the career of the New World's representative man: in a companion piece to "Earth's Holocaust," a fantasy called "The New Adam and Eve." It was the story of a second pair created after "the Day of Doom has burst upon the globe and swept away the whole race of man"—two pure people "with no knowledge of their predecessors nor of the diseased circumstances that had become encrusted around them." Innocent, cheerful, curious, they start forth on their way to discover, as Adam is made to observe, "what sort of world this is, and why we have been sent hither." Holmes, still insisting on the enabling portion of the past, could not have told them much about their fresh and purified world. But Walt Whitman, in *Leaves of Grass*, was ready to tell them everything.

III

Whitman appears as the Adamic man reborn here in the 19th century [JOHN BURROUGHS (1896)].

In his old age, Dr. Holmes derived a certain amount of polite amusement from the poetry of Walt Whitman. Whitman, Holmes remarked, "carried the principle of republicanism through the whole world of created objects"; he smuggled into his "hospitable vocabulary words which no English dictionary recognizes as belonging to the language —words which will be looked for in vain outside of his own pages." Holmes found it hard to be sympathetic toward *Leaves of Grass*; it seemed to him windy, diffuse, and humorless; but his perceptions were as lively as ever. In these two observations he points to the important elements in Whitman which are central here: the spirit of equality which animated the surging catalogues of persons and things (on its more earthy level, not unlike Emerson's lists of poets and philosophers, with their equalizing and almost leveling tendency); the groping after novel words to identify novel experiences; the lust for inventiveness which motivated what was for Whitman the great act, the creative act.

The American Adam

Holmes's tone of voice, of course, added that for him Whitman had gone too far; Whitman was too original, too republican, too entire an Adam. Whitman had indeed gone further than Holmes: a crucial and dimensional step further, as Holmes had gone further than Channing or Norton. In an age when the phrase "forward-looking" was a commonplace, individuals rarely nerved themselves to withstand the shock of others looking and moving even further forward than they. Emerson himself, who had gone so far that the liberal Harvard Divinity School forbade his presence there for more than thirty years, shared some of Holmes's feeling about Whitman. When his cordial letter welcoming *Leaves of Grass* in 1855 was published in the *New York Tribune*, Emerson muttered in some dismay that had he intended it for publication, he "should have enlarged the *but* very much—enlarged the *but*." *Leaves of Grass* "was pitched in the very highest key of self-reliance," as a friend of its author maintained; but Emerson, who had given that phrase its contemporary resonance, believed that any attitude raised to its highest pitch tended to encroach dangerously on the truth of its opposite.

It would be no less accurate to say that Walt Whitman, instead of going too far forward, had gone too far backward: for he did go back, all the way back, to a primitive Adamic condition, to the beginning of time.

In the poetry of Walt Whitman, the hopes which had until now expressed themselves in terms of progress crystallized all at once in a complete recovery of the primal perfection. In the early poems Whitman accomplished the epochal return by huge and almost unconscious leaps. In later poems he worked his way more painstakingly up the river of history to its source: as, for example, in "Passage to India," where the poet moves back from the recently constructed Suez Canal, back past Christopher Columbus, past Alexander the Great and the most ancient of heroes and peoples, to the very "secret of the earth and sky." "In the beginning," John Locke once wrote, "all the world was America." Whitman manages to make us feel what it might have been like; and he succeeds at last in presenting the dream of the new Adam —along with his sorrows.

A measure of Whitman's achievement is the special difficulty which that dream had provided for others who tried to recount it. Its character was such that it was more readily described by those who did not wholly share in it. How can absolute novelty be communicated? All the history of the philosophy of language is involved with that question, from *The Cratylus* of Plato to the latest essay on semantics; and one could bring to bear on it the variety of anecdotes about Adam's naming the animals by the disturbingly simple device of calling a toad a toad.

Hawthorne conveyed the idea of novelty by setting it in an ancient pattern: allowing it thereby exactly to be *recognized;* and reaching a sharpness of meaning also to be found in Tocqueville's running dialectic of democracies and aristocracies. Whitman employed the same tactic when he said of Coleridge that he was "like Adam in Paradise, and just as free from artificiality." This was a more apt description of himself, as he knew:

> I, chanter of Adamic songs,
> Through the new garden the West,
> the great cities calling.

It is, in fact, in the poems gathered under the title *Children of Adam* (1860) that we have the most explicit evidence of his ambition to reach behind tradition to find and assert nature untroubled by art, to re-establish the natural unfallen man in the living hour. Unfallen man is, properly enough, unclothed as well; the convention of cover came in with the Fall; and Whitman adds his own unnostalgic sincerity to the Romantic affection for nakedness:

> As Adam, early in the morning,
> Walking forth from the bower refresh'd with sleep,
> Behold me where I pass, hear my voice, approach,
> Touch me, touch the palm of your hand to my body
> as I pass,
> Be not afraid of my body.

For Whitman, as for Holmes and Thoreau, the quickest way of framing his novel outlook was by lowering, and secularizing, the familiar spiritual phrases: less impudently than Thoreau but more earnestly, and indeed more monotonously, but with the same intention of salvaging the human from the religious vocabulary to which (he felt) it had given rise. Many of Whitman's poetic statements are conversions of religious allusion: the new miracles were acts of the senses (an odd foreshortening, incidentally, of Edwards' Calvinist elaboration of the Lockian psychology); the aroma of the body was "finer than prayer"; his head was "more than churches, bibles and all creeds." "If I worship one thing more than another," Whitman declaimed, in a moment of Adamic narcissism, "it shall be the spread of my own body." These assertions gave a peculiar stress to Whitman's seconding of the hopeful belief in men like gods: "Divine am I, inside and out, and I make holy whatever I touch." Whitman's poetry is at every moment an act of turbulent incarnation.

But although there is, as there was meant to be, a kind of shock-value in such lines, they are not the most authentic index to his pervasive Adamism, because in them the symbols have become too explicit and so fail to work symbolically. Whitman in these instances is stating his position and contemplating it; he is betraying his own principle of indirect statement; he is telling us too much, and the more he tells us, the more we seem to detect the anxious, inflated utterance of a charlatan. We cling to our own integrity and will not be thundered at. We respond far less willingly to Whitman's frontal assaults than we do to his dramatizations; when he is enacting his role rather than insisting on it, we are open to persuasion. And he had been enacting it from the outset of *Leaves of Grass*.

This is the true nature of his achievement and the source of his claim to be the representative poet of the party of Hope. For the "self" in the very earliest of Whitman's poems is an individual who is always moving forward. To say so is not merely to repeat that Whitman believed in progress; indeed, it is in some sense to deny it. The young Whitman, at least, was not an apostle of progress in its customary meaning of a motion from worse to better to best, an improvement over a previous historic condition, a "rise of man." For Whitman, there was no past or "worse" to progress from; he moved forward because it was the only direction (he makes us think) in which he could move; because there was nothing behind him—or if there were, he had not yet noticed it. There is scarcely a poem of Whitman's before, say, 1867, which does not have the air of being the first poem ever written, the first formulation in language of the nature of persons and of things and of the relations between them; and the urgency of the language suggests that it was formulated in the very nick of time, to give the objects described their first substantial existence.

Nor is there, in *Leaves of Grass*, any complaint about the weight or intrusion of the past; in Whitman's view the past had been so effectively burned away that it had, for every practical purpose, been forgotten altogether. In his own recurring figure, the past was already a corpse; it was on its way out the door to the cemetery; Whitman watched it absent-mindedly, and turned at once to the living reality. He did enjoy, as he reminds us, reciting Homer while walking beside the ocean; but this was just because Homer was exempt from tradition and talking at and about the dawn of time. Homer was the poet you found if you went back far enough; and as for the sea, it had (unlike

Melville's) no sharks in it—no ancient, lurking, indestructible evil powers. Whitman's hope was unspoiled by memory. When he became angry, as he did in *Democratic Vistas* (1871), he was not attacking his generation in the Holgrave manner for continuing to accept the old and the foreign, but for fumbling its extraordinary opportunity, for taking a wrong turn on the bright new highway he had mapped for it. Most of the time he was more interested in the map, and we are more interested in him when he was.

It was then that he caught up and set to music the large contemporary conviction that man had been born anew in the new society, that the race was off to a fresh start in America. It was in *Leaves of Grass* that the optative mood, which had endured for over a quarter of a century and had expressed itself so variously and so frequently, seemed to have been transformed at last into the indicative. It was there that the hope that had enlivened spokesmen from Noah Webster in 1825 ("American glory begins at the dawn") to the well-named periodical, *Spirit of the Age* in 1849 ("The accumulated atmosphere of ages, containing stale ideas and opinions . . . will soon be among the things that were")—that all that stored-up abundance of hope found its full poetic realization. *Leaves of Grass* was a climax as well as a beginning, or rather, it was the climax of a long effort to begin.

This was why Emerson, with whatever enlarged "buts" in his mind, made a point of visiting Whitman in New York and Boston; why Thoreau, refusing to be put off "by any brag or egoism in his book," preferred Whitman to Bronson Alcott; and why Whitman, to the steady surprise of his countrymen, has been regarded in Europe for almost a century as unquestionably the greatest poet the New World has produced: an estimate which even Henry James would come round to. European readers were not slow to recognize in Whitman an authentic rendering of their own fondest hopes; for if much of his vision had been originally imported from Germany and France, it had plainly lost its portion of nostalgia en route. While European romanticism continued to resent the effect of time, Whitman was announcing that time had only just begun. He was able to think so because of the facts of immediate history in America during the years when he was maturing: when a world was, in some literal way, being created before his eyes. It was this that Whitman had the opportunity to dramatize; and it was this that gave *Leaves of Grass* its special quality of a Yankee Genesis: a new account of the creation of the world—the creation, that is, of a new world; an account this time with a happy ending for Adam its hero; or better yet, with no ending at all; and with this important emendation, that now the creature has taken on the role of creator.

It was a twofold achievement, and the second half of it was demanded by the first. We see the sequence, for example, in the development from section 4 to section 5 of "Song of Myself." The first phase was the identification of self, an act which proceeded by distinction and differentiation, separating the self from every element that in a traditional view might be supposed to be part of it: Whitman's identity card had no space on it for the names of his ancestry. The exalted mind which carried with it a conviction of absolute novelty has been described by Whitman's friend, the Canadian psychologist, Dr. R. M. Bucke, who relates it to what he calls Whitman's "cosmic consciousness." "Along with the consciousness of the cosmos [Dr. Bucke wrote], there occurs an intellectual enlightenment which alone would place the individual on a new plane of existence—would make him almost a member of a new species." *Almost a member of a new species:* that could pass as the slogan of each individual in the party of Hope. It was a robust American effort to make real and operative the condition which John Donne once had merely feared:

> Prince, Subject, Father, Son are things forgot,
> For every man alone thinks he has got
> To be a Phoenix and that then can be
> None of that kind, of which he is, but he.

Whitman achieves the freedom of the new condition by scrupulously peeling off every possible source of, or influence upon, the "Me myself," the "what I am." As in section 4 of "Song of Myself":

> Trippers and askers surround me
> People I meet, the effect upon me of my early life, or the
>   ward and the city I live in or the nation. . . .
> The sickness of one of my folks, or of myself, or the ill-
>   doing or loss or lack of money, or depressions or
>   exaltations,
> Battles, the horror of fratricidal wars, the fever of doubt-
>   ful news, the fitful events,
> These come to me days and nights and go from me again,
> But they are not the Me myself.
> Apart from the pulling and hauling stands what I am;
> Stands amused, complacent, compassionating, idle, unitary;
> Looks down, is erect, or bends an arm on an impalpable
>   certain rest,
> Looking with side-curved head curious what will come next,
> Both in and out of the game, and watching and wondering
>   at it.

The New Adam: Holmes and Whitman

There is Emerson's individual, the "infinitely repellent orb." There is also the heroic product of romanticism, exposing behind the mass of what were regarded as inherited or external or imposed and hence superficial and accidental qualities the true indestructible secret core of personality. There is the man who contends that "nothing, not God, is greater to one than one's self."

There, in fact, is the new Adam. If we want a profile of him, we could start with the adjectives Whitman supplies: amused, complacent, compassionating, idle, unitary; especially unitary, and certainly very easily amused; too complacent, we frequently feel, but always compassionate—expressing the old divine compassion for every sparrow that falls, every criminal and prostitute and hopeless invalid, every victim of violence or misfortune. With Whitman's help we could pile up further attributes, and the exhaustive portrait of Adam would be composed of a careful gloss on each one of them: hankering, gross, mystical, nude; turbulent, fleshy, sensual, eating, drinking, and breeding; no sentimentalist, no stander above men and women; no more modest than immodest; wearing his hat as he pleases indoors and out; never skulking or ducking or deprecating; adoring himself and adoring his comrades; afoot with his vision,

> Moving forward then and now and forever,
> Gathering and showing more always and with velocity,
> Infinite and omnigenous.

And announcing himself in language like that. For an actual illustration, we could not find anything better than the stylized daguerreotype of himself which Whitman placed as the Frontispiece of the first edition. We recognize him at once: looking with side-curved head, bending an arm on the certain rest of his hip, evidently amused, complacent, and curious; bearded, rough, probably sensual; with his hat on.

Whitman did resemble this Adamic archetype, according to his friend John Burroughs. "There was a look about him," Burroughs remembered, "hard to describe, and which I have seen in no other face, —a gray, brooding, elemental look, like the granite rock, something primitive and Adamic that might have belonged to the first man." The two new adjectives there are "gray" and "brooding"; and they belong to the profile, too, both of Whitman and of the character he dramatized. There was bound to be some measure of speculative sadness inherent in the situation. Not all the leaves Whitman uttered were joyous ones, though he wanted them all to be and was never clear why

47

they were not. His ideal image of himself—and it is his best single trope for the new Adam—was that of a live oak he saw growing in Louisiana:

> All alone stood it and the mosses hung down from the
> branches,
> Without any companion it grew there uttering joyous
> leaves of dark green,
> And its look, rude, unbending, lusty, made me think of
> myself.

But at his most honest, he admitted, as he does here, that the condition was somehow unbearable:

> I wondered how it could utter joyous leaves standing alone
> there without a friend near, for I knew I could not. . . .
> And though the live-oak glistens there in Louisiana solitary
> in a wide flat space,
> Uttering joyous leaves all its life without a friend a lover
> near,
> I knew very well I could not.

Adam had his moments of sorrow also. But the emotion had nothing to do with the tragic insight; it did not spring from any perception of a genuine hostility in nature or lead to the drama of colliding forces. Whitman was wistful, not tragic. We might almost say that he was wistful because he was not tragic. He was innocence personified. It is not difficult to marshal a vast array of references to the ugly, the gory, and the sordid in his verses; brought together in one horrid lump, they appear as the expression of one who was well informed about the shabby side of the world; but though he offered himself as "the poet of wickedness" and claimed to be "he who knew what it was to be evil," every item he introduced as vile turns out, after all, to be merely a particular beauty of a different original coloration. "Evil propels me and reform of evil propels me, I stand indifferent." A sentiment like that can make sense only if the term "evil" has been filtered through a transfiguring moral imagination, changing in essence as it passes.

That sentiment, of course, is not less an expression of poetic than of moral motivation. As a statement of the poetic sensibility, it could have been uttered as easily by Shakespeare or Dante as by Whitman. Many of the very greatest writers suggest, as Whitman does, a peculiar artistic innocence, a preadolescent wonder which permits such a poet to take in and reproject whatever there is, shrinking from none of it. But in Whitman, artistic innocence merged with moral innocence: a preadolescent ignorance of the convulsive undertow of human behavior—something not at all shared by Dante or Shakespeare. Both modes of innocence are present in the poetry of Walt Whitman, and they are not at any time to be really distinguished. One can talk about his image of moral innocence only in terms of his poetic creation.

"I reject none, accept all, then reproduce all in my own forms." The whole spirit of Whitman is in the line: there is his strategy for overcoming his sadness, and the second large phase of his achievement, following the act of differentiation and self-identification. It is the creative phase, in that sense of creativity which beguiles the artist most perilously into stretching his analogy with God—when he brings a world into being. Every great poet composes a world for us, and what James called the "figure in the carpet" is the poet's private chart of that world; but when we speak of the poet's world—of Dostoevski's or Balzac's—we knowingly skip a phrase, since what we mean is Dostoevski's (or Balzac's) selective embodiment of an already existing world. In the case of Whitman, the type of extreme Adamic romantic, the metaphor gains its power from a proximity to the literal, as though Whitman really were engaged in the stupendous task of building a world that had not been there before the first words of his poem.

The task was self-imposed, for Whitman's dominant emotion, when it was not unmodified joy, was simple, elemental loneliness; it was a testimony to his success and contributed to his peculiar glow. For if the hero of *Leaves of Grass* radiates a kind of primal innocence in an innocent world, it was not only because he had made that world, it was also because he had begun by making himself. Whitman is an early example, and perhaps the most striking one we have, of the self-made man, with an undeniable grandeur which is the product of his manifest sense of having been responsible for his own being—something far more compelling than the more vulgar version of the rugged individual who claims responsibility only for his own bank account.

And of course he was lonely, incomparably lonely; no anchorite was ever so lonely, since no anchorite was ever so alone. Whitman's image of the evergreen, "solitary in a wide, flat space . . . without a friend a lover near," introduced what more and more appears to be the central theme of American literature, in so far as a unique theme may be claimed for it: the theme of loneliness, dramatized in what I shall later describe as the story of *the hero in space*. The only recourse for a poet like Whitman was to fill the space by erecting a home and populating it with companions and lovers.

Whitman began in an Adamic condition which was only too effectively realized: the isolated individual, standing flush with the empty universe, a primitive moral and intellectual entity. In the behavior of a "noiseless, patient spider," Whitman found a revealing analogy:

> A noiseless, patient spider
> I mark'd, where, on a little promontory, it stood out, isolated,
> Mark'd how, to explore the vacant, vast surrounding,
> It launched forth filament, filament, filament, out of itself,
> Ever unreeling them—ever tirelessly speeding them.

"Out of itself." This is the reverse of the traditionalist attitude that, in Eliot's phrase, "home is where one starts from." Whitman acted on the hopeful conviction that the new Adam started from himself; having created himself, he must next create a home. The given in individual experience was no longer a complex of human, racial, and familial relationships; it was a self in a vacant, vast surrounding. Each simple separate person must forge his own framework anew. This was the bold, enormous venture inevitably confronted by the Adamic personality. He had to become the maker of his own conditions—if he were to have any conditions or any achieved personality at all.

There were, in any case, no conditions to *go back to*—to take upon one's self or to embody. There is in fact almost no indication at all in *Leaves of Grass* of a return or reversion, even of that recovery of childhood detected in *Walden*. Whitman begins after that recovery, as a child, seemingly self-propagated, and he is always going *forth;* one of his pleasantest poems was constructed around that figure. There is only the open road, and Whitman moves forward from the start of it. Homecoming is for the exile, the prodigal son, Adam after the expulsion, not for the new unfallen Adam in the western garden. Not even in "Passage to India" is there a note of exile, because there is no sense of sin ("Let others weep for sin"). Whitman was entirely remote from the view of man as an orphan which motivated many of the stories of Hawthorne and Melville and which underlay the characteristic adventure they narrated of the search for a father. Hawthorne, an orphan himself and the author of a book about England called *Our Old Home*, sometimes sent his heroes to Europe to look for their families; Melville dispatched his heroes to the bottom of the sea on the same mission. This was the old way of posing the problem: the way of mastering life by the recovery of home, though it might require descent to the land of the dead; but Whitman knew the secret of his paternity.

Whitman was creating a world, even though he often sounds as though he were saluting a world that had been lying in wait for him:

"Salut au monde." In one sense, he is doing just that, welcoming it, acknowledging it, reveling in its splendor and variety. His typical condition is one of acceptance and absorption; the word which almost everyone who knew him applied to his distinguishing capacity was "absorptive." He absorbed life for years; and when he contained enough, he let it go out from him again. "I . . . accept all, then reproduce all in my own forms." He takes unflagging delight in the reproductions: "Me pleased," he says in "Our Old Feuillage"; it is the "what I am." But the pleasure of seeing becomes actual only in the process of naming. It is hard to recall any particular of life and work, of men and women and animals and plants and things, of body and mind, that Whitman has not somewhere named in caressing detail. And the process of naming is for Whitman nothing less than the process of creation. This new Adam is both maker and namer; his innocent pleasure, untouched by humility, is colored by the pride of one who looks on his work and finds it good. The things that are named seem to spring into being at the sound of the word. It was through the poetic act that Whitman articulated the dominant metaphysical illusion of his day and became the creator of his own world.

We have become familiar, a century after the first edition of *Leaves of Grass*, with the notion of the poet as the magician who "orders reality" by his use of language. That notion derived originally from the epochal change—wrought chiefly by Kant and Hegel—in the relation between the human mind and the external world; a change whereby the mind "thought order into" the sensuous mass outside it instead of detecting an order externally existing. Whitman (who read Hegel and who wrote a singularly flatulent poetic reflection after doing so) adapted that principle to artistic creativity with a vigor and enthusiasm unknown before James Joyce and his associates in the twentieth century. What is implicit in every line of Whitman is the belief that the poet *projects* a world of order and meaning and identity into either a chaos or a sheer vacuum; he does not *discover* it. The poet may salute the chaos; but he creates the world.

Such a conviction contributed greatly to Whitman's ever enlarging idea of the poet as the vicar of God, as the son of God—as God himself. Those were not new labels for the artist, but they had been given fresh currency in Whitman's generation; and Whitman held to all of them more ingenuously than any other poet who ever lived. He supervised the departure of "the priests" and the arrival of the new vicar, "the divine litteratus"; he erected what he called his novel "trinitas" on the base of "the true son of God, the poet"; he offered himself as a cheerful, divine scapegoat and stage-managed "my own crucifixion." And to the extent that he fulfilled his own demands for *the* poet—as laid down in the Preface to *Leaves of Grass* and in *Democratic Vistas*— Whitman became God the Creator.

This was the mystical side of him, the side which announced itself in the fifth section of "Song of Myself," and which led to the mystical vision of a newly created totality. The vision emerges from those lyrical sweeps through the universe in the later sections of the poem: the sections in which Whitman populated and gave richness and shape to the universe by the gift of a million names. We can round out our picture of Whitman as Adam—both Adam as innocent and Adam as namer—if we distinguish his own brand of mysticism from the traditional variety. Traditional mysticism proceeds by denial and negation and culminates in the imagery of deserts and silence, where the voice and the being of God are the whole of reality. Whitman's mysticism proceeds by expansive affirmation and culminates in plenitude and huge volumes of noise. Traditional mysticism is the surrender of the ego to its creator, in an eventual escape from the limits of names; Whitman's is the expansion of the ego in the act of creation itself, naming every conceivable object as it comes from the womb.

The latter figure is justified by the very numerous references, both by Whitman and by his friends, to his "great mother-nature." We must cope with the remarkable blend in the man, whereby this Adam, who had already grown to the stature of his own maker, was not less and at the same time his own Eve, breeding the human race out of his love affair with himself. If section 5 of "Song of Myself" means anything, it means this: a miraculous intercourse between "you my soul" and "the other I am," with a world as its offspring. How the process worked in his poems can be seen by examining any one of the best of them. There Whitman skilfully brings into being the small world of the particular poem by introducing a few items one by one, linking them together by a variety of devices, running back over them time and again to reinsure their solidity and durability, adding further items and quickly forging the relations between them and the cluster already present, announcing at the end the accomplished whole and breathing over all of it the magical command *to be*.

Take, for example, "Crossing Brooklyn Ferry":

> Flood-tide below me! I see you face to face!
> Clouds of the west—sun there half an hour high—I see
> you also face to face.

The New Adam: Holmes and Whitman

Crowds of men and women attired in the usual costumes,
how curious you are to me!
On the ferry-boats the hundreds and hundreds that cross,
returning home, are more curious to me than you
suppose,
And you that shall cross from shore to shore years hence
are more to me, and more in my meditations, than you
might suppose.

This is not the song of a *trovatore*, a finder, exposing bit by bit the substance of a spectacle which is there before a spectator looks at it. It
is the song of a poet who creates his spectacle by "projecting" it as he
goes along. The flood tides, the clouds, the sun, the crowds of men
and women in the usual costumes: these exist in the instant they are
named and as they are pulled in toward one another, bound together
by a single unifying eye through the phrases which apply to them
severally ("face to face," "curious to me"). The growth of the world
is exactly indicated in the increasing length of the lines; until, in the
following stanza, Whitman can observe a "simple, compact, well-
join'd scheme." Stabilized in space, the scheme must now be given
stabilizing relations in time; Whitman goes on to announce that
"fifty years hence, others will see them as they cross, the sun half an
hour high" (the phrase had to be repeated) "a hundred years hence,
or ever so many hundred years hence, others will see them." With the
world, so to speak, a going concern, Whitman is able now to summon
new elements into existence: sea gulls, the sunlight in the water, the
haze on the hills, the schooners and sloops and ships at anchor, the
large and small steamers, and the flags of all nations. A few of the conspicuous elements are blessed and praised, in an announcement
(stanza 8) not only of their existence but now rather of the value they
impart to one another; and then, in the uninterrupted prayer of the
final stanza (stanza 9—the process covers nine stanzas, as though it
were nine months) each separate entity is named again as receiving
everlasting life through its participation in the whole:

Flow on river! flow with the flood-tide, and
ebb with the ebb-tide!
Frolic on, crested and scallop-edg'd waves!

And so on: until the mystery of incarnation has been completed.

3

The Fortunate Fall: The Elder
James and Horace Bushnell

There is in short no condition of trial which after all is
seen to be so utterly forbidding and hopeless as just this
state of Adamic innocence.

HORACE BUSHNELL, *Nature and the Supernatural* (1858)

WHITMAN'S favorite identifying word for the creatively expansive
self was "cosmos," and in the cosmos of *Leaves of Grass* hopefulness seemed to have exhausted itself in the plenitude of its own creation. It must have seemed that nothing more could be said about
novelty, innocence, and the construction of a new world; the last word
must have been uttered, especially since every word in the language
had been employed in the utterance. Yet there *was* a dialogue going
on with respect to the Adamic ideal, though Whitman remained deaf
to the other voices in it. The protective agreement of Holmes and
Lowell that the poetry of Whitman was elaborate humbug did not
carry the discussion much further, still less the strictures of the incorrigibly nostalgic or the merely prudish. But the deeper rhythms of a
genuine conversation—a fruitful exchange of insights—may be heard
in the response of a man like the elder Henry James.

When a Mrs. Caroline Tappan asked him why he, too, did not "like
Walt Whitman raise [his] barbaric yawp over the roofs of all the
houses," James tried to explain that "it is because I am not yet a
'cosmos' as that gentleman avowedly is, but only a very dim nebula,
doing its modest best, no doubt, to solidify into cosmical dimensions."
Between the nebular and the cosmic condition, James suggested, there
had to occur a grand tragic transfiguring experience that Whitman
had not sensed or even approached. Cosmoses, he thought, "are destined to a life of such surprising changes that you may say their career
is an incessant disavowal of their birth." Whitman, he hinted, had

after all not gone far enough, though he had probably tried to go too fast. James himself preferred "to be knocked about for some time yet and vastated of my natural vigor, than to commence cosmos and raise the barbaric yawp."

James was perhaps the most energetically hopeful man of his generation, with a hope, so to speak, exploding out of the tensions lying behind it. He was possessed of a transcendent cheerfulness derived from the experience and the full knowledge of tragedy. His cheerfulness was consequently less fragile and more solid than the buoyant innocence of the party of Hope. Along with a very few others, James suggested how the drama of Adam should proceed, or how, to put it differently, the young culture should finally achieve its maturity. James was convinced that the story was not yet finished.

This is to say—and it was the elder James's conscious intention—that he began his account of the representative American spiritual adventure where the professedly hopeful left off. His observations about some of them indicate as much: he referred to Emerson as his fair unfallen friend, and he decided later about Thoreau that he was "literally the most childlike, unconscious and unblushing egotist it has ever been my fortune to encounter in the ranks of manhood." The phrases build into a partial statement of James's program for Adam: for in order to enter the ranks of manhood, the individual (however fair) had to *fall*, had to pass beyond childhood in an encounter with "Evil," had to mature by virtue of the destruction of his own egotism. James's entire intellectual effort—the whole burden of what his wife and his children affectionately and vaguely called "father's ideas"—may be described as an immense salvaging of the American Adam. For unless he were salvaged, James felt, he would never be saved; and, unlike Whitman or Thoreau, James did believe that the moral problem was salvation rather than self-development.

In drawing up his definition of human experience, James frequently employed the metaphor of Adam, and even more of Adam and Eve. His immediate source appears to have been the writings of Emmanuel Swedenborg, who identified the creature prior to moral consciousness as Adam, and that consciousness itself as Eve, reading the Book of Genesis as a darkly mythic report on the psychological history of Everyman. James's relation to Swedenborg was comparable to Melville's involvement with Shakespeare; it was a private understanding rather than an influence; the Swedenborgians excommunicated James regularly. But Swedenborg's use of the Adamic figure appealed to James because he himself was committed to "creation" as the principle and secret of interpretation, so that he too returned time after time to an exegetical wrestling with the first book of the Old Testament—the creation of the world and the story of Adam.

The figure also appealed to James because he was so alert to the Adamic aspirations in the American world around him. This indeed was the world he was primarily talking about; everything he wrote was directed to the urgency of the immediate situation; and it was a daily paradox, which evidently almost never depressed him, that his devoted analyses of the spiritual condition of his readers were so rarely listened to. Reading his pages today, we cannot fail to hear behind those dialectical rumblings the unmistakable sound of a gigantic idea; but in his own time he was drowned out by the hopeful clamor, and the image he reminds us of as he thunders on is that of Mynheer Peeperkorn in *The Magic Mountain*, delivering his oration beside a waterfall.

James's vocabulary was, of course, partly to blame for the blank incomprehension which usually greeted him. One understands the embarrassment of his son William, in his long introductory essay to the *Literary Remains* of his father: "I beseech the reader . . . to listen to my stammering exposition in a very uncritical frame of mind. Do not *squeeze* the terms or the logic too hard!" The same plea should precede even the present brief statement of his notions about innocence and evil: they are close to the center of his thought, but the center is a dense enigma. Yet the very quality of James's "difficulty" helps to make him agonizingly contemporary. He was the intimate friend of Holmes, of Ellery Channing and Theodore Parker, as well as of Emerson and Thoreau; and he has left us one of the most perceptive paragraphs we have about Nathaniel Hawthorne; in several respects, nonetheless, he is closer to us than he was to them. This is not to imply that he was more important than his fellows, for it is in the frustrated violence of his inarticulateness that he most resembles us.

Looking at the hopeful ideal of the solitary innocent, James was struck (as we have been) by its vulnerability; he felt in advance the destitution of the isolated private personality. In attempting to articulate his feeling, he was confronted (as we are) by a swarm of conflicting vocabularies—rival accounts of human nature and human destiny, the religious and the psychological and all the others. For James, there were the systems of Swedenborg, Fourier, and Lamarck, as for us there are, among others, Freud, Marx, and Einstein. And it is precisely in James's attitude toward those various systems with their various symbols that we see ourselves: in his reluctance to choose among them, in his insistence that all symbols from whatever source were veiled and interchangeable metaphors, faint signs of a true fact about humanity. So by "history" he did not exactly mean history as the historians use that term; nor by "sin" and "evil" did he think to denote sin and evil as the theologians do; and "God" was not, strictly speaking, God, but humanity, though not humanity either in its customary sense.

In the eighteen fifties, when there was a revival of faith in the relation of language to reality and terms were still believed to determine something, James's language seemed to his readers to be pushing the equivocal to the point of the irresponsible. A century later, when the multiplication of languages has led to the general uselessness of any one of them, and to a public distrust of all public language as such, when we resort more and more to fables, gestures and parables, the method of the elder James may be recognized at once and has a claim on our sympathy. For he too took every collection of conventional signs as an indistinct fable. And the fable he most passionately returned to was that of the birth, death, and rebirth of the new Adam.

James looked forward with no less assurance than Emerson and Whitman to a human achievement of perfection; but the signal difference between James and his unfallen friends is indicated by his statement (in the letter about Whitman) that the perfection he had in mind was one "to which manifestly no one is born, but only *re*-born." His italics emphasized the same conviction in the sentence which followed: "We come to such states not by learning, only by *unlearning*." What had to die, what had to be unlearned, was the proposition, writ so extensively in *Leaves of Grass*, that the individual was the source of his own being. "He lived and breathed," William was to say about his father, "as one who knew he had not made himself." This was the knowledge which led him to his major principles: principles which, like the impulse behind them, were less intellectual concepts than (in William's words) "instinct and attitude, something realised at a stroke and felt like a fire in the breast." Such knowledge, moreover, was an accomplishment, gained through a kind of suffering so comprehensive that it might accurately be called a kind of death. Of his many narrations of this liberating tragedy, perhaps the most succinct occurs in *Society the Redeemed Form of Man* (1879):

The only hindrance to men's believing in God as a creator is their inability to believe in *themselves* as created. Self-consciousness, the sentiment of personality, the feeling I have of life in myself, absolute and underived from any other save in a natural way, is so subtly and powerfully atheistic, that, no

matter how loyally I may be taught to insist upon creation as a mere traditional or legendary fact, I never feel inclined personally to believe in it, save
as the fruit of some profound intellectual humiliation or hopeless inward
vexation of spirit. My inward afflatus from this cause is so great, I am conscious of such superabounding personal life, that I am satisfied, for my own
part at least, that my sense of self-hood must in some subtle exquisite way
find itself wounded to death—find itself *become death*, in fact, *the only death I
am capable of believing in*—before any genuine resuscitation is at all prac-
ticable for me.

This was the view of human development that motivated James's
repeated observation that "the first and highest service which Eve
renders Adam is to throw him out of Paradise." James regarded the
contemporary ideal of man as Adam in Paradise as adolescent rubbish;
"every man who has reached even his intellectual teens," he wrote,
"begins to suspect that life is no farce . . . that it flowers and fructifies
on the contrary out of the profoundest tragic depths"; and he trained
his most trenchant rhetoric on the Adamic figure. The heroic and win-
some hero of the idealists appeared, under the eye of the elder James,
as "a dull, somnolent, unconscious clod," as an "innocent earthling,"
as "imbecile, prosaic, unadventurous." James clung to the older ending of the story of creation, just as he continued to prefer the old
"virile" pessimistic spirit of religion to the "cuddling-up-to-God" of
the "feeble Unitarian sentimentality." In the Book of Genesis he
found an allegory of every individual's spiritual adventure, of everyone, that is, who had the energy to grow up. Growing up required the
individuating crisis which in Genesis is dramatized as the fall of Adam:
the fatal, necessary quickening within the unconscious chunk of innocence of the awareness of self.

The capital sin in the Jamesian universe was just this exclusive
self-consciousness, egotism, "proprium," or "selfhood," as he variously labeled it. This was about as far as many personalities had the
power to travel; this was, for example, the limit of Thoreau's accomplishment; it was about as far as the American culture had come: but
James watched expectantly for that "transformation-scene in human
affairs" (in his son Henry's phrase) which would affect the drama of
the culture and which might be observed in the private history of certain individuals. That transformation-scene, the second and greater
crisis in experience, led from total self-distrust to a rebirth of the personality as a *social* being: one might say, to rebirth as a citizen of the
holy and glorious city of James. The new form of man, "the redeemed
form of man," was society; only the sin made possible the rebirth;

and, for all its tragedy, it was a necessary sin, and a subject for rejoicing.

James himself had undergone the entire complex experience, from an early self-assertiveness, through the fearful evening in England in the spring of 1844 when he was smitten by "a perfectly insane and abject fear" which reduced him "from a state of firm, vigorous, joyful manhood to one of almost helpless infancy," to a far more vigorous new life dedicated to preaching his own brand of socialism. It was in the light of his own recollections that James could announce the ineluctable requirement of a tragic *fall* in such robustly hopeful accents.

He examined the alternative hypothesis, which seemed to motivate the expressions and the conduct of the Adamists. Supposing, James asked, that their dream was a true dream and that men, in America or anywhere else, were truly sinless, truly exempt from the temptation and the fall. The condition they would enjoy would in that case, however pleasant, be aimless and "horticultural"; there would be no rise and no ambition to rise to the nobler condition of genuine manhood. The inadequacy of Adamism was eloquently set forth:

In Adam, then, formed from the dust and placed in Eden, we find man's natural evolution distinctly symbolized—his purely instinctual and passional condition—as winning and innocent as infancy no doubt, but also, happily, quite as evanescent. It is his purely genetic and *premoral* state, a state of blissful infantile delight unperturbed as yet by those fierce storms of the intellect which are soon to envelope and sweep it away, but also unvisited by a single glimpse of that Divine and halcyon calm of the heart in which these hideous storms will finally rock themselves to sleep. Nothing can indeed be more remote (except in pure imagery) from distinctively *human* attributes, or from the spontaneous life of man, than this sleek and comely Adamic condition, provided it should turn out an abiding one: because man in that case would prove a mere dimpled nursling of the skies, without ever rising into the slightest Divine communion or fellowship, without ever realising a truly Divine manhood and dignity.

That paragraph (it is from *Christianity the Logic of Creation* [1857]) condenses one of the most telling critiques ever formulated of an enduring phase of the American cultural temperament. And its tone is no less revealing than its content. There was nothing in James of that inverted pride in evil that has become almost the national counterpart of the continuing claim of innocence. Someone remarked to a friend of his that James puzzled him because "if he has a preference it is for evil"; but James's response to the conventional embrace of despair was summed up in a comment on Carlyle (Carlyle who, according to James's correspondent, pronounced "his usual putrid theory of the universe" in a series of remarks "interpolated with convulsive laughter"): "Never was anything more false than this worship of sorrow by Carlyle; he has picked it up out of past history and spouts it for mere display . . . it is the merest babble." James escaped the sterilities of both sides—the arrested development of infantile innocence and the premature old age of a paralyzing absorption with sin—by seeing the moral problem in unvaryingly dramatic terms: as a process, a story, with several grand climacterics.

It was this sense of a plot in experience that gave manifest sincerity to his account of the Fall—of Adam's fall and the fall of "every son of Adam"—as essentially fortunate. "Any one with half an eye," he wrote, "can see . . . that 'Adam's fall,' as it is called, was not that stupid lapse from the divine favor which it has vulgarly been reputed to have been, but an actual rise to the normal human level." He went on: "We certainly may, if we like, continue to vote this manly act of Adam disastrous . . . but to the deathless immortal part of man . . . it is anything but disastrous. It is an every way upward step indeed, pregnant with beatific consequences. . . . And accordingly every son of Adam . . . welcomes this puny, silly death, which inwardly *is* his proper consciousness, as his inevitable and unconscious resurrection to life." James's picture of the falling and the fallen was lit up at each instant by the radiance of the *vita nuova* which the "silly death" alone made possible.

But as we read these passages, we recover some of our original regret over the perverseness of his language. It was an extraordinarily private language; in his manipulation of it, James shows us the Emersonian man, spontaneously marking great truths with no regard whatever for their diversified historical formulations. His friend Garth Wilkinson indicated an important difference between himself and James when he acknowledged his own insistent attention to history. And we are not helped by James's habit of assaulting past doctrines in terms that suggest he must be thinking about their opposites. Even his son William, not the most dependable guide to intellectual history, had to comment upon his father's remarkable ignorance of the past: an ignorance which partly prevented him from communicating his analysis of the present.

For what James had hit on by the sheer force of his speculation was a variation on a very ancient theme: the theme of the "fortunate fall." In the history of Christian theology, the theme can be traced back almost to the fourth century A.D., and its most enduring formulation came in the medieval hymn which is sung during the Holy

The Fortunate Fall: James and Bushnell

Saturday Mass.[1] The hymn is exultant; it is known, indeed, as the "Exultet"; it is the most poetic and the most transcendently hopeful answer that Christianity ever contrived to the old puzzle about the existence of evil in a world created by a benevolent God. "O felix culpa!" the hymn exclaims; "quae talem et tantum meruit habere redemptorem" ("O happy sin! to deserve so great a redeemer"). The theological implication is: that happiness may be predicated of the sin because, as a consequence of it, the world was enlarged and enlightened through the figure of the Redeemer and the joy of the Atonement. It is the imputation to the human event of the quality of the divine action. And the hymn thus paradoxically rejoices in the enforced departure of Adam from Eden: "O certe necessarium Adae peccatum"— certainly Adam's sin was necessary.

The Christian suggestion teeters on the verge of heresy, and, for all its cheerfulness, it has always made its proponents uneasy. But as a metaphor in the area of human psychology, the notion of the fortunate fall has an immense potential. It points to the necessary transforming shocks and sufferings, the experiments and errors—in short, the experience—through which maturity and identity may be arrived at. This was just the perception needed in a generation that projected as one of its major ideals the image of man as a fair unfallen Adam. The claims of newborn innocence for the individual in America inevitably elicited the response that innocence is inadequate for the full reach of human personality; that life, in James's words, "flowers and fructifies . . . out of the profoundest tragic depths." The ancient theme of the fortunate fall might have conveyed James's meaning with weight and authority.

How it might do so has been demonstrated in a later day by the extraordinarily dense little statement of dreaming Earwicker in Joyce's *Finnegans Wake:* "O foenix culprit! ex nickylow malo comes micklemassed bonum." Some of the nearly endless suggestions and combinations there are the following: that out of evil (malo), though it is related to the devil (nick) and is itself a nothingness (nickylow— *nihilo*), comes a vastness (mickle, mass) of good; a good symbolized

1. See the essay, "Milton and the Paradox of the Fortunate Fall," in Arthur O. Lovejoy, *Essays in the History of Ideas* (Baltimore, 1948). Professor Lovejoy begins by quoting some lines from *Paradise Lost* (Book XII, ll. 462 ff.), beginning with Adam's response to the Archangel Michael: "O Goodness infinite, Goodness immense! / That all this good of evil shall produce, / And evil turn to good. . . . Full of doubt I stand, / Whether I should repent me now of sin / By me done or occasioned, or rejoice / Much more that much more good thereof shall spring." Professor Lovejoy then traces the history of this paradox from the early centuries up to the writing of Milton.

by Michaelmas. Through the experience of evil, the perpetrator of the *culpa*, the culprit, is reborn like the phoenix; and thus the culprit is happy after all (*felix*).

Joyce was the very type of imagination in total communion with the whole of a many-stranded past. Henry James the elder, sharing his age's enthusiastic rejection of the past, was quite the opposite type. He had vaulted to the insight; but he lacked the language to articulate it. James had none of the dour nostalgic belief in inherited depravity; he accepted the principle that men began like Adam. But he went on to ask whether men must remain in the state of Adam—whether life had not more to offer than "this sleek and comely Adamic condition." He could not clearly and finally answer his own question: perhaps just because the insight he had seized upon was essentially dramatic and could therefore be better described in action than argued in syllogisms. The vocabulary he really needed was, one may hazard, the language of narrative literature. But James apparently never realized that something like a "fortunate fall"—explained and justified in terms much like his own—was central to the fiction of his friend Hawthorne and of Hawthorne's friend Melville. And he did not live long enough to read in his son Henry's novels a very comparable principle spelled out in extraordinary dramatic detail.

But James was a philosopher and had a philosophic prescription for the troubles of the day. "I believe," he wrote Emerson in 1843, "Jonathan Edwards redivivus in true blue would after an honest study of the philosophy that has grown up since his day make the best reconciler and critic of philosophy."

We can only dimly imagine the celestial indifference of Emerson to that sentence, which he perhaps took as some kind of misprint. No period could have seemed less hospitable to Jonathan Edwards than the age Emerson presided over. Edwards, who by 1858 had been dead for a century, was an alien figure in his own lifetime, and never more than when, in a document published in the year of his death, he undertook a defense of *The Great Christian Doctrine of Original Sin*. Edwards' statement of that doctrine had appeared bleak enough even to his contemporaries; and the hundredth anniversary of the publication was celebrated, not with demands for a revival of Edwardsean theology, but with the jaunty assurance that the whole of Edwards' machinery had finally and irrevocably broken down. This was the burden, in that year 1858, of Holmes's poem, "The Deacon's Masterpiece," in which the system of Edwards was likened to a "one-hoss shay" which collapses once and for all.

The Fortunate Fall: James and Bushnell

Nevertheless, it was in 1858 that there was printed a volume which went far to answer the prescription of the elder James: *Nature and the Supernatural*, the major work of a Hartford theologian called Horace Bushnell. Bushnell, in so far as he would be known at all, was to be known as a sort of genial Jonathan Edwards; and his book did in fact proceed from a critique of the two parties—the hopeful and the nostalgic, the idealists and the orthodox Calvinists—to a reconciliation of their conceptions of individual morality. Less splendid a rhetorician than Henry James, but a good deal steadier and better grounded, Bushnell gave the soundest analysis of his age, for those who felt that Adamism was both the pre-eminent and the most dangerous illusion in contemporary thought.

But the force of Bushnell's analysis of original sin and original innocence should be measured against the achievement of Edwards himself.

II

The theology of Edwards (1703–58) was a virile reaffirmation of the radical Protestant doctrines of the relation between God and man, grace and nature, dependence and freedom.[2] But it was a reaffirmation looking forward, not backward, rooting itself, not in the language and principles of scholasticism, but in the psychology of John Locke and the physics of Isaac Newton. Edwards took these "late improvements in philosophy," as he called them, not in order to adjust them to religious principles adhered to by everybody, but in order to restore a tough-minded body of beliefs which the hopeful of his time had long been softening and sweetening. This audacious and double-edged enterprise was what lent drama to Edwards' role: which was not only that of the tragic hero (with something like a tragic fall, when, due partly to his stubborn arrogance, he was expelled from his Northampton pulpit in 1750), but that of the mediator; it was perhaps his attempt to mediate that gave rise to the drama. Confronted by a decaying Puritanism, on the one hand, and the new theories of knowledge and of nature, on the other, Edwards accepted the stupendous assignment of revitalizing the former by the insights gained from the latter. Edwards was not trying to set the clock back, he was trying to set it right. And it is exactly in this endeavor, and in the quality and scope of it, that we may locate his enduring importance, however we judge

2. Every present and future student of Edwards must be primarily indebted, as I am, to Perry Miller's volume in the "American Men of Letters Series": *Jonathan Edwards* (New York, 1949). I have expressed my own admiration for this book in *Hudson Review*, spring, 1950, from which many of the remarks here are taken.

the arguments by which he sought to carry it out. It was the *design* of the enterprise, more than its fulfilment, that the elder James must have had in mind as he meditated on the need for an Edwards redivivus.

Edwards stood for wholeness at a moment when heresy was becoming all the fashion. His opponents, of course, won the day, and even his satellites tended to betray him. The latter, over succeeding decades, managed to preserve his system (which was really a system of tensions and balances) only by letting it congeal around a group of doctrines far less adventurous than those argued by Edwards; they introduced alternative modifications and fell to accusing one another of pantheism. They were the precursors of the party of Memory, but Edwards—like James and Bushnell—had the more flexible outlook of the *tertium quid*. The decline of Edwardseanism was due to the futile effort to combat the more appealing theories of the precursors of the party of Hope: men (like Charles Chauncy) whom Edwards coldly identified by their "talk of a prevailing innocency, good nature, industry and cheerfulness." He ironically ascribed to them the following claim: "It must be understood that there is risen up now at length, in this happy age of light and liberty, a set of men of a more free and generous turn of mind, and of a more inquisitive genius, and of better discernment."

Both these remarks occur in Edwards' last completed work, *The Great Christian Doctrine of Original Sin Defended*. Edwards did in all sincerity consider the doctrine "great," just as he could honestly regard the doctrine of God's sovereignty in "choosing whom he would to eternal life, and rejecting whom he pleased" as "exceedingly pleasant, bright and sweet"; to understand original sin was to grasp so much more of the total structure and motion of the universe, a great thing to do. As he defends it, consequently, he gives us less the impression of gloomy satisfaction in reducing a tentative sprightliness to renewed despair than of a bold extension of vision which insists upon despair as the way toward "comfort and exceeding joy." Edwards implicitly charges the view of his opponents with a lack of richness, with being content with too little: this, he suggests, is true of the document he was particularly disputing (the *Free and Candid Examination* of Edward Taylor, an English theologian), and more generally of the "free and generous men" who spoke about good nature and innocency.

One of the typical arguments of that school was that, after all, men performed more good actions than evil ones, that mankind on the whole displayed a fairly good disposition, that the emphasis on sin was therefore exaggerated. To which Edwards replied that it was like declaring a servant *good* because "he did not spit in his master's face as often as he performed acts of service," or a wife because, "although she committed adultery . . . with the slaves and scoundrels sometimes, yet she did not do this so often as she did the duties of wife." The trouble with the free and generous men, Edwards contended, was that they had not perceived the true grandeur of the question.

Hawthorne would remark that reformers were one-eyed; Edwards indicated a beam even in the eye they had. Sin itself, he kept saying with every verbal device at his disposal, was nothing else than the operation of nature apart from grace: a condition into which nature relapsed at the moment of the Fall. Man's proper role was to act in every instance out of an entire communion with God: whatever he did of himself and for himself was sinful. This was not a threat, but a sheer definition, a definition which St. Paul and St. Augustine had also attempted. God, Edwards argued, originally implanted "two kinds of principles" in man: the inferior principles, such as self-love and normal human appetites—principles collected under the word *flesh*—and the superior principles, "wherein consisted the spiritual image of God, and man's righteousness and true holiness"—which may be called *supernatural*. It was these higher principles which departed, or were withdrawn, at the Fall; what remained was "flesh without spirit." As for the principles of the lower kind, "they are like *fire* in a house; which we say is a good servant, but a bad master; very useful while kept in its place, but if left to take possession of the whole house, soon brings all to destruction." Normal human appetites are perfectly healthy when they are bound to the higher principles; turned loose on their own, they fester at once. To be satisfied merely with the natural powers was wantonly to give up the very answers to the mysteries of existence.

It is a special irony that precisely Edwards' mediating intention—his strategy of "reconciliation and criticism"—helped to defeat him in his own day. The doctrine which he defended was outdated and out of harmony with the dominant view and so increasingly unpalatable to the enlightened; and the scientific principles he urged in support of the doctrine were too far advanced for his opponents' conservative understanding.

There is irony also in the failure of Edwards' attempt to answer persuasively the already popular arguments against the "imputation" to the very whole of mankind of a sin attributable only to the race's founder. The arguments of the opposition were perhaps surprisingly like those Oliver Wendell Holmes and his colleagues were to bring forward a century later: they rested on the moral differentiation of one individual from another, and of one moment in time from another. How could the entire race, including generations not to be born for thousands of years, be involved with the behavior of Adam in Eden? In replying to the question, Edwards got into a metaphysical phase which he had thus far been able to avoid, having promised to stick to the verifiable facts, "lest any cry out *metaphysics!* as the manner of some is." But the aim of his brief metaphysical excursion was to demonstrate the substantial unity or identity of the race, in certain respects and for certain purposes. "The race," of course, taken as a progressive accumulation of individuals, comes into being bit by bit, moment by moment, year by year; but "the race" is nonetheless a meaningful phrase, and it is also true that the racial "many" exist as a unit everywhere and all the time. Indeed, its continuing existence is itself the gift of God, who is therefore fully warranted in treating the race as a unit, as something entirely present (for punitive purposes) in the one man Adam and at the instant of his fall. Edwards was chiefly expounding the justice of God's so treating the race; but it was probably his vision of the unity, the wholeness, of mankind that his readers were least inclined to share.

Nonetheless, Edwards was exploiting his view to reach an intolerably bleak conclusion. The unity he was asserting was a "oneness by virtue whereof *pollution* and *guilt* from *past* wickedness are derived," a oneness that "must account for guilt and an evil taint on any individual soul, in consequence of a crime committed twenty or forty years ago, remaining still, and even to the end of the world and for ever." A temperament working under different pressures and responding to other needs would be able to find in the fact of racial unity an assurance not so much of guilt as of comfort: an antidote to loneliness, a stimulus to self-understanding. A hundred years after the publication of *Original Sin Defended* and the death of its author, Horace Bushnell reconsidered the relation between human imperfection and the need for communion with history. Bushnell probed the resources of memory to discover an inviolable hope.

III

Bushnell was born in Litchfield, Connecticut, in 1802, resided for the major portion of his life in Hartford, where he was pastor of the North Church, and died in Hartford in 1876. His career, with a few exceptions, can be associated almost exclusively with Hartford, where he worried the theologians, won an impressive following among his congregation and became the city's first citizen, and wrote his two most important treatises: *Christian Nurture* (1847) and *Nature and the Supernatural* (1858).

What Bushnell had to say is less striking in isolation than in context. What is impressive is the dialectical power he brought to bear upon the contemporary discussion, a power which in fact helped to disclose the actual existence *of* a discussion. Bushnell saw it and helps us see it as a dialogue written in collaboration by many persons: a dialogue in which, as in a dialogue of Plato, attitudes and concepts were introduced, supported, tested, opposed, and eventually transformed. In the American dialogue too, as in a dialogue of Plato, the conception at issue has a sort of dramatic career, as though it were a surrogate for the hero of a ritual drama—something to be challenged, purged, and renewed. That analogy has added force, since the most controversial conception in Bushnell's generation was precisely the heroic image of the American as Adam. The career of that image, and the discussion it stimulated, become clear to us when we encounter a disputant who really had listened to what others had been urging. Few men in the century listened as thoughtfully and patiently as Horace Bushnell; and when the opposing sides had finished their speeches, he offered himself as mediator.

His mediating enterprise, like that of Edwards, was expansive rather than reductive. He opposed unity, as he said in another connection, which aimed "either to be huddled into a small inclosure, or to show the world how small a plot of ground we can all stand upon." He was a good dialectician, moving nimbly from the many to the one and back again, "questioning whether all parties were not in reality standing for some one side of the truth"; thus he was a bad party man and managed to vex all the parties at once. He was not surprised, having noticed in himself a "vein of comprehensiveness," when his most ambitious book, *Nature and the Supernatural*, was "pelted all around" —one periodical condemning it for forsaking "the New Haven theology," while another "makes me a ninny for being *in* the New Haven theology." But, by 1858, Bushnell was more than accustomed to such partial readings and partisan attacks.

He had understood the situation from the day of his ordination as pastor of the North Congregational Church in Hartford in 1833, when he saw himself being "inserted delicately between an acid and an alkali"—the so-called Old School and New School of New England Protestantism—"having it for [my] task to keep them apart and save [myself] from being bitten of one or devoured by the other." His strategy for escaping either disaster was nicely suggested even earlier. N. P. Willis, the poet and journalist, who knew him as an undergraduate at Yale in 1827, recalled Bushnell teaching him the proper technique for sharpening a razor, "drawing it from heel to point both ways," and thus making "the two cross frictions correct each other" —an excellent method, Willis was to think, "for making the roughness of opposite sides contribute to a mutual fine edge."[3]

Bushnell's capacity for making the cross-frictions correct each other was, of course, the measure of his ability to disturb or disappoint everyone. "We never," he insisted, "come so near to a truly well-rounded view of any truth as when it is offered paradoxically": a statement calculated to keep him in trouble. This is no doubt one of the several reasons why Bushnell has never been better known; for our intellectual and literary histories have for the most part been written by members of one or the other of the major parties—Hope or Memory—and Bushnell incorrigibly employed each to extend its opposite.

If the nostalgic were listening, he had hard words for them: "No man was ever inspired through his memory. The eye of genius is not behind. Nor was there ever a truly great man, whose ideal was in the past. The offal of history is good enough for worms and monks, but it will not feed a living man. Power moves in the direction of hope." That was delivered at Yale in 1843, by the man already known to have been seduced, like the infidels at Concord, by Coleridge's *Aids to Reflection* and by the suspect German theologian, Schleiermacher. He was capable of declaring, too, in the midst of his colleagues' most strenuous scholastic term-splitting that "poetry is the real and true state of man," and to produce some of his best points by quoting, not from Calvin, but from Shakespeare, and setting them forth, not in syllogisms, but in metaphors. When he urged his congregation to "embrace the destiny of hope," it might have been Emerson speaking. But in speaking *about* Emerson, he had quite another text:

Who is a finer master of English than Mr. Emerson? Who offers fresher thoughts, in shapes of beauty more fascinating? Intoxicated by his brilliant creations, the reader thinks, for the time that he is getting inspired. And yet, when he has closed the essay or the volume, he is surprised to find—who has ever failed to notice it?—that he is disabled instead, disempowered, reduced

3. For these and other anecdotes see Theodore T. Munger, *Horace Bushnell* (Boston, 1900), also the book by his daughter, Mary Bushnell Cheney, *Life and Letters of Horace Bushnell* (New York, 1880). Among the very few studies of Bushnell, I would mention the brief analysis of his theory of language, in *Symbolism and American Literature* by Charles Feidelson (Chicago, 1952).

in tone. He has no great thought or purpose in him; and the force or capacity for it seems to be gone. Surely, it is a wonderfully clear atmosphere that he is in, and yet it is somehow mephitic.

Bushnell's situation was not unlike that of Jonathan Edwards, except that by 1850 the free and generous spirit (the professors of "innocency") was greatly in the ascendance and found its only opposition in an immobile orthodoxy. Bushnell composed a penetrating critique of both parties, taking into account the "late improvements in philosophy" over the century since the death of Edwards and proposing a new scheme for reconciliation. His two most interesting books dovetail skilfully. In *Christian Nurture* he exposed the defects of orthodoxy, with asides to remind the reader of the contrasted dangers of simple hopefulness. *Nature and the Supernatural* examined the inadequacies of idealism, with footnotes on the chilliness of orthodoxy.

Bushnell's purpose was to show that the human personality fulfilled itself only through a classic drama of a fall and a regeneration, and that regeneration depended crucially on an organized and living tradition. Orthodoxy insisted so heavily on the Fall that it held the creature wholly passive in the process of redemption. Redemption, for the orthodox, was effected by a single shattering blast from heaven; nature was saved by being destroyed, and grace did everything. But if the orthodox gave too little credit to nature, the party of Hope gave it too much. The latter denied the Fall altogether, and so saw no need for those "organic powers"—family, society, church—which might co-operate in the regeneration of human nature. The two parties connived at a radical error: they took "every man as if he existed alone," without any "vital connection with the ties and causes, and forms, and habits, which constitute the frame of our history." One party explored the purgatorial terror of the human condition; the other rejoiced in the self-expansion which that condition allowed. Orthodox and idealist alike thrust forth the individual moral nature to stand alone beneath the silent spaces: to be frightened by them, like Pascal, or to vanish lovingly into them, like Emerson. It is not easy to name a contemporary of Horace Bushnell who so shrewdly located the major American theme of loneliness at the crossroads of the two antithetical strains of the culture.

Bushnell's critique of the Edwardsean view admitted its original merit in displacing "an era of dead formality" and in bringing in "the demand of a truly supernatural experience." But the nature of that experience, Bushnell felt, was nothing more than "a miraculous epidemic, a fireball shot from the moon," and entirely on the outside of life. He was quick, however, to distinguish his doctrine of "nurture" from the current enthusiasms for self-culture, the program of those "many who assume the radical goodness of human nature" and whose program, as Bushnell saw it, resembled a mere "vegetable process," the limp opposite extreme to Edwardseanism. Even if a child "was born as clear of natural prejudice or damage as Adam before his sin," Bushnell remarked, "spiritual education . . . would still involve an experiment of evil, therefore a fall and a bondage under the laws of evil." The drama of human life "involves a struggle with evil, a fall and a rescue"; maturity involved "a double experience . . . the bitterness of evil and the worth of good."

Those remarks are taken from *Christian Nurture*, a book aimed principally at the supernaturalists and concerned with the *tactics* of regeneration: that is, with the way in which "history" could contribute to the process, and nature collaborate with grace. The judgment of Adamism it briefly suggests was expanded throughout the five hundred pages of *Nature and the Supernatural*, for this latter volume was aimed at the most innocently hopeful and was thus concerned less with the tactics than with the factual necessity of redemption. Bushnell explored the whole body of what he called "naturalistic literature," ancient and modern—all literature in which "nothing supernatural is to be admitted," however lofty the sentiments or idealistic the doctrine. The naturalistic tradition had culminated, Bushnell thought, in mid-nineteenth-century America with the publication of Emerson's little book *Nature*. This was its perennial premise: "Redemption itself, considered as a plan to raise man out of thraldom under the corrupted action of nature . . . is a fiction. There is no such thraldom, no such deliverance."

Rightly identifying that premise as the characteristic one of the day, Bushnell set out to refute it: to expose innocence as a dangerous fiction, sin and the consequent need for rebirth as the vital facts. The first half of *Nature and the Supernatural* comprises a dialectical scrutiny of the many varieties of currently hopeful opinion, examined within a carefully established framework. Bushnell's framework included an elaborated distinction between the natural and the supernatural, between what Bushnell called "things" and what he called "powers," between necessity and freedom, evolution and regeneration. His terms suggest how much use he was making of "the philosophy that has grown up since [Edwards'] day": Bushnell was applying a post-Kantian vocabulary to problems he had grasped with the assistance of Coleridge.

The Fortunate Fall: James and Bushnell

But "sin" became meaningful, Bushnell argued, only within such a framework. The conception of supernature was essential to the definition of sin: "the very sin of the sin is that it is against God." And since sin is a free lapse from the supernatural, only a power could act sinfully—only a free agent, as against a "thing" controlled by necessity. Naturally speaking—and everyone outside the orthodox camp *was* speaking naturally—there was and could be no such thing as sin. From his larger viewpoint, Bushnell found three fatal flaws in the "naturalistic" outlook which propagated the ideal of human sinlessness: it made life uninteresting; it was false; it was pragmatically dangerous.

The denial of the Fall—the hopeful insisted—was supposed to make life more cheerful; Bushnell was sure it succeeded only in making it duller. It was a denial of that human potential for evil which had made life adventurous precisely by making genuine moral crisis possible. It was a failure to understand tragedy. The sustained American aversion for tragedy, then as now, was based upon an obscure connection between tragedy and low spirits. Bushnell, pointing to the most enduring tragic dramas and tragic heroes, suggested that tragedy, by posing a real opposition and a real choice in human experience, was an affirmation of human dignity, and fundamentally optimistic. Adamism, Bushnell argued, by dissolving the opposition or absorbing it into a purely natural scheme, rendered life flat, colorless, undramatic, and boring.

Like Jonathan Edwards, Bushnell brought forward a little of the enormous evidence, in the recurring disorders of the world, for a radically imperfect human nature. The facts, of course, had to be admitted by anyone entering the discussion; but they had been explained in a number of ways, some of them contradictory but all tending to protect the individual from any imputation of inherent and inherited evil. Fourier, for example, had traced all wrongdoing to faultily constructed societies and had recommended not more regenerative pressure but more political science. Strauss, the German theologian who was enjoying a brief popularity among the hopeful, had diagnosed the trouble as springing from individual mistakes; the race was absolved, the atmosphere was cleared, and an intensive course of progressive education was proposed. Bushnell was not hostile either to political science or to improvements in education; he had preached about the former and composed *Christian Nurture* in support of the latter. But he retained enough of the Edwardsean logic to believe that the causes indicated were hardly adequate to the cosmic, "steady" effects admitted; the causes were not to be dismissed lightly, but they were derivative, stemming from a single and a steady source.

At this point Bushnell knew very well that he was confronted by the peculiarly dynamic American brand of Adamism: by the cumulative force of the living legend. For the party of Hope was often willing to grant the gloomy picture of the world and its history; it did so all the more cheerfully, exactly because it lent excitement to its claim that the New World was emancipated from the Old. It had long been a pleasure, in the fresh air of the new garden, to look across at a stale, corrupt, and dying Europe and to count up its burdens, as Noah Webster had done, contending that "in that country, laws are perverted, manners are licentious, literature is declining and human nature is debased." The very motive force of the native enthusiasm was the assumption that, in Webster's next phrase, "American glory begins at the dawn"; that the individual in America was untouched by history and had somehow been created immediately, and not mediately or by way of the whole sorry race. He was not the most recent descendant of Adam, but rather a new Adam.

Bushnell took note of these claims and regarded them with a wise and skeptical eye. In the first place, he reasoned, the probable condition of the hypothetical first Adam, which the hopeful were so bent on rehearsing, was not at all so enviable as had been supposed. The condition was without doubt an uncorrupted one, pure and innocent and indescribably new. But it was, at the same time, an unsatisfactory condition, a "condition privative," lacking in the vast store of knowledge accumulated by man in the course of very long experience, happy and unhappy.

The first Adam must have been limited in his nature by the "necessary defect of knowledge and consequent weakness of a free person or a power considered as having just begun to be"; and anyone who pretended to himself that he had just begun to be would be no less defective, no less feeble. What Adam could not have known were those insights "as are gotten historically, one by one, and one after another, under conditions of time." Emerson, who believed the conditions of time to be transparently unreal, would have answered at once that the only knowledge worth having existed out of time altogether; it had, he would have said, nothing to do with history and was as instantly available to Adam as to anyone else, to the boy reading in the corner, or to Horace Bushnell. Bushnell admired the eternal laws almost as much as Emerson, but he did not follow the assumption that a mere glimpse of those laws made men virtuous. "The eternal law of justice makes no one just, that of truth, no one true," Bushnell wrote, anti-Platonically. What those timeless principles required, in order to make them humanly effective, was "a drill, in the field of experience."

If the condition of innocent newness was wilfully devoid of understanding, it was likewise woefully exposed to disaster. Supposing men were created "like so many Adams . . . to exist independently and apart from all reproductive arrangements." Would their no doubt perfectly uncorrupted character be strong enough to hold its own in the world as it was constituted? For the real world was already fouled and disordered by the actions of the countless generations of men. It must therefore be "a frame of being wholly inappropriate to their new-created innocence." In that atypical awkward phrase, Bushnell pointed to the dramatic situation which Hawthorne, Melville, and the younger Henry James would erect into a dominant *mis-en-scène* of so many of their narratives: the helplessness of the innocent in a world infected by ancient evil, the helplessness of the innocent abroad.

Innocence would inevitably be struck down by the actual forces of such a world; and the very illusion which precipitated the catastrophe would work against recovery. The plight of the fallen innocent was sketched by Bushnell in merciless language: "Self-centered now, every man in his sin, and having no ligature of race and family affection to bind them together, the selfishness of their fall would be unqualified, softened by no mitigations. . . . Society there is none. Law is impossible. Society and law suppose conditions of organic unity. There is in short no condition of trial which after all is seen to be so utterly forbidding and hopeless as just this state of Adamic innocence." Thus the dreary destiny of the individual behaving as though he were created at a new first moment of time; thus the ultimate cheerlessness of the ambition of primal purity. Bushnell moved on rapidly to explain that the hypothesis was luckily false, that the actual state of affairs was a great deal more hopeful.

Fortunately, as it turned out, there had been a fall. Happily, there had been a sin. And, consequently, there had followed the long story of educative experience. All of that experience was at the disposal of each new member of the race. The new member inherited the corruption, but he likewise shared in the wisdom. If he could never regain Adam's radical innocence, he need never regress to Adam's ignorance. Conscience was, after all, higher than innocence. Moral history and the energies of tradition gave Bushnell grounds for a more substantial hope.

II
The Narrative Image

The master-at-arms was perhaps the only man in the ship intellectually capable of adequately appreciating the moral phenomenon presented in Billy Budd. And the insight but intensified his passion, which assuming various secret forms within him, at times assumed that of cynic disdain—disdain of innocence—to be nothing but innocent! Yet in an aesthetic way he saw the charm of it, the courageous free-and-easy temper of it, and fain would have shared it, but he despaired of it.

HERMAN MELVILLE, *Billy Budd*

4

The Fable of the Critics

The admirers of poetry, then, may give up the ancient
mythology without a sigh. Its departure has left us what is
better than all it has taken away; left us the creatures
and things of God's universe.

WILLIAM CULLEN BRYANT
"Lectures on Poetry" (1825)

THE hopeful were ready to support and anxious to illustrate the
proposition in Emerson's *The Poet* (1844) that "the man is only
half himself, the other half is his expression." An inseparable half of
the hopeful program—along with the renovation of the man—was the
refreshment of the word: so that it might utter the Adamic secret and
contribute thereby to the Adamic career. Over the first half of the
century there was a great deal of confused and repetitious talk about
a "new literature," a "national literature." But the voices, discordant
as they were, held a note of understandable urgency: for there was
much at stake. It was not merely a matter of prestige; poets and
novelists were not merely being summoned, in response to jibes from
abroad, to enlarge the national supply of the beautiful. The new literature was to be a reflection in language of the novel and healthy facts
of immediate life. It was to be a poetic equivalent of the life for which
it would also be a revelation, providing, like *the* Revelation, some clues
by which to plot a course of actual conduct.

In the critical probings of the hopeful, we may recognize a favorite
undertaking of the present generation: the quest for myth, as it is
called. But the myth being sought for was a sort of antimythic myth.
The critics—in Arnold's sense of those who prepared the ground for
creative artists—no doubt did call upon native writers to construct
imaginative statements about the new world and disclose that world's
transcendent meaning. To this extent there was a conscious search
for myth. But as the world and its representative hero were fresh and

underivative, so also was to be the account of them. Artists were forbidden to define their subject by analogies or recurrences; our Joyce, our Eliot, even our Yeats, would have been outlawed. In the new earthly paradise, a cleansing of the memory was prerequisite to the imaginative spokesman.

The other manner of proceeding may be represented by James Russell Lowell, who even in his jauntiest days, when he was hot from Harvard, shared the European habit of defining the present by noting its affinity with some portion of the past: of finding release for energies stifled by one tradition in the liberating life of another. It was Lowell who made the most of the historic claim that the true predecessor of the Yankee was not the Augustan Englishman, but the Jacobean; and Lowell's invocation of a fresh and underivative literature was a command to his countrymen that they "become my new race of more practical Greeks." This is the more familiar strategy of renaissance. It was exactly the strategy of that group in the European Renaissance that most resembled the party of Hope: the French poets calling themselves "The Pléiade." Those colleagues of Pierre Ronsard, "signing off" from a traditional church and championing a national literature concerned with the natural man, reverted for aid, almost as a matter of course, to the imitable masterpieces of Greece and Rome. Du Bellay's *Deffense et illustration de la langue francoyse*, the sixteenth-century French version of *The American Scholar*, compiled check lists of ancient themes, genres, and even verbal devices for the aspiring native poet. And when neoclassicism had had its long day, the strategy proposed next (in an essay by Stendhal) was another backward shift of allegiance, from Racine to Shakespeare.

Emerson, of course, in his dedicated effort to extend the horizon of his provincial listeners, spoke on many occasions of the value of the books of the past. But it turned out, under pressure, to be a pretty limited value, discoverable almost entirely on the level of talent and of "the understanding," a minor solace during "the humble Junes and Novembers of the soul," and not essential to the creative spirit. His most resonant advice to the American scholar, concluding the lecture bearing that name, was that he had "listened too long to the courtly muses of Europe" and that it was high time to listen now to the new and natural music of the new continent. These were the lines in the address that won it the title of the "declaration of literary independence." But that very phrase suggests that it was independence which was being declared, and not alternative new cultural alliances.

The instinct of the hopeful in so posing the creative problem may well have been fundamentally sound. Foreign observers, anyhow, from Tocqueville to Auden have regularly reminded us that the European practice of apprenticeship and imitation in the arts—so right and necessary *for* the European—can be fatal in this country. In America, they tell us, any work that tries to draw nourishment from any other is apt to choke to death in the process, though that reminder is itself a foreign judgment, and behind it there stirs a familiar anxiety lest we spoil for Europeans the image they comfortably possess of us. This much is obvious: that the serviceable relation between the individual talent in America and the European tradition is extremely delicate and painfully ambiguous.

And the historic case is that the search for forms and fables by the party of Hope began with the assumption that new ones would have to be devised, after the old ones had all been discarded. "The old sources of intellectual excitement seem to be well-nigh exhausted." This—in the words of the editor of the first competent anthology of American prose (1847)—was the dominant attitude. And this—in Emerson's graceful variation on the prevalent figure: "Adam in the garden, I am to new-name all the beasts of the fields and all the gods in the sky."

II

The task of the new Adam as poet was at once grandiose and simple. According to one listener (in 1849), this is what the hopeful seemed to be saying: "We want a national literature commensurate with our mountains and rivers. . . . We want a national epic that shall correspond to the size of the country. . . . We want a national drama in which scope shall be given to our gigantic ideas and to the unparalleled activity of our people. . . . In a word, we want a national literature altogether shaggy and unshorn, that shall shake the earth, like a herd of buffaloes thundering over the prairies."

The speaker is not Walt Whitman, though the speech is a fair caricature by anticipation of some of the sentences in the Preface to *Leaves of Grass*. The speaker is Longfellow; or rather, it is a person named Hathaway in Longfellow's novel *Kavanagh*. And his interlocutor—a Mr. Churchill—also anticipates one of the famous responses to Whitman, when he reminds Hathaway that "a man will not necessarily be a great poet because he lives near a great mountain."[1] In the chapter-long exchange between the two men—the brash

1. Cf. Carlyle's remark that Whitman thought he was a big man because he lived in a big country.

spokesman for an "honest" and uninhibited nationalistic magazine and the genteel schoolmaster who is all his life to be on the verge of composing a romance in the great tradition—Longfellow has given us an image of the typical failure of communication between the literary representatives of hope and memory.

He has also, very likely, given us an image of the contradictory tendencies he noticed in himself. For if Churchill is no doubt closer to the familiar Longfellow, Hathaway was a part of him too, and so was the novel's hero, young Kavanagh, who was busy at that moment learning from the old masters in Italy that great art consists in the imaginative heightening of the immediate. These were the conflicting elements in the emergent culture, and we may expect to find symptoms of each of them even in so nostalgic a writer as Longfellow; all the elements were at work in *Hiawatha*. This may be why Longfellow (surprisingly, as the story is usually told) remained friendly toward Margaret Fuller, even after she reduced him to the status of a minor figure, on the grounds that "he sees life through the windows of literature"; for this is exactly what Kavanagh returns to say about Churchill. *Kavanagh* is in some small degree confessional, as well as satiric; there is a little wistful sincerity in the otherwise clownish exaggeration of the nationalist's table-thumping conclusion: "We do not want art and refinement. We want genius—untutored, wild, original, free."

No one outside Longfellow's novel was talking quite like that— unless it was Bronson Alcott, who talked as unguardedly as the English language permitted. But Hathaway was merely a distortion and an extension of many a hopeful critic; and if he sounds a trifle ridiculous, it is because his raucous voice has lost the bold seriousness of much of what actually *was* being said. Emerson's appeal, for example, to the giant striding down from "unhandselled savage nature," to destroy the old culture and to build the new, was similar in kind to Hathaway's view; and so was the question explored at the first meetings of the transcendentalists: why "on this titanic continent, where nature was so grand, genius should be so tame." Longfellow may have had in mind the unmodulated lines of Lowell, published the year before (1848), in an all-out attack upon derivative writing launched at the peak of Lowell's hopefulness:

> You steal Englishmen's books and think Englishmen's thoughts,
> With their salt on her tail, your wild eagle is caught:
> Your literature suits its each whisper and motion
> To what will be thought of it over the ocean. . . .
> Forget Europe wholly, your veins throb with blood,
> To which the dull current in hers is but mud.

The Fable of the Critics

Lowell's program (he was to change his mind in a couple of years) for a total replacement of memory by hope—"Forget Europe wholly"—had been enunciated for more than half a century, though it had accumulated nervous intensity over the years. Similar sentiments had been advanced endlessly on lecture platforms and in the little magazines; they reached summits of pride, anger, and hope in Fourth of July orations. It was estimated somewhat drily, by Duyckinck's moderate *Literary World* (in 1847), that if all the documents relating to "this prolific text . . . of a native authorship" were collected, they would constitute "a very respectable library." Lowell, in his *Fable for Critics* the following year, only contrived a sprightly digest of that library.

The critical noise, however, was not all denial and protest; the content of the new song was being hinted at simultaneously. A typical summary and message of hope may be drawn from the editorial introduction to Rufus Griswold's anthology, *The Prose Writers of America* (1847). Griswold was the very type of insecure and uncreative hanger-on in the literary world; even his contemporaries recoiled from the shrillness of his support of novelty; Duyckinck commented that "the thought [of nationality in literature] seems to have entered and taken possession of [Griswold's] mind with the force of monomania." Griswold tried to dissociate himself from the "absurd notion . . . that we are to create an entirely new literature." "The question between us and other nations," he went on, "is not who shall most completely discard the past, but who shall make the best use of it." His summary, however, was an inventory of themes to be discarded: "Courage, such as is celebrated by the old poets and romancers, is happily in disrepute; Religion, as it has commonly appeared in the more elegant forms of literature, has not been of a sort that ennobles man or pleases God; and Ambition, for the most part, has been of a more grovelling kind than may be looked for under the new forms of society." Under the new forms, Griswold wound up, the principle of letters, as of life, religion, and politics, was to be—and his volume illustrated the theme—"Peace on earth and good will to men."

The ease of the formula reflected the assurance Griswold shared with the hopeful that the period of protest was over, the creative moment at hand. Yet in a peculiarly exasperating paradox, the very abundance of peace and good will in the new Eden seemed to be making creative activity almost impossible. The contention long had been that the new scene had been all too thoroughly cleansed of the old evils and the literature they produced. Without either the evils or the traditions, the new poet was having a hard time—as hard, we may judge in retrospect, as the new Adam striving to grow up.

III

American critics who have worried the question of the adequacy of American life for art have regularly looked at the same evidence and returned the same verdicts. To take only a single instance: a relatively early exchange in the *North American Review* between Edward Tyrell Channing (in 1819) and William Howard Gardiner (in 1822). Their subject was the possibility of fiction in the new country; but what they had to say was relevant to narrative in the broadest sense, and it partook of the same disquiet and the same hope that others would bring to the general discussion of "poetry." It is narrative or story that primarily concerns us: the dramatic value of the Adamic vision.

Edward Tyrell Channing expressed his doubts about fiction in America on the occasion of a review of William Dunlap's biography of Charles Brockden Brown. Channing (1790–1856) may be reckoned as hovering on the fringe of the hopeful—as much, anyhow, as his older brother, Dr. William Ellery.[2] It was Edward Tyrell Channing who, as Boylston Professor of Rhetoric and Oratory at Harvard, introduced Emerson, Thoreau, Parkman, and Holmes to an eloquence more supple and more suited to the temper of the day than the conventional flourishes he made a point of rejecting in his inaugural discourse (1819). Channing's own style had little of the sense of urgency which would kindle the rhetoric of Thoreau and Emerson; but he was a mildly resolute guide to new directions; and his reservations about fiction did not arise from any nostalgic regret over the foreseeable drift of contemporary society.

In Brockden Brown, Channing acknowledged a novelist of power and ingenuity, and for the sake of those qualities he was willing to put up with Brown's taste for the bizarre—with the combustion and ventriloquism of *Wieland* and the assorted somnambulisms of *Edgar Huntly*. In view of Brown's talents, Channing wanted to know why, only a decade after his death, he was already "so far from being a popular writer." He decided that it was because Brown had tried to get his effects out of native materials. And this led Channing to explore the hypothetical reasons why the novel might not ever be born

2. William Ellery Channing (1780–1842), the so-called "apostle" of Unitarianism, also had his say on the declaration of American literary independence in *Remarks on American Literature* (1830), published in "Old South Leaflets," Vol. VI. Dr. Channing rested his belief in a national literature on religious grounds.

The Fable of the Critics

in this country. A century later, Lionel Trilling explored in much the same way the hypothetical reasons why the novel might finally be dead.[3] The reasons tendered for both speculations are suggestively close and provocatively opposite.

The difficulty, Channing thought, lay partly in the nature of actual experience; but it lay even more in the *sense* of experience in the minds of readers—in the characteristic expectancy about the condition and behavior of men in the New World. Channing reflected on the absence of "romantic associations" in the American mind; the phrase had a technical origin in Scottish aesthetics, but it stood for what would later be called the "tragic sensibility." "The difficulty of succeeding in Brown's kind of fiction," wrote Channing, was due "not to the entire absence of romantic incident, situation and characters, but . . . to the want in his reader of romantic associations with the scenes and persons he must set before us." Romance for Channing was closely allied to darkness. What he regretted was the lack of the sense of darkness in the imagination of readers: moral darkness, and not merely the darkness of dungeons and pits. Americans, he felt, were unable to recognize, in the dungeons they read about, an image of spiritual imprisonment which a man might experience in the Hudson Valley or on the banks of the Schuylkill. Americans, Channing observed, did not like to think about "the terrible power, dark purposes and inextricable toils of the contriver." For, as Channing went on in an especially luminous sentence: "The actions we esteem great or are prepared to witness and encourage, are the useful rather than the heroic, such as tend to make society happier, not such as disturb or darken it." In American eyes, life appeared to be fresh and flourishing, unincrusted by history and undistracted by doubts: "the laboring and the happy are seen everywhere and not a corner or a recess is secret."

Though Channing underestimated the continuing pull of Puritanism as well as the steady attraction of the Gothic, there were examples enough to substantiate his main thesis: among them, Emerson's uneasy failure to make any sense of Hawthorne's stories and the noisy misunderstanding of *Moby-Dick*. The Adamic temper was usually not satisfied by such dark and desperate adventures. But alongside Channing's apprehensions of 1819 we may place the suggestion made in the mid-twentieth century by Lionel Trilling that the novel may be dead—not because of an excess of peace, good will, happiness, and innocence, but because the image of evil is so overpow-

3. "Art and Fortune," in *The Liberal Imagination* (New York, 1950).

eringly at work in our affairs that it has crowded every other image out of our vision. The imitation of an action (as Aristotle defined dramatic poetry) is an unrewarding undertaking whether life reveals too much good will or too much evil; for in the former case, action is unnecessary; in the latter, it becomes impossible.

Channing pursued his inquiry to ask about the chances for fiction devoted to the society as it actually existed, the kind of fiction "which makes the fable subservient to the developing of national character, or of the manners, usages, prejudices and conditions of particular classes," and takes as its purpose "to present what exists." Channing felt that if romantic fiction would probably not get very far because of a lack of shadows, the novel of manners was equally improbable because Americans did not yet have any. Romance stumbled over hope and innocence, realism was rebuffed by novelty.

Channing wanted to be able to say, as Scott Fitzgerald *could* say, that the very rich were different from everyone else; but he had to admit that, up to date, they were only richer; they manifested none "of the exclusive spirit of an established order." This was to be the judgment of Henry James and a reason for his departure to the ar-tistically useful exclusiveness of European circles. Lionel Trilling makes the same point, suggesting that the class distinctions which Fitzgerald was able to exploit did not survive the financial disaster of 1929. Channing, in 1819, thought it possible that the rich could in time become rich and strange and impure enough to be identifiable; but certainly they were not so yet. And as to the lower classes, they were merely the less rich. There were those sensible and industrious and indistinguishable men of whom he said that "to visit in their own home would please us more than to read of them in a novel." And, finally, there were the simply queer: those whose peculiarity "would not be found in character so much as in vulgarity of manners and narrowness of opinion."

The sharpness of Channing's perception was, here as elsewhere, to some extent limited by the conventional terms of his discussion. He was quite right in supposing that the American scene was deficient in materials for an eighteenth-century English or Continental novel; he was wrong in suggesting that the scene contained no story at all. What his analysis reveals is not the lack of tension in the new society but a special kind of tension. It was a tension—and Channing unknowingly makes us see it—between the eccentric, on the one hand, and the un-differentiated lump of solid citizenry, on the other: the very stuff of Sherwood Anderson's poignant tales of the "grotesques." And it would not require much development or shuffling of the elements for that tension to assume the more impressive shape of the one distinctly American narrative theme: that of the solitary hero and his moral engagement with the alien tribe. Such was to be the enduring fable of the American Adam.

IV

It was toward that theme that W. H. Gardiner, in a fumbling way, directed a reply to Channing, in an essay based on a review of the recently published novel by Cooper, *The Spy* (1821). Gardiner (1797–1872) is not remembered at all, except by very close students of the life of his friend William Prescott, the historian. But from Gardiner's few articles it seems that he was the most meticulous commentator on fiction before Poe. Like Poe, Gardiner was tireless in exposing errors in diction or slovenliness of narrative technique. Unlike Poe, however, Gardiner's interest was principally in the creation of character, and not with the perfectly fulfilled fable. Faults of diction were failures in the presentation of persons, not breaches in a total design. And so, despite pages of minute strictures, he was very heartily disposed in favor of James Cooper (who would not adopt the middle name Fenimore for another five years); for, even in his second novel, Cooper appeared to be vindicating American society for the artist, by finding in it the prototypes for living and memorable fictitious characters.

Gardiner began his response to Channing by granting one of the latter's premises: that "the power of creating interest in a work of fiction, so far as it arises from the development of character, lies in this generalising principle which substitutes classes for individuals." But he flatly denied Channing's charge that America, having no classes, could provide no such individuals. In America, Gardiner boasted, there could be found "a greater variety of specific characters" than anywhere else in the world, and he illustrated the claim by listing a number of fruitful possibilities, in a passage less alive and sweeping but not much less cogent than the lines (in *The Poet*) in which Emerson paraded before readers and writers the teeming ingredients for a great new poetry ("Our log-rolling, our stumps and their politics, our fisheries, our Negroes and Indians . . . the northern trade, the southern planting, the western clearing," etc.).

Here are some of Gardiner's potential "characters": "the high-minded vainglorious Virginian, living on his plantation in baronial estate"; "the active, enterprising moneygetting merchant of the East"; "the Connecticut pedlar . . . vending his *notions* at the very

ends of the earth"; "the long shaggy boatman 'clear from Kentuck' "
who traverses the Mississippi or the Ohio; "the Dutch burgomaster";
"the white savage who roams over the remote hunting tracts of the
West"; "the red native of the wilderness that crosses him in his path."
It would be interesting to support that list and Gardiner's faith in the
value of American life for art, by mentioning the works of fiction that
since have centered on the adventures of one or another of the types
suggested.[4]

But partly because of his subordination of action to character,
Gardiner did not emphasize one recurrent aspect of these characters
which we, today, are bound to notice: that is, the number of them who
are outside society or detached from it. His peddler, his boatman, his
white hunter, and his red Indian are essentially solitary individuals.
Gardiner sees them in such settings as the East, "the ends of the
earth," the wilderness; but he does not attempt to outline the representative experience in which any one of them might be caught up
—in which character might have the opportunity to announce itself.

That was to be the very essence of the problem of American fiction:
the invention of a story or plot imitating, as plots traditionally do, a
genuine action. And since action, in this context, is the name we give
to significant psychological or moral change, the problem can be stated
thus: What kind of change is possible for the solitary figure surrounded
by space? What is the imaginable *career* of Whitman's live oak? Or
how—it is the same question—can character be brought into being
and presented when the character is not primarily conceived as the
perfection of widely shared qualities, good or bad, but rather as something propelled by lonely, personal, and self-generated energy? In so
far as American writers have solved these problems, we have had an
authentic American fiction: a fiction which passes the condition of
man through the perspective of a new society's potent solitude.

4. We have, for instance, been given a broad choice among southern barons, by
novelists from Simms to Faulkner and Robert Penn Warren; Dreiser has most effectively dramatized the money-getting hero in his chronicles of Frank Cowperwood. Cooper's
spy himself, Harvey Birch, was the first of the peddlers, and the career of the later
peddlers, or traveling salesmen, has been traced by writers as different as Eudora Welty
and Arthur Miller. The shaggy boatman was already moving into legend, as Gardiner
wrote, in the form of Mike Fink (died 1823?), while his image lies close beneath the
surface of *Huckleberry Finn* and turns up again, maddened, in "the shaggy old whale-
hunter" Ahab. The white savage and the red native were to battle their way through a
whole series of novels, Cooper's tales of Natty Bumppo and Robert Montgomery Bird's
Nick of the Woods (1837) being among the most readable of them—and Faulkner has
added his own curious and private history of their relations in his saga of the Chicasaw
Indians and the McCaslin family.

V

Cooper himself, by no means so optimistic about the native resources for fiction as his admiring critic Gardiner, gave back one kind of answer to this question. In language highly reminiscent of Channing and anticipative of Henry James, he observed the absence of materials in the New World ("no annals . . . no manners . . . no obscure fictions . . . no gross and hardy offences") and noted that the few limited successes to that date (1831) were derived, not from the image of individuals in conflict, but from an engagement of "the universal laws of nature." A few writers "have succeeded," he wrote, "precisely in proportion as they have been most general in their application." Cooper was emphasizing the difficulties as a way of gaining praise for any American writer who managed to get by them; it was so much easier to turn the trick in Europe.

It was possible, however, to rejoice in the empty blankness of the American scene as the ideal condition for new writers: just as the ethical commentators could sometimes rejoice in the nonhistoric morning blankness of the moral atmosphere. Such was the happy argument of William Cullen Bryant, lecturing in 1825 at the New York Athenaeum on "Poetry in Its Relation to Our Age and Country." After rehearsing the complaints of the faithless critics—"Our country is described as peculiarly barren of the materials of poetry"—Bryant went on to admit as a matter for good cheer that "this is not an age to give birth to new superstitions, but to explode and root out old." The admirers of poetry, he counseled, could give up the ancient myths without a sigh; for what remained was nothing less than life itself: "men and women . . . the creatures and things of God's universe." It was a response suggestively close in spirit to that given by Howells in the face of Henry James's inventory of American deficiencies for the writer.[5]

Bryant felt that the new literature could get along well enough not only without the ancient mythology, but without any mythology at all; the new myth would be devoid of myth. Nor was he alarmed at the thought of poetry dealing with "the universal laws of nature"; he was sure that those laws were the new Adam's closest neighbors. "Let the fountain tell me," he intoned, "of the flocks that have drunk at it . . . let it speak of youth and health and purity and gladness . . . let it murmur of the invisible goodness that fills and feeds its reservoirs."

5. Howells replied that what was left was simply life itself and that the writer was therefore better off without that paraphernalia.

Bryant's fountain (he wrote a poem about it in 1838) may be graphed at the opposite pole from the magic well in Hawthorne's *The House of the Seven Gables*, with its ancient images and cunning reminders. And we may feel about his poetry in general, as Emerson did, that it was "a vase to receive and not a fountain to impart character"; that, in Emerson's deft exploitation of the metaphor, the poetry was "feminine." Yet we must allow that Bryant was not indulging in mere sentimentality—to any greater degree, anyhow, than other critics in the party of Hope. Bryant, faithful to his generation's vision, was interpreting that vision to the party, explaining what might be demanded of a literature divorced from history and purged of memories. The hopeful fable, according to the vision, would deal with generalized man, invested with the generalized qualities of purity and gladness and invisible goodness: a sort of rarefied and beautiful blank.

VI

There yet remained something of a question about the shape of the fable, the story which would dramatize purity and goodness. There was still the question of what was the underlying action to be imitated. Perhaps the soundest guess about this was made by Tocqueville, when, after listening to manifestoes like Bryant's and expressions of concern like those of Channing and Cooper, he formulated the fable which he foresaw the American writer limited to.

Tocqueville's achievement, especially in his discussion of "Some Sources of Poetry among Democratic Nations," was essentially that of an uncommonly gifted reporter rather than of an inspired prophet; his prophecies, indeed, leave something to be desired. He put together, with remarkable lucidity, only what he heard on all sides; and it amounted to this: "Among a democratic people poetry will not be fed with legends or the memorials of old traditions," since democracy—so Tocqueville inferred from a hundred interviews—"gives men a sort of distaste for what is ancient." He detected all the difficulties that so resolute a rejection of traditions, conventions, and literary habits would produce; but he saw that when all those elements and aids had disappeared, something yet remained: man himself. The new subject, in Tocqueville's words, was to be "Man himself, taken aloof from his country and his age and standing in the presence of Nature and God."

The career of man—homeless, timeless, and alone—came to this, as Tocqueville formulated the universal adventure: "Man springs from nowhere, crosses time and disappears forever in the bosom of God; he is seen but for a moment, wandering on the verge of the two abysses, and there he is lost." That was perhaps as apt a summary of the fable which the critics were looking for as the evidence made possible. Tocqueville was not entirely easy about so abstracted a story, and he feared that the literature resulting might be too cloudy for comfort. But he very clearly exposed what remained when conventions had been set aside and the past forgotten. Something very like his brief story of the human adventure did indeed become the essential and recurring anecdote of American fiction: that story or—in the case of our greatest writers—the story of that story. For what some novelists were to discover was that the story implicit in American experience had to do with an Adamic person, springing from nowhere, outside time, at home only in the presence of nature and God, who is thrust by circumstances into an actual world and an actual age. American fiction grew out of the attempt to chart the impacts which ensued, both upon Adam and upon the world he is thrust into. American fiction is the story begotten by the noble but illusory myth of the American as Adam.

5

The Hero in Space: Brown, Cooper, Bird

And you O my soul where you stand
Surrounded, detached in measureless oceans of space,
Ceaselessly musing, venturing, throwing, seeking the
    spheres to connect them. . . .

WALT WHITMAN

IN SKETCHING the emergent fable urged by the critics on American writers, I have largely followed the hopeful line. According to the hopeful, "youth and health and purity" were suitable themes for the New World artist; man himself, seen in a time-free perspective, was the representative character; and as for materials and resources, the American was instructed to "forget Europe wholly" and draw exclusively from the scene around him. Criticism, interpreted as a marshaling of resources for future purposes, is primarily a forward-looking affair, and a century ago that meant a fervently hopeful affair. The issue, moreover, was not very sharply drawn within criticism itself: the demand for underivative writing about the healthiness of American life did not noticeably conflict with the continuing lectures and essays by Harvard professors on the unrecoverable splendors of the classical texts. And alongside both kinds of criticism, there lay in unintrusive alertness the multiplying corpses of the imitative poems and stories stillborn almost daily in the newspapers and magazines of the country. These items were rarely scrutinized and rarely even attacked by the hopeful evangelists, who simply brushed them aside as they pressed for freshness and originality: "when," ran the recurring refrain, "will our literature achieve *its* national independence?"

In fiction it was quite the other way, at least in the only fiction which can still command our attention. If the liveliest criticism, as it developed, was persistently and even repetitiously hopeful, the best of our fiction has from the outset been neither exclusively hopeful nor exclusively nostalgic, because it has been both. There were many dreary examples of fiction of both extremes. But the quality of anything like a genuine and enduring fiction could not help being "ironic": in the sense that all genuine fiction is, by nature, ironic. For fiction, whether comic or tragic, dramatizes the interplay of compelling opposites: the real peeping around the corner of the illusory, or the real exploding in the midst of the apparent, in whatever terms of manners, psychology, or sheer picaresque adventure the novelist has seized upon. Forward-looking criticism asked for a narrative or poetic image of the grand illusion of the day: a new kind of hero in a new kind of world, to be characterized in new language. The novelists of power—Hawthorne and Melville, above all—did not so much meet that request as comment upon it dramatically. They responded as the elder James and Bushnell responded; they found the narrative means to say: Supposing there were such a figure—young, pure, innocent—what would happen if he entered the world as it really is?

The dialogue, within the realm of literature, was consequently *between* theory and practice, between the critic and the creative artist. This is perhaps as it should be and as it undoubtedly still is.

If there was a fictional Adamic hero unambiguously treated—celebrated in his very Adamism—it was the hero of Cooper's *The Deerslayer:* a self-reliant young man who does seem to have sprung from nowhere and whose characteristic pose, to employ Tocqueville's words, was the solitary stance in the presence of Nature and God. But after Deerslayer, there begins the march of those more complex and sometimes tragic Adams of Hawthorne and Melville and Henry James—those bright personalities who first come at us as Deerslayer does, but whose subsequent adventures dramatically test the Adamic fable of the critics, who pay the price of their own innocence, while revealing, as though by unconscious compensation, what could after all be made of those scanty original materials.

The evolution of the hero as Adam in the fiction of the New World —an evolution which coincides precisely, as I believe, with the evolution of *the* hero of American fiction generally—begins rightly with Natty Bumppo. I call such a figure the hero in *space*, in two senses of the word. First, the hero seems to take his start outside time, or on the very outer edges of it, so that his location is essentially in space alone; and, second, his initial habitat is space as spaciousness, as the unbounded, the area of total possibility. The Adamic hero is discovered, as an old stage direction might have it, "surrounded, detached in *measureless oceans* of space."

The American Adam

That phrase of Whitman's, intended to describe his own soul, is a happy one, since it announces that same affinity between the ocean and the prairie—the "wide, open spaces"—which Cooper and Melville would remark on and exploit, and on which Parkman also commented. At the same time, Whitman invests his metaphor with the note of sadness and loneliness which the spatial position must contain: the romantic yearning, authenticated and concretized by the solid facts of geographical and social life in America. The yearning, the ceaseless musing, venturing, and seeking, the uncertain gestures of the spirit which Whitman perceived, would eventually define the hero in space, after Deerslayer; and it was a small step from this loneliness to a darker fearfulness—when hidden hostilities began to expose themselves in the previously benevolent surrounding. Tragedy, in American fiction, was generated by the impact of hostile forces upon the innocent solitary, who had sprung from nowhere, and his impact upon them.

The next three chapters trace such a development, by looking rather closely at the half-dozen-odd novels wherein the successive moments of the evolution are clearest because the novels themselves have, at least in some degree, the independent life of art. The present chapter concentrates on James Fenimore Cooper and especially on *The Deerslayer*; with that central emphasis followed by a rapid glance at a considerably less-well-known writer and novel—Robert Montgomery Bird's *Nick of the Woods* (1837)—a faint and fitful anticipation of *Moby-Dick* and perhaps the first work of fiction which at all effectively suggested the ominous features of the spatial condition. But in order to assess the contribution of Cooper (and hence, later, the splendid alchemy of Hawthorne and Melville), it seems useful to begin with a much earlier, Gothic version of the representative hero—Charles Brockden Brown's *Arthur Mervyn* (1799). For in this novel, both the hero and his representative experience make their appearance while still entangled in Continental literary conventions. This was one of the novels named by Edward Tyrell Channing as of the genre which would never catch on in the New World. In fact, its story and its genre were the ones which American novelists would return to again and again.

I

Arthur Mervyn is a guileless young man of eighteen who comes in 1793 from his country farm into the city of Philadelphia, and there discovers the prolific reality of evil in every imaginable moral and physical form. When we first encounter him at the close of his second descent into the city, he is propped up against a wall and apparently dying of the plague; but even then there can be detected behind his "decayed visage" a "simple and ingenuous aspect" and "traces of uncommon but manlike beauty." The burden of the novel's first volume is Arthur's somewhat incoherent report on the events which have so wasted, yet never destroyed, his manly simplicity. A few of the details, however gory or preposterous, are worth mentioning; for the very crudeness of *Arthur Mervyn* allows us to see all the more plainly the rhythm and the typical ingredients of the story in question.

Arthur has left home after his father has remarried, taking to wife a buxom and illiterate servant girl. Arthur's only living relative is his father (he lets it slip later that the only other Mervyn child to attain maturity, a sister, had been seduced by a wandering schoolmaster and had instantly killed herself); now, alienated from his father, Arthur finds himself entirely alone in an unknown world. He makes his solitary way into the city, being properly gulled en route by a youth of sportive taste, who leaves him wedged in a closet in the bedroom of a strange house, just as the owner and his wife are arriving to go to bed for the night. Arthur manages to creep safely out (without his shoes); and, proceeding anxiously along the streets in the dawn, he approaches the first person he sees to beg of him enough money to get back to the country again. The person accosted, however—a handsome elderly man, with a prosperous and cultivated air, calling himself Welbeck— invites Arthur to his home; and there, evidently with some private scheme in mind, clothes and feeds him, instructing him to act as a secretary, say nothing about his origins, and show no astonishment at anything which may happen.

Arthur gropes about in this dark and ominous world for several days, regularly shaken by inexplicable new disturbances. The mysteries reach their climax in the midnight murder by Welbeck of a strange man who has entered the house in a fury and challenged him to a duel. Arthur stumbles onto a scene composed of a dead body and a desperate Welbeck and listens in stupefaction to an evil and intricate tale. That tale defies summary: sufficient that the dead man, a sea captain named Watson, has once befriended Welbeck, rescued him from an unsavory dilemma in Liverpool, and taken him to the Watson home in Charlestown; and that, in Watson's subsequent absence, Welbeck has seduced the married sister, who became pregnant and vanished; upon this, the husband shot himself and the father went mad. Escaping south, Welbeck ran into new occasions for crime and profit and was about to put his ideas to work (with Arthur's innocent assistance) when Watson turned up to accuse him and be killed.

Welbeck hurries away, plunges into the Delaware River, and presumably drowns, while Arthur recovers his scattered wits only enough to flee the city, taking cover in the country with a friendly family, the Hadwins. This new set of strangers provides much comfort, but the Hadwins have their terrors too; and Susan, the elder daughter, has been reduced at a stroke to suicidal hysteria over fear for the life of her fiancé, trapped in the newly plague-ridden Philadelphia. Before long, Arthur braves a second entrance into the city, on a chivalric quest for Susan's betrothed. He does find him at last, after moving through a series of dreadful spectacles—Philadelphia has become a city of the dead and the dying; and he recognizes in the object of his search the same young man (Wallace) who had tricked him on the first visit. This affair barely ended, Arthur meets up again with Welbeck, who has risen from seeming death by water to look for some banknotes secreted in the house. Welbeck declares the notes to be forgeries, and Arthur, who chances upon them, throws them into the fire, whereupon Welbeck disappears, out of his head with fury, and Arthur, exhausted and infected with the plague, totters through the city to fall senseless in the street.

All this, mind you, is merely a contraction of the main plot of Volume I; I have omitted the many minor characters and the multiplying subplots, and I can simply mention the second volume, wherein further pitfalls and triumphs are prepared for the recovered and, to some degree, matured hero. Brown was, of course, manipulating the only literary conventions he knew: the conventions of the emergent Gothic novel and of the sentimental romance; his seductions, betrayals, perversions, his midnight rivers, and his shrouded, frenzied figures—these were the commonplaces of what Mario Praz has called "the Romantic agony."[1] That agony was the agony of the chaste innocent appalled by unspeakable evil; but Brown exploited the conventions in a fable which managed to convey his personal sense of human experience and which—since his sense coincided with many another response to life in the following decades—we may in retrospect accept as distinctly native in outline.

It is, to begin with, a matter of emphasis. Brown's favorite fictional subject, as he told a French correspondent, was "great energies em-

---

1. In the title of his book, *The Romantic Agony* (London, 1933). The author's own Italian title was *La Carne, la morte e il diavolo*, but Professor Praz tells me that the English title is perfectly apt for his subject.

ployed in the promotion of vicious purposes"; "give me," he said, "a tale of lofty crimes rather than of honest folly."[2] In *Wieland* and *Ormond*, consequently, he centered on the dreadful accomplishments of the villain-heroes after whom the novels were named, with the helpless virtue of Clara and Constantia serving to enlarge the frightfulness. In *Edgar Huntly*, we are invited for much of the time to follow the lunatic peregrinations of the eventually self-destroying Clithero Edny. Even Arthur Mervyn on occasion mirrors his creator's ethical interests, when, for example, he confesses to the pleasure stimulated by the "terrific images" he conjures up of the plague. He realizes that there is no necessity for dwelling upon them, and he concludes that the images must contain "some nameless charm"—that the horrible is akin to the sublime. That very realization, coming after Arthur's first involvement with the vicious energies of Welbeck, is a sign that Arthur is growing up. For *Arthur Mervyn* differs a little from Brown's other more Europeanized novels in the attention it gives not so much to lofty crimes as to the modifying effect of such wickedness upon an honest and foolish character. It is the American theme.

Still, Brown remained to some extent of Welbeck's party, at least as a novelist. He tried to conceal his absorption with evil under a good deal of sententious moralizing, but the absorption was always evident. It had to be: since for Brown, who looked upon existence as a continuous dull ache, creative writing was consciously therapeutic, and a part of the illness to be cured was an overactive awareness of the living reality of the world's Welbecks. The ache was physical: Brown had tuberculosis all his life and died of it, in 1809, at the age of thirty-eight. But it was psychological as well, the product of a profound self-distrust which expressed itself repeatedly to the dismay of his pedestrian friends: "I am sometimes apt to think that few human beings have drunk so deeply of the cup of self-abhorrence as I have."

It is not our business here to probe to the source of Brown's condition; perhaps it partook of the same wilful expense of powers which seems to have touched off the steady self-dislike that Hawthorne was to record in his Salem notebook. Brown's fiction—all the best of it, four long novels, crowded incredibly into the eleven months from September, 1798, to August, 1799—constituted a deliberate symbolic

---

2. Most of the biographical information about Brown and the quotations from him may be found in Harry R. Warfel's valuable *Charles Brockden Brown* (Gainesville, Fla., 1949). Anyone interested in Brown, however, should start with the biography begun by Paul Allen and finished by William Dunlap, *The Life of Charles Brockden Brown* (2 vols.; Philadelphia, 1815).

action. It was writing alone, as Brown said explicitly during an aside in *Arthur Mervyn*, which "blunted my vexation, hushed my stormy passions, turned my peevishness to soothing, my fierce revenge to heart-dissolving pity." And so, in novel after novel, he annihilated in narrative those hard clusters of evil inclination he appeared so intimately to understand.

But there was more to the story than that; there always is. Brown was an early American illustration of the alliance between art and illness—between art, moreover, and the knowledge, which may derive from the experience, of evil. But he illustrates at the same time the special intensity—indeed, the sense of outrage—with which the American has characteristically acknowledged that alliance. Brown gives us the impression (as Melville does) of furious disillusion. He had been and very likely he remained a utopian idealist. Paul Allen, in the biography of Brown, spoke of "his favorite prospect of a perfect system of government." And in his first published writing—sketches composed when he was eighteen and presented under the title of *The Rhapsodist*—he enacted a self-appointed role as the perfect individual: relaxing, in the Ohio wilderness, into a perfecting sympathy with nature. The rhapsodic strain was muted, as Brown discovered in the life about him and, more painfully, in his own heart a refutation of the dream of primal purity—muted, but not altogether silenced. The incompatibility of the dream and the fact led where it might be expected to lead: the mature Brown, as his faithful friend Dr. Elihu Hubbard Smith told him worriedly, "affected to be mysterious and made ambiguity [his] delight." The curve of Brown's complex development is a kind of preview in actuality of the career of Melville's Pierre Glendinning, hero of a novel subtitled *The Ambiguities:* an account of the loss of Eden and the tragic inability to accept the loss.

Brockden Brown attempted, like Pierre, to master his divided condition by dramatizing it, in his various pairs of devil-and-innocent. His artistic achievement can scarcely have been enough to assuage him, but some intermittent achievement there was, and of a revealing kind. The weaknesses are obvious: *Arthur Mervyn* betrays them at every turn. The plot, as any summary of it must show, is ludicrous and often unintelligible. Brown employed the method of narration which William Faulkner has managed with far greater skill: the method of packing one story inside another, and a third inside that. Indeed, at one moment in *Arthur Mervyn* we are at not less than four removes from the immediate—a device which expands the book's dark and violent cosmos, but which also confuses us intolerably. The style, which varies not a jot from one autobiographical speech to another, seems usually to be imbedded in a kind of Latinate glue; Arthur's recollection of his first erotic response is as follows: "I had been a stranger to what is called love. From subsequent reflection I have contracted a suspicion that the sentiment with which I regarded this lady was not untinctured from this source." The world of the novel is singularly sparse and shadowy, as though Brown composed only when he was half-asleep. There is no surprise in Arthur's coming upon Welbeck, after scrambling out of the closet; Welbeck was apparently the only living inhabitant of the city that day. As a matter of fact, by a telling paradox, the city of Philadelphia enjoys in the pages of the novel a far more dense and richly populated existence during the plague than in its better days. The hordes of suffering victims and the masses of corpses are (as Henry James might say) intensely *there* in a way that supposedly healthy citizens had never been.

The clear superiority of the plague scenes is a mark of Brown's deepest preoccupation and the area of his genuine talent; for the world that he could quite artfully bring into being and explore with the greatest assurance was the land of the dead. This was something which also would become a Romantic commonplace, but in Brown's occasionally compelling prose we may recognize it as a land of spiritual crisis, a hell in which moral consciousness is either overwhelmed or transformed into the toughness of conscience. In the world of *Arthur Mervyn*, the average destiny is violence and horror—crime, treachery, rape, suicide, murder; plague-ridden Philadelphia (like Faulkner's Jefferson) is a concentration of that world and an "objective correlative" to what Brown seems to have inwardly envisoned.

Contemplating the novel in these terms, we can find in *Arthur Mervyn* that same universe of dissociated embodiments of malignity into which Horace Bushnell was to follow his own hypothetical Adam. For Philadelphia is an exclusive and impenetrable network of secret and corrupt liaisons—but a network, at the same time, of mutually destructive, hateful individuals, each craftily on his own. Brown gets this effect by what appear to be clumsy coincidences: the owner of the house Arthur is lured into by Wallace is, for example, none other than the business associate of the man he next encounters, Welbeck—a schemer Welbeck would betray in a second, and vice versa.

Moving blindly toward that world, that city, coming fresh from the country, getting partly inside and becoming nearly destroyed (alienated from home, squeezed into a closet, caught in a criminal web, stricken by the plague), is the foolish young innocent: the first of our Adams.

He is not, to be sure, entirely naturalized; in Arthur, we discover the young hopeful from the provinces of many a European country, anxious to make good in the capital city. The theme is universal, and it has been universally dramatized. Arthur resembles his American successors in so far as he is genuinely solitary. Indeed, he does seem to have no relations in time; he has no past and no inheritance to help or to hinder him; he brings with him nothing but a pure and empty heart and a mind like a *tabula rasa*. In the typical Gothic novel of Europe—such as *The Mysteries of Udolpho* by Mrs. Ann Radcliffe—the plight of the hero or heroine is a family affair: it is exactly the shock of evil emanating from one's close kin which energizes the tale. In *Arthur Mervyn*, as in most comparable fiction after it, it is the very unrelatedness of the hero to the centers of evil or to anything else which first stimulates the great unease. And as to Arthur's competence to deal with evil, "Less can be said," as Welbeck remarks in a nice understatement, about one of his own female conquests, "in praise of [his] understanding than of [his] sensibility."

It is the end of the first phase of the initiation: that is, of the process of maturing, as formalized and made ethically meaningful. In the chaotic second volume of the novel, Arthur demonstrates his maturity in the traditional way by putting his new knowledge to the service of others—rescuing this person from a brothel, that one from a prison. Though Brockden Brown had few means, in the available vocabulary of his day, to identify his story—the cheerful expectancies of his audience, as E. T. Channing would observe, working quite against him—he nonetheless offered in *Arthur Mervyn* a muffled version of an adventure to be located by later fiction in the very heart of American life.

II

Brown gives us a wavering glimpse of the new hero's features; but it was Cooper's contribution to bring the hero fully to life by taking him out of the cities and cellars and putting him where he belonged—in space. The "scene" is the distinguishing element in Cooper's best compositions: whenever, that is, the scene is spacious enough, whenever it is the forest or the sea.[3] "It is on the sea and in the forest," as

3. Here and in my discussion of Hawthorne, I use the word "scene" in the manner suggested by Kenneth Burke, in *The Grammar of Motives* (New York, 1945). As used by Mr. Burke, the word means, first of all, not the simple geographical *location* of some thing, person, or act, but rather the qualitative and qualifying context. In the hands of the expert, the "scene" can thus *contain* the act or the character—and can be substituted for either, or become a metaphor for either. Thus the blasted heath in *Macbeth* is not

The Hero in Space: Brown, Cooper, Bird

Francis Parkman said, "that Cooper is most at home. Their spirit inspired him, their images were graven on his heart"; and for Parkman this meant that Cooper was the first undeniably New World writer.

Cooper was a sailor—actually, during five of the earlier years of his life (1806–10) and in his typical enthusiasms and behavior during the rest of his life, whether writing another romance of the sea or drawing up a history of the American navy (1839) or in rancorously prosecuting one of his libel suits. But like two other sailors, Melville and Conrad (both of whom admired him enormously), Cooper meditated the symbolic value of the sea and went on, like Melville in particular, to penetrate its affinity with the uncreated world beyond the frontier. For Cooper the forest and the sea shared the quality of boundlessness; they were the *apeiron*—the area of possibility.

But Cooper differed radically from either Conrad or Melville in his refusal to perceive any evil, overt or hidden, in the magnificent world of space, or in any of its creatures. *His* most memorable creatures come into moral being in the environmental influence of that world; they draw their breath in it; they reflect its firm and simple purity; they share its aloofness from time. Natty Bumppo is, of course, its representative *par excellence*, along with Chingachgook, the noble Mohican, especially in their youthful friendship as described in *The Deerslayer;* Canonchet, the Narraganset in *The Wept of Wish-ton-Wish*, belongs there too; and to some extent Harvey Birch, the lonesome and heroic peddler who doubles as *The Spy;* and perhaps even Long Tom Coffin in *The Pilot*—Tom Coffin who has forgotten how to act in the land-world.

The drama Cooper constructed for these actors on the spatial scene resulted from his trick of poising that scene upon the very brink of time. In the characteristic adventure of a Cooper novel (it is not to be confused with the "plot": see below), the personality of the Adamic hero is made to impinge upon the products of time: the villages lying a little inland, or on the safer side of the frontier; social institutions, with their precedents and established practices; relationships inherited through the years, thick with intimate histories; complexities, involvements, and corruptions. These appear concretely as the game laws, for example, in *The Pioneers;* as the secret, suspect, early career of Judith Hutter in *The Deerslayer;* as the mixed domestic, erotic, and

---

merely a place where some witches happen to foregather: it is their rightful habitat, it is the kind of context which produces witches; it is a symbol of the same order as the witches, within the symbolic pattern of the play.

military Anglo-American relations in *The Spy*. These are things the hero has to cope with in the course of his dramatic life, but which he must eventually stay clear of, if he is to remain faithful to the spatial vision. In *The Bravo* (1831), where the setting is the ancient city-state of Venice, the bravo himself is fixed inside the heart of corruption and maintains his own purity literally at the cost of his head; there was no place for him to escape to. But in those novels where the setting is the untracked American forest, the world always lies all before the hero, and normally, like Huck Finn, he is able to light out again for the "territories."

The principle of survival in his essential character requires him constantly to "jump off" (this was the current phrase)—to keep, as it were, two jumps ahead of time. This was the notion carried by the popular anecdote whereby Daniel Boone, Natty's historic cousin, was made to complain that "I had not been two years at the licks before a d——d Yankee came and settled down *within an hundred miles of me!*"[4] It is in obedience to that principle that Deerslayer logically, though gracelessly, turns down Judith's proposal of marriage. The mission of poor Harvey Birch, in *The Spy*, at once forces him into dealing with the affairs of the Wharton family and prohibits him from forming bonds with them or with anyone else. And more typically still, in the first of the *Leatherstocking Tales* to be written, *The Pioneers* (1823), Natty Bumppo—like Billy Budd, in the tale composed sixty-eight years later but springing from almost identical tensions—innocently runs afoul of the law by shooting a deer out of season and, after inspecting the situation, wisely takes off from the town and community of Templeton for the freer country to the west.

These instances and a dozen more like them, though by no means the usual focus of Cooper's tiresome, conventional plots, are the index to his real achievement. For in the universe of Cooper, as against that of Brockden Brown, space so-to-speak asserts itself against the onslaught of time, with a vigor that is articulated in the new hero's impregnable virtue—and indeed makes that hero's birth and survival possible. These instances are also the mark of Cooper's one great gift, possibly the one gift indispensable to the narrative artist who aspires to transmute American experience into story: the gift for seeing life dramatically as the measurement by conduct of institutions and the measurement by institutions of conduct.

4. Quoted by Henry Nash Smith, *Virgin Land* (Cambridge, Mass., 1950), p. 54. Professor Smith's book, which I came across when the present study was largely completed, is rich in suggestive information about the historic notions of the new Eden and the new Adam.

The Hero in Space: Brown, Cooper, Bird

The whole vexatious problem of art and experience in the New World, in the age of hope and very probably ever since, is related to that difficult double process. Henry James, speaking as a writer of fiction and speaking about the stuff of fiction—i.e., "experience"—defined experience as "our apprehension and our measure of what happens to us as social creatures." It was an acute formulation of the traditional view; but, in America, experience in that social sense has not always been so easily come by. Experience cannot always be the stuff of fiction, but rather its climax—the ultimate achievement or the ultimate disaster. The individual in America has usually taken his start outside society; and the action to be imitated may just as well be his strenuous efforts to *stay* outside as his tactics for getting inside; and if he does get inside, it makes a difference whether he is walking into a trap or discovering the setting in which to realize his own freedom. So the lesson for the writer anxious to be honest with the American scene has often been this: that what has to be measured and apprehended is painfully twofold—the elements appraise each other. The success of James Fenimore Cooper in apprehending the lesson is the precise equivalent of his success as an artist. And his success was marginal precisely in the sense that the most illuminating clashes and insights occur on the margins of his plots.

This is no doubt why it is always so hard to locate the source of Cooper's power: we look for it in the wrong places and, not finding it there, are inclined to deny its existence, wondering the while at the taste of our ancestors. Looked at squarely, Cooper's novels betray an astonishing lack of co-ordination between the classical ingredients of narrative: plot and character and thought and diction. Frequently these seem to have nothing to do with one another; they are not related organically, or set deliberately at odds; they are, in a phrase of Eliot's, in the same book only by accident. The stylized romances which weigh down most of the pages in books like *The Spy*, *The Pioneers*, and *The Bravo* have a very slight connection with the characters who engage our attention on the peripheries. The incidents in *The Last of the Mohicans* are violent and incredible, and the style is unbearably sentimental.

One is sometimes tempted to say that Cooper has no style at all—unlike Charles Brockden Brown, who has a marked style, and a poor one. Cooper's attempts at style are all too often just that: attempts at *style*—random linguistic inflations, verbal excitements, neither expressing nor even adorning, but very nearly destroying the life that is yet at work in the fragments and corners. We are lucky, as Yvor

The American Adam

Winters has hinted, when the style is so monotonously bad that we can forget it. Where the events or the characters may independently engross us, "thought," speculative or dramatic, is usually absent; and the other way around. There is a good deal of political thought to be chewed on in *The Monikins* (1835); but it is a kind of punishment to try to follow its allegory and its deadly prose, while few, if any, ideas disturb the responses of the Whartons or the Munroes. If we look to Cooper's letters for revelation, we are smothered by the notes on some dinner party, the endless arithmetic of publishing, the analyses of the libel law—by lifeless gossip and a humorless, constricted egotism. Yet, for all the surface awkwardness and the nonsense, not less than half a dozen of Cooper's novels possess an amount of indestructible power: something we answer to even before we have spotted it; some image of experience we know to be fundamentally our own, or at least could wish that it were.

This was even truer in Cooper's more wishful generation; for what Cooper was doing for his readers was to grasp the expectancies of the day and project them in narrative. This does not mean that Cooper was a "realistic" reporter of his age, though he liked to think of himself as a realist and chided Brockden Brown for a lack of verisimilitude —for putting side by side, in the cave scene of *Edgar Huntly*, "an American, a savage, a wild cat and a tomahawk in a conjunction that never did nor ever will occur." But Cooper failed to see that Brown was not aiming at literal accuracy, but at the special effect of terror by incongruity: the terror implicit in the hero's solitary condition in an unknown world. Cooper was immune to the terror and rather relished the position; but he in turn was charged with tampering with the actual facts and making them not too frightful but too comforting. Parkman, who loved and resembled him, thought his Indians too kindly; Poe regarded Cooper's fiction as "remarkably and especially inaccurate"; and Mark Twain traced in the inconsistencies of Natty Bumppo the profile of a vaudeville comic. But Cooper's fiction—the *Leatherstocking Tales* anyhow—moved consciously away from a semi-historic authenticity (framing, in the early novels, those romantic posturings at mid-stage) toward a sort of sustained fantasy, in many respects much *more* authentic: a re-creation in story of the dream-legend of his contemporaries. The peak of that development was *The Deerslayer*.

There has been an interesting difference of critical opinion about *The Deerslayer*. Yvor Winters is not alone in judging it inferior to many other novels "in plot and in movement," and in thinking that it has "few . . . serious merits." My own high relative estimate coincides with the one expressed by D. H. Lawrence—"the most fascinating Leatherstocking book is the last, The Deerslayer"—because I agree with Lawrence in seeing the novel as the culmination of a process which exemplifies the American myth. Lawrence's words seem to me at once exact, poetic, and inimitable: "The Leatherstocking novels . . . go backwards from old age to golden youth. That is the true myth of America. She starts old, old, wrinkled and writhing in an old skin. And there is a gradual sloughing off of the old skin, towards a new youth. It is the myth of America."

It is. Cultural and individual self-renewal was the aim of the day's most magnetic metaphors; it was the principle of Thoreau's celebration of the molting season and Whitman's giant leap to the beginning of time—varieties of the great surge of motion from memory to hope. Cooper completed that motion a number of years before either *Walden* or *Leaves of Grass*—the journey from Natty Bumppo's old age and death in *The Pioneers* and *The Prairie* to his birth and golden youth in *The Deerslayer*—and he completed it in terms of the character of his hero and the experience which shaped it—when both were settled in the scene that became them.

Cooper felt the myth at a greater depth than did most of his trend-following colleagues (who served up innumerable tales of retreats to the wilderness Eden); and he bodied it forth with all the ardor of a declining conviction. His hero and his hero's friend, in *The Deerslayer*, are all the more timeless and sturdily innocent, their world all the more fresh, free, and uncluttered, as Cooper's own hope for his historic world grew fainter. He was beginning to realize, as a posthumous fragment expressed it, that "there is no such thing on earth" as the perfect community his fellows still schemed about; and that anyone who understood the cruelty and stupidity inherent in a democratic society like America's—who had perhaps been wounded by that society—would have to "look beyond the limits of his earthly being for consolation and support." For a novelist, one promising area to look to might be the invulnerable world of myth, as an enduring model for the actual.

The plot of *The Deerslayer* recounts a series of skirmishes between a group of white trappers and frontiersmen on Lake Otsego and a local band of marauding Iroquois. The whites include old Thomas Hutter and his two "daughters," Judith and Hetty, and the huge, amoral Harry March—Hurry Harry. Moving in and out of their circle, with them but never of them, helping them, instructing them, saving them, and always keeping at some ethical and psychic distance from them are young Natty Bumppo and his Indian ally Chingachgook. The plot is little more than a medley of captures and rescues, scalpings and shootings, tactics and countertactics; except for the final episode, when Judith Hutter, a raven-haired charmer of doubtful background, tries to talk Natty round to marrying her, in language he modestly fails to grasp. But the "action" of the story as distinct from the plot—what is really going on in the novel—is something far more significant: it is the birth of an archetypal, still finely individualized character, which Lawrence identifies as "*the* essential American soul . . . an isolate, almost selfless, stoic, enduring man." Natty Bumppo is the full-fledged fictional Adam. He is born with all due ceremony during an incident that has every self-conscious quality of a ritual trial. The incident, which is one of the greatest moments in all Cooper's fiction, is in the seventh chapter, when Deerslayer kills his first Indian. It is dawn on a spring morning, as Deerslayer— "entirely alone"—glides in his canoe to the lake's bank, is shot at by an Iroquois hidden among the trees, hastily takes cover, and enters a duel of skill which is carried on like a deadly dance. The adversaries, peering around from behind trees, bow courteously to each other; they exchange words and proposals; each gesture and act of preparation has an air of solemn formality. They fire simultaneously—it is like a kiss—and, while "Deerslayer dropped his piece and stood, with head erect, steady as one of the pines in the calm of a June morning, watching the result," the Iroquois plunges forward into the opening, hurls his tomahawk with a fearful howl, and falls dying to the ground. The trial successfully passed—the trial of honor, courage, and self-reliance —Deerslayer earns his symbolic reward of a new name.

"What we call him?" [asks the dying Iroquois].
"Deerslayer is the name I bear now. . . ."
"That good name for boy—poor name for warrior. He get better quick. No fear *there*"—the savage had strength sufficient, under the strong excitement he felt, to raise a hand and tap the young man on his breast—"eye sartain— finger lightning—aim, death—great warrior soon. No Deerslayer—Hawk- eye—Hawk-eye—Hawk-eye. Shake hand."

The new hero rejoices in his new name and status: "Hawkeye! That's not a bad name for a warrior, sounding much more manful and valiant than Deerslayer." Like his closest equivalent in recent fiction, Isaac McCaslin, on the occasion of his first ritualistic encounter with Old Ben in William Faulkner's *The Bear*, Hawkeye could reflect (he virtually does) that "he was witnessing his own birth"—or rebirth as the

American Adam: accomplished appropriately in the forest on the edge of a lake, with no parents near at hand, no sponsors at the baptism; springing from nowhere, as Tocqueville had said, standing alone in the presence of God and Nature.

The rest of the novel completes the process, as Hawkeye becomes secure in his characteristic virtues: largely by opposition to the habits of the others around him. Less important than the melodrama of the capture and rescue of Hurry Harry and Tom Hutter is Hawkeye's growing awareness that, while they fight and collect scalps for profit, his own "gifts" require him to come to terms with his forest home, to kill solely in order to live there. And beneath the comedy of poor Hetty's visit to the Iroquois camp and her attempt to preach the captors into releasing their prisoners is a profoundly suggestive distinction between the quality of Hetty's innocence and that of Hawkeye's; Hetty has an innocence which is, in fact, a self-delusive helplessness, a half-witted conviction of universal goodness, which exposes her to every physical and moral danger and finally kills her. It is partly by contemplation of that hapless girl, by conversations with Hetty and about her, that Hawkeye arrives at a more durable kind of innocence and at the insight that it must be bounded by an observation of ethical differences. Cooper skilfully exposes the solid core of Hawkeye's Adamism by setting it alongside the flimsy hopefulness of Hetty Hutter.

Cooper was wise to tell no further tales of Hawkeye, to leave him alone at the close of *The Deerslayer*, in his spatial world unencumbered by wife and family, and to conclude the entire *Leatherstocking* series with the hero's birth and young manhood. For according to the vision Cooper shared, the end was paradoxically a fresh beginning, and no transforming experience was envisaged or desired beyond it. Only an imagination of a quite different order would seek to carry the story further: an imagination which perceived the possible dependence of moral growth on evil and which could draw from that tragic irony a more widely ranging narrative. Hawthorne and Melville had such an imagination; but as a rehearsal for their imaginings and as a minor, yet notable, moment in the history of Adam as fictional hero, we may glance briefly at *Nick of the Woods* by Robert Montgomery Bird.

III

Robert Montgomery Bird of Philadelphia (1806–54) was a physician of restless temperament with a flair for storytelling, a man of minor talent and blunted perceptions, who yet, in *Nick of the Woods*

(1837), came closer than he knew to breaking through the conventions of fiction and producing a novel of honesty and stature. In his Preface to *Nick of the Woods*, which was written during the second wave of interest in literature about the Revolution and the Indian wars, Bird claimed that his treatment of the Indian character was more realistic than Cooper's. But he claimed too little; he is another instance of the American novelist insufficiently aware of what most vitally engages him.

There was some truth in Bird's critique of Cooper for throwing a "poetical illusion over the Indian character" and in the contention that he himself had portrayed them "as . . . they existed . . . ignorant, violent, debased, brutal." The major adversary of *Nick of the Woods*, Wenonga, the Black Vulture, chief of the terrifying Shawnees of Kentucky, is first discovered lying hopelessly drunk in the bushes outside his encampment; and in an effective twist to the customary attribution of great courtesy, the first Indians encountered step through the door of the white men's cabin with the ironic greeting, "Bozhoo [*bon jour*] brudders—Injun good friend"—and advance for the kill with a hoot of "malign laughter." But his view of Indian morality, while derived from a rational conviction about the eternal superiority of civilization to barbarism, was also symptomatic of some deeper response to experience: a moral realism not clearly enough recognized by Bird to command his narrative at all points or to sustain its initial drive, but something yet powerful enough frequently to color it.

It affected, for example, those conventional elements and persons Bird was unable to keep out of his story. Romance and social intrigue, borrowed from English popular fiction, occupy, as usual, too many pages; but an attitude of fresh skepticism about the mores of such romance continues to creep in: into the tone describing the dead faint in which the heroine passes most of the adventure; into the ridicule the title-figure pours upon the juvenile hero's stagy lament over the girl's worse-than-death situation. "Would that twenty bullets had pierced her," cries Roland Forrester, "rather than she should have fallen alive into the hands of Braxley" (the white deceiver, now conniving with the Shawnees)—and Nathan: "Is thee wretched because thee eyes did not see the Injun axe struck into her brain? Friend, thee does not know what such a sight is." The notion of ethical reality lying half-suppressed beneath such moments was what gave life to Bird's one really distinguished characterization, the highly ambiguous Nathan Slaughter.

The Hero in Space: Brown, Cooper, Bird

Nathan is the innocent man of love transformed by a collision with evil. He had once been, quite genuinely, a pacifistic Quaker, living a quiet, pastoral life along the frontier, behaving according to the tenets of universal friendliness; so he is still regarded by the frontiersmen, who mock at him as a futile old man; so, in some contradictory way, he still partly remains. But the core of his character has undergone a radical change—the result of an unutterable shock. After Nathan had opened his arms to a visiting band of Shawnees and even handed his rifle over to them as a gesture of trust, the Indians had promptly murdered his wife and his five children before his eyes and inflicted a terrific wound on his own scalp. Nathan, dragging himself back to life, is turned into the frontier's most ferocious Indian-hater and -killer, the scourge of the Shawnees—called by his enemies, with unconscious propriety, the Jibbenainosay, the "Dead Man Who Walks."[5] For so he is, hiding the scar of an almost deadly wound beneath a broadly flapping hat made of tanned skins, hiding his mission of revenge beneath the conduct of the suffering servant. The diabolic conversion of his energies is symbolized in the sign of the cross he carves into the corpses he has already brutally mangled; this is why the whites refer to the unknown killer as Nick (*Old* Nick) of the Woods. The shock which motivates Nathan's secret warfare reverberates and ripples through the novel and comes close to lifting it out of its mediocre genre.

It is tempting to guess that that shock is the correlative of some psychic shock experienced by the author, the wound the correlative of some trauma; but nothing in the author's life, so far as we know about it, permits us to say so. Bird lived in Philadelphia and Delaware, practiced medicine for a couple of years, wrote a series of moderately successful plays, and three other novels (hardly worth remembering) before *Nick of the Woods* in 1837. In his later years he became depressed by ill health and a belief that he was unappreciated; but at the time of writing *Nick*, his fortunes and spirits were generally on the

---

5. Francis Parkman took note both of the theme and of Bird's use of it, in an aside in *The Conspiracy of Pontiac* (*The Works of Francis Parkman* [Boston, 1902], XVII, 127). "It is not easy for those living in the tranquillity of polish-life," wrote Parkman, with his customary very faint curl of the lips, "to conceive the depth and force of that unquenchable, indiscriminate hate which Indian outrages can awaken in those who have suffered them. The chronicles of the American borders are filled with the deeds of men, who, having lost all by the merciless tomahawk, have lived for vengeance alone." Then, in a footnote, he adds, "So promising a theme has not escaped the notice of novelists, and it has been adopted by Dr. Bird in his spirited *Nick of the Woods*." One of Parkman's special gifts was for spotting the dramatic theme in given historical incidents and conditions (see chap. 8).

rise; and the absence of any pain for him in the creative process is indicated by his reflection: "How blessedly and lazily, making a novel, a man may go spinning and snoozing over his quires." The source of the book's partial achievement must be left unaccounted for, except for an unexplorable hunch about unrecorded disturbances.

Bird's notion about the writing of fiction is unhappily mirrored in the major portion of the book's narrative, and in the shape the story finally assumes—a slackening from potential tragedy to melodrama. The incidents of the book take place in the Salt River Valley of Kentucky during the last years of the Revolution; they include the journey of Roland Forrester and his cousin Edith through the forest, the attacks upon them by the Shawnees, their various imprisonments and rescues, and the conspiracy to defraud them by the villainous Braxley. The incidents are not unexciting—the book is a good yarn and is easy to read; but, as in a Cooper novel, we have to disentangle from the surface plot the more important action unfolding itself almost in spite of the plot: in this case, the revelation of a complex character which is at once the manifestation of a complex moral sensibility. Nathan Slaughter belongs to the cluster of heroes in space; but he has turned sour; he throws his environment into relief by being at odds with it.

On the first page of the novel there are quoted the final lines of *Paradise Lost:* Adam and Eve, the world lying all before them, taking through Eden their solitary way: those lines so apt to the contemporary dream and so often invoked in it, those lines so central to the later ironic purposes of Henry James. On the same page we are introduced to the Kentucky frontier in terms of the current Eden imagery: "It was not unnatural, indeed, that men should regard as an Eden the land in which the gallant Daniel Boone, while taking his 'pleased rambles' on the 22d of December, 1769, discovered 'myriads of trees, some gay with blossoms, others rich with fruits.' " The proper inhabitant of such a frontier Eden is, of course, the unmodified American Adam: innocent, vigorous, bright with hope, trustingly intimate with his surroundings. Bird's accomplishment was to place upon that scene a figure who formerly had possessed many of the Adamic qualities; who possesses some of them still, and continues to believe they are the supreme qualities in a better world; but for whom the scene has become intolerably darkened.

Nathan's public behavior, during the early chapters of the novel, is in some sort a mimicry of Adamism: with the innocence not of Hawkeye but of Hetty Hutter—that innocence which hopes to turn away wickedness by the expression of lofty sentiments. But within him,

The Hero in Space: Brown, Cooper, Bird

Nathan has become the outraged Adam, hurled out of Eden by a visitation of the devil, venting his outrage in a ferocity of revenge with the extravagant emotion that only the original native illusion could engender. Nathan indeed almost rises, for an instant or two, to the great fictional stature that the matched forces made possible: the stature of the inverted Christ—the stature reached in one motion by Melville's Ahab. For, like Ahab, Nathan is a member of the gentle Quaker sect who has been wounded beyond all physical and psychological endurance, who has been scorched by experience, and who returns from death to a private mission of revenge—a revenge similarly conceived as the salvation of that little world which simultaneously rejects him.

Of course, any comparison of *Nick of the Woods* and *Moby-Dick*, of Nathan's quest for the Black Vulture and Ahab's for the White Whale, must be an exercise in literary judgment and must conclude by observing that the paradoxes of Nathan's character are gradually drained of tension as the story proceeds, until toward the end they verge on mere comic incongruity. Wenonga is killed by Nathan, the young persons are saved and duly married, every person who deserves it lives happily thereafter. The strength of imagination with which Bird took hold of his story at the outset could not be sustained; but in the figure of Nathan Slaughter, he began to suggest what might happen when the hero became alienated from space, when the conditions which rendered him solitary succeeded at the same time in driving him mad.

6

The Return into Time: Hawthorne

Adam saw it in a brighter sunshine, but never knew the shade of pensive beauty which Eden won from his expulsion.

HAWTHORNE, *The Marble Faun*

THE shift from a Natty Bumppo to a Nathan Slaughter was a process of aging and embittering; it reflected a shift in setting, as the actual frontier scene pushed beyond the forests to the plains and the western mountains. In fact and in the garish and transient frontier fiction which the facts encouraged, the new representative adventurer —the plainsman and the mountaineer—now found himself surrounded by a more ominous and drearier kind of space. The character of the hero changed in response to the new environment. Professor Henry Nash Smith, in his excellent study of "the American west as symbol and myth" (*Virgin Land* [1950]), has remarked that, as "the scene has been shifted from the deep fertile forests . . . to the barren plains," the figure in frontier literature becomes one who "no longer look[ed] to God through nature, for nature [was] no longer benign; its symbols [were] the wolves and the prairie fire." Kit Carson replaced Daniel Boone, Hawkeye's prototype. Contemplating the condition of Carson, Professor Smith concludes that "the landscape . . . throws the hero back in upon himself and accentuates his terrible and sublime isolation. He is an anarchic and self-contained atom—hardly even a monad—alone in a hostile, or at best a neutral, universe."

A comparable change in the constituent elements of dramatic literature—in the character of the hero and the quality of his "universe"—was taking place simultaneously in the developing fiction of the East. Other personal and cultural factors were at work in this fiction; yet American fiction has regularly registered through its own peculiar symbols the changing contours of the continent and its history. In Hawthorne and after him in Melville, we come upon dramatic structures which probe more deeply the changes foreshadowed by Bird in the Adamic fable of Cooper.

The isolated hero "alone in a hostile, or at best a neutral, universe" begins to replace the Adamic personality in the New World Eden. The essential continuity of American fiction explains itself through this historic transformation whereby the Adamic fable yielded to what I take to be the authentic American narrative. For much of that fable remained in the later narrative: the individual going forth toward experience, the inventor of his own character and creator of his personal history; the self-moving individual who is made to confront that "other"—the world or society, the element which provides experience. But as we move from Cooper to Hawthorne, the situation very notably darkens; qualities of evil and fear and destructiveness have entered; self-sufficiency is questioned through terrible trials; and the stage is set for tragedy. The solitary hero and the alien tribe; "the simple genuine self against the whole world"—this is still the given, for the American novelist. The variable is this: the novelist's sense of the initial tension—whether it is comforting, or whether it is potentially tragic; whether the tribe promises love, or whether it promises death.

Hawthorne was perhaps the first American writer to detect the inevitable doubleness in the tribal promise. For he was able by temperament to give full and fair play to both parties in the *agon:* to the hero and to the tribe as well. And, having done so, he penetrated to the pattern of action—a pattern of escape and return, at once tragic and hopeful—which was likely to flow from the situation as given. In addition, Hawthorne felt very deeply the intimacy between experience and art, and he enacted a change as well in the resources and methods of the narrative art: something which mirrored, even while it articulated, his heroes' and heroines' adventures. Finally, it was Hawthorne who saw in American experience the re-creation of the story of Adam and who, more than any other contemporary, exploited the active metaphor of the American as Adam—before and during and after the Fall. These are the three aspects of Hawthorne that I shall consider.

I

The opening scene of *The Scarlet Letter* is the paradigm dramatic image in American literature. With that scene and that novel, New World fiction arrived at its first fulfilment, and Hawthorne at his. And with that scene, all that was dark and treacherous in the American situation became exposed. Hawthorne said later that the writing of *The Scarlet Letter* had been oddly simple, since all he had to do was to get his "pitch" and then to let it carry him along. He found his pitch in an opening tableau fairly humming with tension—with coiled and covert relationships that contained a force perfectly calculated to propel the action thereafter in a direct line to its tragic climax.

It was the tableau of the solitary figure set over against the inimical society, in a village which hovers on the edge of the inviting and perilous wilderness; a handsome young woman standing on a raised platform, confronting in silence and pride a hostile crowd whose menace is deepened by its order and dignity; a young woman who has come alone to the New World, where circumstances have divided her from the community now gathered to oppose her; standing alone, but vitally aware of the private enemy and the private lover—one on the far verges of the crowd, one at the place of honor within it, and neither conscious of the other—who must affect her destiny and who will assist at each other's destruction. Here the situation inherent in the American scene was seized entire and without damage to it by an imagination both moral and visual of the highest quality: seized and located, not any longer on the margins of the plot, but at its very center.

The conflict is central because it is total; because Hawthorne makes us respect each element in it. Hawthorne felt, as Brown and Cooper and Bird had felt, that the stuff of narrative (in so far as it was drawn from local experience) consisted in the imaginable brushes between the deracinated and solitary individual and the society or world awaiting him. But Hawthorne had learned the lesson only fitfully apprehended by Cooper. In *The Scarlet Letter* not only do the individual and the world, the conduct and the institutions, measure each other: the measurement and its consequences are precisely and centrally what the novel is about. Hester Prynne has been wounded by an unfriendly world; but the society facing her is invested by Hawthorne with assurance and authority, its opposition is defensible and even valid. Hester's misdeed appears as a disturbance of the moral structure of the universe; and the society continues to insist in its joyless way that certain acts deserve the honor of punishment. But if Hester has sinned, she has done so as an affirmation of life, and her sin is the source of life; she incarnates those rights of personality that society is inclined to trample upon. The action of the novel springs from the enormous but improbable suggestion that the society's estimate of the moral structure of the universe may be tested and found inaccurate.

The Scarlet Letter, like all very great fiction, is the product of a controlled division of sympathies; and we must avoid the temptation to read it heretically. It has always been possible to remark, about Hawthorne, his fondness for the dusky places, his images of the slow movement of sad, shut-in souls in the half-light. But it has also been possible to read *The Scarlet Letter* (not to mention "The New Adam and Eve" and "Earth's Holocaust") as an indorsement of hopefulness: to read it as a hopeful critic named Loring read it (writing for Theodore Parker's forward-looking *Massachusetts Quarterly Review*) as a party plea for self-reliance and an attack upon the sterile conventions of institutionalized society. One version of him would align Hawthorne with the secular residue of Jonathan Edwards; the other would bring him closer to Emerson. But Hawthorne was neither Emersonian nor Edwardsean; or rather he was both. The characteristic situation in his fiction is that of the Emersonian figure, the man of hope, who by some frightful mischance has stumbled into the time-burdened world of Jonathan Edwards. And this grim picture is given us by a writer who was skeptically cordial toward Emerson, but for whom the vision of Edwards, filtered through a haze of hope, remained a wonderfully useful metaphor.[1] The situation, in the form which Hawthorne's ambivalence gave it, regularly led in his fiction to a moment of crucial choice: an invitation to the lost Emersonian, the thunder-struck Adam, to make up his mind—whether to accept the world he had fallen into, or whether to flee it, taking his chances in the allegedly free wilderness to the west. It is a decision about ethical reality, and most of Hawthorne's heroes and heroines eventually have to confront it.

That is why we have the frantic shuttling, in novel after novel, between the village and the forest, the city and the country; for these are the symbols between which the choice must be made and the means by which moral inference is converted into dramatic action. Unlike Thoreau or Cooper, Hawthorne never suggested that the choice was an easy one. Even Arthur Mervyn had been made to reflect on "the contrariety that exists between the city and the country"; in the age of hope the contrariety was taken more or less simply to lie between the restraints of custom and the fresh expansiveness of freedom. Hawthorne perceived greater complexities. He acknowledged the dependence of the individual, for nourishment, upon organized society (the city), and he believed that it was imperative "to open an intercourse with the world." But he knew that the city could destroy as well as

---

1. Cf. the fine observation and the accompanying discussion of Mark Van Doren, in *Nathaniel Hawthorne* (1949), p. 162: "Hawthorne did not need to believe in Puritanism in order to write a great novel about it. He had only to understand it, which for a man of his time was harder."

nourish and was apt to destroy the person most in need of nourishment. And while he was responsive to the attractions of the open air and to the appeal of the forest, he also understood the grounds for the Puritan distrust of the forest. He retained that distrust as a part of the symbol. In the forest, possibility was unbounded; but just because of that, evil inclination was unchecked, and witches could flourish there.

For Hawthorne, the forest was neither the proper home of the admirable Adam, as with Cooper; nor was it the hideout of the malevolent adversary, as with Bird. It was the ambiguous setting of moral choice, the scene of reversal and discovery in his characteristic tragic drama. The forest was the pivot in Hawthorne's grand recurring pattern of escape and return.

It is in the forest, for example, that *The Scarlet Letter* version of the pattern begins to disclose itself: in the forest meeting between Hester and Dimmesdale, their first private meeting in seven years. During those years, Hester has been living "on the outskirts of the town," attempting to cling to the community by performing small services for it, though there had been nothing "in all her intercourse with society . . . that made her feel as if she belonged to it." And the minister has been contemplating the death of his innocence in a house fronting the village graveyard. The two meet now to join in an exertion of the will and the passion for freedom. They very nearly persuade themselves that they can escape along the forest track, which, though in one direction it goes "backward to the settlement," in another goes onward—"deeper it goes, and deeper into the wilderness, until . . . the yellow leaves will show no vestiges of the white man's tread." But the energy aroused by their encounter drives them back instead, at the end, to the heart of the society, to the penitential platform which is also the heart of the book's structure.

In no other novel is the *agon* so sharp, the agony so intense. But the pattern is there again in *The Marble Faun*, as Miriam and Donatello flee separately from the city to the wooded Apennines to waste their illicit exultation in the discovery that they must return to Rome and the responsibility for their crime. It is true that Zenobia, in *The Blithedale Romance*, never does return from her flight: because her escape consummates itself in suicide, and she drowns in the river running through the woods near the utopian colony. Zenobia, who is often associated in the narrator's fancy with the figure of Eve, is too much of an Eve to survive her private calamity. The more usual outcome—more usual, that is, with Hawthorne—is realized in a sort of tremulous parody by the abortive train ride of Hepzibah and Clifford Pyncheon in *The House of the Seven Gables*—"the flight of the two owls," who get only a station or so along the line into the country before limping back to town to confess to a crime which has not after all been committed.

It is poor Clifford who most blatantly gives voice to the contemporary aspirations imitated in these journeys, as he babbles on in an echo of the hopeful language he must have heard from Holgrave, the daguerreotypist. Homelessness, he explains to an embarrassed fellow-passenger, is the best of conditions; "the soul needs air: a wide sweep and a frequent change of it." He sees "the world and my best days before me" and is sure the flight has restored him to "the very heyday of my youth." These exclamations comprise the first principles of Adamism; Clifford trembles in the untenable belief that he has fulfilled the action attributed (by Lawrence) to Cooper's Hawkeye—the motion "backwards from old age to golden youth." The ironic context for his babbling and the total collapse that it rapidly leads to reveal that here, for the first time in American fiction, the story of Adam has become an element of the story actually being narrated—and so begins to suffer serious modification. Clifford, too, wants to make that leap from memory to hope; his Adamic ambition is an ingredient in the novel; but his leap is Icarian.

Many things are being *tested* as well as exemplified in these circular journeys, in the pattern of escape and return. Among them, the doctrine inherited from Edwards that "an evil taint, in consequence of a crime committed twenty or forty years ago, remain[s] still, and even to the end of the world and forever." Among them, too, the proposition, implicit in much American writing from Poe and Cooper to Anderson and Hemingway, that the valid rite of initiation for the individual in the new world is not an initiation *into* society, but, given the character of society, an initiation *away from it:* something I wish it were legitimate to call "*de*nitiation." The true nature of human wickedness is also in question. Hawthorne's heroes and heroines are almost always criminals, according to the positive laws of the land, but Hawthorne presumed all men and women to be somehow criminals, and himself not the least so. The elder James reported to Emerson how Hawthorne had looked to him at a Saturday Club meeting in Boston: "like a rogue who finds himself in the company of detectives"; we can imagine him there: furtive, uneasy, out of place, half-guilty and half-defiant, poised for instant flight. No doubt it was because he appraised his personal condition this way that Hawthorne so frequently put his characters in the same dilemma: James's comment is a droll version of the opening glimpse of Hester Prynne. And no doubt also this was why Hawthorne so obviously sympathized with what he nevertheless regarded as an impossible enterprise—the effort to escape.

But if he customarily brought his sufferers back *into* the community; if he submitted most of his rogues to ultimate arrest; if the "evil taint" does turn out to be ineradicable, it was not because Hawthorne yielded in the end to the gloomy doctrine of Edwards. It was much rather because, for all his ambivalence, Hawthorne had made a daring guess about the entire rhythm of experience and so was willing to risk the whole of it. His qualifications as a novelist were at stake; for if the guess had been less comprehensive, he would have been a novelist of a very different kind: an inferior Melville, perhaps, exhausting himself in an excess of response to every tragic, new, unguessed-at collision. But if the guess had been any more certain, he might scarcely have been a novelist at all, but some sort of imperturbable tractarian. As it was, he could share some part of the hope motivating the flight; he could always see beyond the hope to the inevitable return; and he could even see a little distance beyond the outcome of surrender to the light and strength it perhaps assured.

Beneath the sunshine that illuminates the soul's surface, he once wrote, there is a region of horror that seems, to the inward traveler, "like hell itself," and through which the self wanders without hope; but deeper still there is a place of perfect beauty. He was not often so certain, but that was the substance of his guess about experience. And this is why there is always more to the world in which Hawthorne's characters move than any one of them can see at a glance. There is more than the surface sunshine covering the whole horizon of the hopeful of his day or his fiction—his "new Adam and Eve," the comfortable customers of his "Celestial Railroad," in their untested faith in human purity and in a new world all the braver because it had stamped out the past. But there is more too, much more, than the darkness, the monsters, and the divers shapes which tormented the souls of the lost and the guilty—Mr. Hooper behind his black veil, Reuben Bourne of "Roger Melvin's Burial," young Goodman Brown. There was still some fulfilment of the spirit, some realization of the entire self which it was worth losing one's self to find; only the lost, indeed, were likely to find it on their return journey, though a soul might shrivel, like young Brown's, in the process.

The Return into Time: Hawthorne

II

The nature and prerequisites of the achievement Hawthorne envisaged are best illustrated by *The Marble Faun*—though that novel sometimes gains its clarity at the expense of its poetry. The achievement in question was, of course, a kind of salvation: Hawthorne's kind. And his kind seemed to depend upon an individual perception which was in great part artistic. *The Marble Faun* is a novel explicitly about the hero as Adam; but it is no less a novel about the heroine as artist. In it, Hawthorne's sense of the analogy between human creativity and human conduct—so evident elsewhere in his fiction—receives its most thorough and complex expression. The artistic dimension of *The Marble Faun* is neither secondary nor peripheral; it is precisely the dimension in which the story's chief "epiphany" is clinched.

There is, for example, a moment in the novel when the pattern of escape and return is conducted entirely in terms of artistic creation. Miriam, the dark-haired heroine of the book and the spokesman for both ethical *and* creative freedom from the past, discovers that her self-portrait is a very recognizable, though unconscious, copy of a stylized portrait of the sixteenth century. The shock of that recognition sets off a chain reaction. Miriam's acknowledgment of the resemblance between her own portrait and that of a long-dead lady helps her later to perceive the resemblance between the action she has shared with Donatello and the adventure of a long-dead pair—of Adam and Eve, in fact. It is a saving shock, for salvation by recognition is the heart of the book's epiphany. It is the kind of perception, Hawthorne suggests, which restores the self to its right relation with the world; it is the great means of control both in art and in life.

Here, as in a number of his other writings, Hawthorne presents a judgment about Adam as artist (the hopeful ideal) which spilled over into a judgment of Adam as moral agent. He always had a good deal to say about the problems of the artist in America; and as to the available materials for literature, he shared the misgivings of Channing and Cooper about their meagerness. In the little notes with which he took to introducing his novels—as though bracing himself in advance for a poor reception—Hawthorne contended that human relations cast too slight a shadow in America for the artist's purpose; that there was too little texture in American life; and that, besides, the temper of his countrymen contained too little tragic expectancy. Those were his discursive pronouncements; but Hawthorne delivered his most cogent opinions and his principal doubts by the more artful means of stories about writers and artists.

There are a surprising number of the latter; and, indeed, in Hawthorne's tales and novels the moral agents—persons of no stated vocation who are simply vessels of ambition or guilt or wayward desire—seem almost to alternate as main characters with those who are artists by profession: the unnamed painter of "The Prophetic Pictures"; Drowne, the carver of the wooden image; Owen Warland, the goldsmith in "The Artist of the Beautiful"; Kenyon, the sculptor, and Miriam and Hilda, painters, in *The Marble Faun;* Coverdale, the poet in *The Blithedale Romance;* Holgrave, the daguerreotypist in *The House of the Seven Gables.* The number of them testifies to the curious significance that Hawthorne attributed to his own profession; and the alternation testifies to his deep sense of the analogy.

Something further was probably at work in the bundle of artistic anecdotes: namely, a certain perplexity on Hawthorne's part, prompted by the same misgivings he spoke of in the Preface. In more recent fiction the ubiquity of the artist as hero has meant one of two things: that the writer (like Joyce) has hit upon the artist as the representative figure in the modern world or that the writer (like Gide) has found it so difficult to cope with the shadowless fragmentations of the immediate scene that he is forced to take that difficulty as the only subject he can bear living witness to. In the latter case, one is presented less with the imitation of an action than with the trials of the imitator; the artist in the work is not so much a hero as an apology for the absence of a hero; literature doubles back on itself and becomes obsessed with the task of exploiting its own tribulations.

A century ago, the American scene—not because it was falling apart, but inversely because it had not yet come together—gave some warrant to the self-consuming anxiety which issued in poetry about poetry and the troubled self-portrait. Hawthorne exhibited an uneasy awareness of the almost wilful contemporary impoverishment of artistic resources; perhaps this accounts for the proportion of artists among the characters he invented—or at least for the proportion of frustrated artists, like Miriam and Owen Warland and Coverdale. Hawthorne's anxiety was increased by his conviction that creativity was an analogous, possibly even an alternate, route to salvation. For Hawthorne could neither share the belief of his Puritan ancestors that the artistic enterprise was at best a mere trope for the really impressive work of the rescue of the human soul; nor could he arrive at the later romantic avowal that what had formerly been described as the rescue of the soul was in reality a concealed metaphor for the greatest human accomplishment—that is, for art.

It was a matter, for Hawthorne, of an analogy almost amounting to an equivalence—and, on the whole, an equivalence of difficulty and frustration. Thus, in "The Artist of the Beautiful" (1843), Owen Warland is willing to seek fulfilment either in "life" (via love and marriage and acceptance within the village community) or in the making of beautiful objects. Frustrated in life, he turns to art; and when he has fashioned an object of supreme beauty, it is destroyed by the clumsy hands of those same persons who had previously rejected him. The story closes with a reflection much admired by Melville and seeming to point to a resolution: "When an artist rises high enough to achieve the beautiful, the symbol by which he made it perceptible to mortal sense became of little value in his eyes, while his spirit possessed itself in the enjoyment of the reality." But I think we should take this as ironic, since the story it concludes is itself a perceptible symbol and indestructible; the conclusion is, in fact, a knowing description of the habitual recourse of the thwarted transcendentalizing imagination.

The hopeful, and especially the transcendental, critic pinned his faith on the Now, as the subject of fiction and poetry: the Now purged of accretions from the past. Hawthorne remarked, in another but relevant context, that the "visionary and impalpable Now . . . if you once look closely at it, is nothing." And, indeed, the stuff of the Now did tend to evaporate, under artistic scrutiny. Yet the hopeful critic continued to insist that the Now was the only portion of *time* important to the writer, because if the immediate could be jostled long enough, beams of the Eternal would begin to show up in it; and it was with the Eternal that poetry had to deal. This was the tactic of writers like Emerson and Thoreau, and occasionally even of Herman Melville: they manipulated the concrete and transient to the point where, in the climaxes of paragraphs, they could set off metaphysical sky-rockets. And the creative spirit thereupon possessed itself in the enjoyment of the higher "reality." This was the procedure proper to what Allen Tate has called the "angelic imagination": the imagination prompted by the assumption that humans, like angels, can have direct perception of timeless essences. Now if anyone was certain that men were not in any respect like angels, it was Nathaniel Hawthorne; though he was restless and heretical enough to wish sometimes that they were and to tell, as in the tale of Owen Warland or of Aylmer in "The Birthmark," the sad story of someone who thought so. Given his conviction, however, Hawthorne could never rest in Owen Warland's complacency; he had to do what, according to Mr. Tate, "the symbolic imagination" always had to do: "to return to the order of temporal sequence—to *action*."

Hawthorne returned to "the order of temporal sequence" for the purpose of getting beyond it. He wanted to be in touch with the eternal as much as did the transcendentalists; but he suspected that men, imperfect animals that they were, saw *through* time rather than over it or around it. When he forgot this suspicion, he tended to indulge in those *concetti* which Henry James rightly regarded as his greatest weakness.[2] When he remembered, he enlisted his language on the side of the actual in such a way that he was able to look within occurrences for signs of *re*-currence, to probe the action for what it *re*-enacted. He listened for echoes. For Hawthorne at his best, it was a question of the right quotation: a very hard question in an age which thought it slavish to quote. The moral and artistic awareness Hawthorne was struggling to realize has been expressed in our generation by Thomas Mann: "Life so to speak in quotation is a kind of celebration, in that it is a making present of the past." But the awareness urged upon Hawthorne's generation was indicated in Emerson's abrupt little sentence: "I hate quotations. Tell me what you know." This was a painful utterance for anyone who felt that telling what he knew was precisely what quotations were good for. It was just that contempt for the past—as the source of symbols explanatory of the present—which led to Hawthorne's anxiety about the profession he had chosen; his anxiety was dramatized in his stories about artists. But in *The Marble Faun*, Hawthorne tackled the job of exploiting even the anxiety: of finding the right quotation for the hatred or ignorance of quotation itself.

III

The Marble Faun describes a double or perhaps a triple return into time: the return of art itself as expressed by analogy in the enforced and tragic return of the hero and the hero's artist-lover. On the literal level there is simply the return of a young man to the city of Rome to surrender himself to justice. The vibrations of that return bear testimony to Hawthorne's expert sense of the right relation between character and setting. Cooper was right to place his Adamic hero, at the moment of his rebirth, in the benign and timeless forest beyond the frontier. Hawthorne was no less astute to lead his own Adam to

2. In a little-known essay on Hawthorne, contained in *Library of the World's Best Literature*, edited by Charles Dudley Warner (New York, 1897), XII, 7055.

his transfiguring experience in an environment dense with the linked histories of several scores of generations. Donatello in *The Marble Faun* is the most innocent person and the figure least conscious of the force and challenge of time in nineteenth-century American literature, with the exception of Billy Budd. And he is introduced in the midst of an immeasurable and continuously influential antiquity—an antiquity which touches him not at all, until he has sinned.

The novel's plot verges more than once on incoherence and wanders somewhat helplessly for about a dozen chapters, while we wonder whether Hawthorne will find the sustaining power to finish it. *The Marble Faun* is not the best and probably not even the second-best of Hawthorne's novels; but its deficiencies are deficiencies of talent rather than of genius. The incoherence, that is, remains for the most part superficial and in the execution; it only slightly impairs our view of the classical design of the action. With an eye on the action, we may reduce the plot to the following incidents:

Donatello, a young Italian nobleman of great simplicity and charm, encounters in Rome a group of visiting artists: two Americans, Kenyon and Hilda, and a beautiful dark-haired Anglo-Jewish woman, Miriam. Falling in love with Miriam, Donatello becomes aware of some mysterious event in her early private history, and of the continuing pressure exerted by a Capuchin monk, evidently a participant in the event, who now lurks menacingly on the the periphery of Miriam's new life.

Incited by Miriam's fear of the Capuchin, her violent desire to be free of him, and perhaps an actual gesture of encouragement, Donatello murders him. Donatello flees Rome to his country estate at Monte Beni in the Apennines, to brood on the meaning of his act and upon his own muddled responses to it. Miriam follows him. They meet and agree that neither of them may escape the consequences of the crime. Donatello returns to Rome and gives himself up; he is last heard of in the depths of a civil prison. But the experience has transformed him into a man.

Miriam returns to give *her*self up to a life of penance, entering upon a pilgrimage to last as long as Donatello's imprisonment, which may be lifelong. Their friends, Kenyon and Hilda, having in some degree shared in the tragedy, are its survivors; and the gloom of the conclusion is faintly lit by the subdued joy of their discovery of each other and their belief—however faltering—in the value of the adventure they have all of them shared.

Thus the plot: an assortment of rather melodramatic incidents with those Mysteries-of-Udolpho overtones later complained of by Eliot. Donatello's resemblance to the marble faun of Praxiteles gave the novel its American title. *The Marble Faun* is apt enough as regards the plot; but *Transformation*, the title supplied by the English publishers, is a better index to the action; and it may be because Hawthorne knew that action only becomes realized in plot that he referred to the English publishers as pigheaded. That action is the transformation of the soul in its journey from innocence to conscience: the soul's realization of itself under the impact of and by engagement with evil—the tragic rise born of the fortunate fall. It is a New World action—my supposition is that it is *the* New World action, the tragic remainder of what Lawrence called the myth of America. It is what has to happen to "golden youth" if it is to mature; and the novel is the kind of novel which had to be written if the young literature was to mature. Donatello, though purportedly an Italian aristocrat, is nonetheless the hero of the hopeful, seen in a tragic perspective: the figure who, in approaching experience, comes up against the social world under the great, appealing illusion that (in the words of Horace Bushnell) he is "a free person [who has] just begun to be."

The outline of Donatello's personality is made known to us through the recurring imagery of Eden: imagery employed in the beginning only by Hawthorne; then, after the "Fall," by Kenyon and Hilda; and only at the last by Miriam. This progression of insight and recognition is the core of the story. To Miriam, stifled by her own enveloping history, Donatello appears as "a creature in a state of development less than what mankind has attained"; less than mankind, yet oddly more perfect; a "creature of simple elements," part animal and part child, manifesting a kinship to "that wild, sweet, playful, rustic creature" whose marble image he resembled, and manifesting, too, the unreasoning variability of animals—the docility of the pet spaniel, the tenacity of the bulldog. The action of *The Marble Faun* is the assumption of total manhood by this child-animal. The young innocent becomes entangled (in the way Bushnell predicted that, given the world, he would have to be) with the net of pre-existing relationships —involvements which, like those between Miriam and the Capuchin, the hero's very character makes it impossible for him to intuit or guard himself against. The action concludes not only with the hero's assumption of manhood but with the imaginative grasp by Miriam and more uneasily by Kenyon of the meaning and the value of the sin and suffering which manhood requires.

The action has to do with the discovery of *time* as a metaphor of the experience of evil. Rome is thus the best imaginable setting; nothing in the New World could match it. What was wanted, for the maximum effect, was maximum antiquity—a symbol coexistent, if possible, with the temporal order itself; and Rome is identified in the story as "the city of all time." The seven-gabled home of the Pyncheons had reached back a century or so to the Puritan period, and Hawthorne did all he could with it. But Rome, Hawthorne remarks on the opening page of *The Marble Faun*, reaches back through a "threefold antiquity"—Christian, Roman, Etruscan. And it is in dramatic contrast to such massive age that the hero is then promptly introduced as an "Arcadian simpleton." The tension between the simpleton unconscious of time and the infinitely history-laden environment parallels the introductory tension of *The Scarlet Letter:* between Hester Prynne and the hostile community. The action in *The Scarlet Letter*, discharged by that opening tableau, follows Hester's effort to escape from the community and her eventual return into it, to spend her life there as an increasingly revered member. In *The Marble Faun*, the action unfolds from its starting point: in terms of Donatello's consciousness of the quality, the content, the pressures of time. It is thus only *after* the sin and the flight that Donatello seems to grow aware of his own ancestry—explaining to Kenyon, at Monte Beni, that his family history goes back beyond the Middle Ages to earliest Christendom and perhaps to a time before that. Donatello's family, like the city of Rome, has a multiple antiquity; and his acceptance of the burden of inheritance may be his way of coming to terms with all that Rome represents in the novel: with the world.

The degree of actual tension in *The Marble Faun* is the degree of Hawthorne's divided sympathies toward the contending factors. And he was not less ambivalent toward time than he had been toward the Puritan community. His involvement with time, always profound, had always been notably ambiguous. It was not a metaphysical interest; Hawthorne had been concerned not with the ontological status of time, but with its contents and effects: not with time as a concept, but with the coloration it lent to the things it perpetuated and with the value or the misfortune of sustained temporal relations. He had a passion for sources and beginnings, for traditions and continuities, and resented in America the scantiness of histories. Though Tocqueville was unduly impressed by the claims of the hopeful and had doubted that American poetry would "be fed with legends or the memorials of old traditions," Hawthorne never seemed able to get hold of legends and traditions enough. He wore out the few he could find; and it may have been to refurbish his stock that in 1853 he consented to go to Europe as his government's representative. In Europe, where he tripped over unchanging traditions and customs in appalling abundance, his resentment veered around toward the ancient.

"At home," Henry James remarked (1895), "he had fingered the musty; but abroad he seemed to pine for freshness." Both sides of the observation can be matched by its opposite. Even in the American days, the musty needed the fresh in the shaping of rewarding experience: this is the very formula that somewhat tamely concludes *The House of the Seven Gables*. And while, in England, Hawthorne consigned to the flames the accumulated treasures ("rubbish") of the British Museum and wondered how human aspiration could tolerate English social immobility, nonetheless in Paris he lamented fluidity and thought that nothing worth while could take root there.

Hawthorne himself had identified his generation's major ideal in the image of Adam, and he both celebrated and deplored it. The individual divorced from his racial or family past seemed to Hawthorne at once a liberated person and a lost son: an orphan, as he also had been. Such an ambivalence, the very stuff of drama, stayed with Hawthorne to the end; even in the inchoate and unfinished *Dr. Grimshawe's Secret* (posthumous, 1883), the hero, Redclyffe, is an orphan cast afloat in the American world, who travels to England, motivated by "a great deal of foolish yearning for a connection with the past." Redclyffe's nostalgia is for the kind of "density" he finds in the atmosphere of an English country estate: a thickening of life and character caused by the hidden vitality of the past. In such a place, Redclyffe supposes, "the life of each successive dweller was eked out with the lives of all who had hitherto lived there . . . so that there was a rare and successful contrivance for giving length, fullness, body, substance, to this thin frail matter of human life." Yet Redclyffe stubbornly votes for America and returns there; America's homes were mere "tents of a day, inns of a night"; but, though its atmosphere was much thinner, it was also much freer. That was Hawthorne's personal conclusion, too, after a comparable meditation in Florence.

The Marble Faun was a dramatization on a large scale of these many fertile contradictions. The question of density was as relevant to art as to life. Fulness and substance for his thin, frail materials was just what the American artist needed, according to Hawthorne; and Rome offered the narrative artist every contrivance for giving such substance to the events recounted. Rome's "very dust . . . is historic," it is noted; and every fragment of church or temple is "a great solid fact out of the past." Hawthorne extended himself to exploit each indication of the past as the source of life in the present: newly built houses are "perched on the lofty delapidations of a tomb"; the Capuchin, for a Gothic moment, is confused with a legendary Wandering

Pagan, lost in the Catacombs for fifteen hundred years; life feeds on death; Christianity is bolstered by paganism; the past is everywhere the exemplar or the substructure of the present. But the cumulative force of those associations, strained as some of them may be, is precisely to give maximum meaning to Miriam's cry of desperate and ebbing hope: "Is the past so indestructible, the future so immitigable?" The tension of the novel is provided by the vigor of Miriam's effort to escape the consequences of her private past and the solidity of the "fact" of the past in general.

The tension is illuminated by analogous oppositions within the field of artistic creation. Hilda, after a brief attempt at original creation, yields entirely to the work of copying the old masters; but her honesty and her heightened enjoyment of the beauty contrived by others are contrasted with the pretenses of an English sculptor who cooks up lifeless imitations of the antique and is an effete slave (Kenyon thinks) to something "whose business or efficacy in our present world, it would be exceedingly difficult to define." Miriam turns her back altogether on the art of the past, claiming to paint wholly from the self and about the self; and her self-portrait becomes an unconscious imitation of the very painting—the "Beatrice" of Guido—which Hilda is currently engaged in copying.

This is one of the major "epiphanies" in the book—one of the major moments of reversal and recognition—and a crucial event in Miriam's education. It makes possible a recognition by her of the mythic model for the adventure she has shared with Donatello; and *that* recognition is the means of accepting it, appraising the experience, and knowing what to do about it. It is Donatello who acts and is acted upon, but it is Miriam who is gifted with the perception that controls the action at last and rounds out the novel. *"The story of the fall of man! Is it not repeated in our romance of Monte Beni?"*

The value of the identification is a sudden tremendous deepening of insight. Miriam explores the analogy further: the authentic manliness of the former child-animal Donatello may, she believes, offer a clue to an ancient mystery. "Was that very sin—into which Adam precipitated himself and all his race—was it the destined means by which, over a long pathway of toil and sorrow, we are to attain a higher, brighter, and profounder happiness, than our lost birthright gave?" If the Fall was, after all, immensely fortunate, so then was Donatello's re-enactment of the Fall. Miriam is saved by the analogy: by her grasp of the analogy.

And so, perhaps, is Kenyon. A little later, he confronts Hilda with the novel's concluding ambiguity: that the adventure has proved life too "deadly serious" for anyone, like Donatello, "compounded especially for happiness"; or that Donatello's adventure illustrates the fact that "Adam fell that we might ultimately rise to a far loftier paradise than his." Hilda is far too "hopeful and happy-natured" to settle for either. A small shudder runs through the final pages at the suggestion of a fortunate fall; yet the lingering, uneasy impression remains that there has been demonstrated in action what the elder James had argued in theory. Hilda, and all the world, may call Donatello's action a crime or a sin. But his fall was in many serious respects an upward step—an entrance into that true reality which, for Hawthorne, is measured by time.

Wandering through the vineyards near Donatello's country estate, Kenyon speculates on Donatello's action and the astonishing mental and moral maturity it has bred in him. In the physical scenery about him Kenyon senses an answer by metaphor to the speculations that trouble him. He looks upon the setting "with somewhat the sensations of an adventurer who should find his way to the site of ancient Eden, and behold its loveliness through the transparency of gloom which has been brooding over those haunts of innocence ever since the fall." The gloom is there, but perhaps it has a greater beauty than the original. "Adam," reflects Kenyon, "saw it in a brighter sunshine, but never knew the shade of pensive beauty which Eden won from his expulsion." The language and the response suggest that here is an adjustment to time which offers a control for life. To the eye of the artist, the color of time was very much richer than the blankness of the original sunshine. For such was the nature of man.

7

Melville: The Apotheosis of Adam

I bless his story,
The Good Being hung and gone to glory.

HERMAN MELVILLE[1]

THE *Marble Faun* completed a cycle of adventures carrying a representative American fictional hero from his ritual birth (in Cooper) through a "fall" which can be claimed as fortunate because of the growth in perception and moral intelligence granted the hero as a result of it. If we abstract an anecdote, in this hazardous way, from a series of novels taken in sequence, we find something dealt with so often and so variously by American writers after Hawthorne that it may be regarded as the major (if not the only) "matter" by which they have sought to advance their craft. We can call it "the matter of Adam," since for those who have recognized it—Hawthorne, Melville, James, and Faulkner at the least—it was as usable as "the matter of France" or "the matter of Troy" once was for poets in the medieval world. It has been the primary stuff by which the American novelist has managed to articulate his sense of the form and pressure of experience and by which he has extended the possibilities of the art of fiction. In this chapter we consider how the one novelist in nineteenth-century America gifted with a genuinely myth-making imagination was able to elevate the anecdote to the status of myth, and so give it a permanent place among the resources of our literature.

The matter of Adam: the ritualistic trials of the young innocent, liberated from family and social history or bereft of them; advancing hopefully into a complex world he knows not of; radically affecting that world and radically affected by it; defeated, perhaps even de-

1. From a fragment contained in the so-called "Daniel Orme manuscript," i.e., an unfinished anecdote, intended to be part of *Billy Budd* and presumably dealing with the life of the old Dansker in that *novella*. The fragment seems a variation on the ballad, "Billy in the Darbies," which closes *Billy Budd* (*Melville's Billy Budd*, ed. F. Baron Freeman [Cambridge, Mass., 1948], p. 282).

stroyed—in various versions of the recurring anecdote hanged, beaten, shot, betrayed, abandoned—but leaving his mark upon the world, and a sign in which conquest may later become possible for the survivors. *In hoc signo vince:* the analogy is inescapable, and it was Herman Melville who first made it manifest.

The Adamic hero is the equivalent, in American fiction, of the prince or king in the long tradition of classical drama. The telling distinction is one of strategic distance: the distance at the outset between the hero and the world he must cope with. For the traditional hero is at the center of that world, the glass of its fashion, the symbol of its power, the legatee of its history. But the American hero as Adam takes his start outside the world, remote or on the verges; its power, its fashions, and its history are precisely the forces he must learn, must master or be mastered by. Oedipus, approaching the strange city-world of Thebes, was in fact coming home; the hero of the new world has no home to begin with, but he seeks one to come.

The Adamic hero is an "outsider," but he is "outside" in a curiously staunch and artistically demanding manner. He is to be distinguished from the kind of outsider—the dispossessed, the superfluous, the alienated, the exiled—who began to enter European fiction in the nineteenth century and who crowds its almost every page in the twentieth. A distinguished critic of Conrad, Morton Zabel, has listed the major causes of "alone-ness" for Conrad's heroes, and the list will serve, I think, for many another European writer obsessed with the same theme: "A man may be alone because he is a banished wastrel who has made life a law unto himself . . . because he is young and irresponsible . . . because fate has estranged him from the ties of normal life . . . because he has become disgraced in the eyes of society or betrayed by a false confidence or idealism . . . because he has betrayed a trust . . . because he fosters the intolerance and arrogance of self-willed pride . . . or because . . . a fatal vein of skepticism in his nature has induced a nihilism of all values."[2] Most of the outsiders in European fiction of the past century may be catalogued under one or another of those heads, from Turgenev's superfluous men to Gide's bastards and Mann's artists, to the hero of the existentialists and the restless spiritual prowlers of Kafka and Greene (especially if we allow a theological flavor to words like "fate" and "society" in the quotation). But there is no satisfactory category there for Donatello or Redburn, Pierre or Billy Budd, for Huck Finn or Daisy Miller, Isabel Archer or even Jay Gatsby. These are, by some magic of art, morally

2. Morton D. Zabel, Introduction to the Viking Portable *Conrad* (New York, 1947).

prior to the world which nonetheless awaits them; as between them and the world, it can be questioned who is outside of whom. It is not, as with the European characters, that the realities of social experience and action catch up with them; but it is they who approach and enter into those realities, with alternative comic, disastrous, or triumphant consequences. Their creators seem ready to proffer their private dignity and their very amount of being as worthy to compare with the dignity and being of the public world—something demanding a special gift of artistic duplicity. And even if Mr. Zabel's *loci* can contain Hester Prynne, Captain Ahab, and Faulkner's Joe Christmas, it cannot contain the whole of them; for they are tormented extensions and distortions of their Adamic prototypes.

What is perhaps surprising is the regular recurrence of the hero as Adam, long after his story had been brought to its logical conclusion by Hawthorne and Melville. Two possible but opposite explanations for the endurance of the hero and the story suggest themselves. We may suppose that there has been a kind of resistance in America to the painful process of growing up, something mirrored and perhaps buttressed by our writers, expressing itself in repeated efforts to revert to a lost childhood and a vanished Eden, and issuing repeatedly in a series of outcries at the freshly discovered capacity of the world to injure.

On the other hand, when the narrative account of the hero as Adam is lit by the author's awareness of the American habit of resistance to maturity, then the continuing life both of the hero and of his story are evidence rather of cultural manhood. It has been said that America is always coming of age; but it might be more fairly maintained that America has come of age in sections, here and there—whenever its implicit myth of the American Adam has been a defining part of the writer's consciousness. When this has happened, the emergent mythology of the new world has been recognized and exploited as a stable resource; the writer has found means, at hand and at home, for a fresh definition of experience and a fresh contribution to the culture. This is what is meant, I take it, by cultural maturity.

Melville is our most revealing example of both the contradictory inferences here suggested. He may or may not, as Professor Thompson has argued,[3] have engaged in a lifelong quarrel with God; but he certainly engaged in a long quarrel with himself—the kind of quarrel which, as Yeats said, makes poetry. For Melville took the loss of innocence and the world's betrayal of hope as the supreme challenge to

3. Lawrence Thompson, *Melville's Quarrel with God* (Princeton, 1952).

understanding and to art. He wanted not to accept that betrayal; and for a while he kept going back over the ground of the experience as if to prove the betrayal untrue or avoidable. That illusory effort is part of the meaning of *Redburn* and most of the meaning of *Pierre* and *Clarel*. But in the course of his deeply vexed odyssey, Melville found the resources for coming to terms with his losses: terms of extraordinarily creative tension in *Moby-Dick* and terms of luminous resolution in *Billy Budd*. His resources were moral and intellectual ones, but they were available to him only as he discovered the artistic resources. Experience fulfilled and explained itself for Melville only and finally in language. He was the writer above all others who could have asked Forster's question: "How do I know what I think till I see what I say?"

What Melville thought at the end, when he saw everything he had said, was, curiously enough, a dialectically heightened value in something he had supposed irretrievably destroyed. He found a new conviction about the saving strength of the Adamic personality. When this conviction became articulate in *Billy Budd*, the American hero as Adam became the hero as Christ and entered, once and for all, into the dimension of myth.

II

Only so much of Melville and his writing is relevant here as bears upon the history of the American Adam: as symbol of a possible individual condition, as type of hero for fiction. But it is in the nature of Melville's achievement that any fragment of his writing, or all of it together, can seem to respond directly to any serious question we ask of it. Any set of symbols, as Mark Van Doren gracefully remarked about *The Tempest*, "lights up as in an electric field" when moved close to a novel or *novella* of Herman Melville. The best of him corresponds to the "substances" mentioned in *White-Jacket*, which "without undergoing any mutations in themselves, utterly change their colour, according to the light thrown upon them." Critical light, pumped out all too dazzlingly these latter years, has thus been able to disclose a multitude of Melvilles: the God-hating Melville, the father-seeking and castration-fearing Melville, the traditionalist-and-quasi-Catholic Melville; Melville the cabalistic grubber in obscure philosophies, Melville the liberal democrat and defender of the vital center, and Melville the jaunty journalist of the adventures of boys at sea. Such proliferating multisidedness is an evidence of genius, but not, in my opinion, of the very highest genius; and if there are already more Melvilles than there have ever been Dantes, it is partly because Dante's poetry is firm in an inner coherence and is not totally plastic to the critic. But a certain lack of finish was a deliberate element in Melville's aesthetic as well as his metaphysic; and criticism can always finish the story according to its private enthusiasms. With this *caveat*, we may consider Melville the myth-maker at work upon the matter of Adam.

We may begin with a passage from chapter 96 in *Moby-Dick*, "The Try-Works"—taking the passage as a summary of Melville's attitude to innocence and evil; as an example of Melville's way with the material (attitudes, tropes, language) available to him; and as a guide for the rest of this chapter.

The incident of "The Try-Works" will be recalled. Ishmael falls asleep at the tiller one midnight, as the "Pequod" is passing through the Java seas heading northward toward the haunts of the great sperm whales. Waking up, but not yet aware that he has been asleep, Ishmael finds himself staring into the mouth of hell: "a jet gloom, now and then made ghastly by flashes of redness," an infernal scene through which giant shadow-shapes like devils are moving about some dreadful work. He is "horribly conscious of something fatally wrong"; "a stark bewildered feeling as of death" comes over him. Then he realizes —just in time to swing about, grasp the tiller, and save the ship from capsizing—that he has turned in his sleep and is facing the two furnaces, or "try-pots," amidships, and the three black harpooners stoking the masses of whale blubber from which the oil is extracted ("tryed-out"). The moral follows, the felt analogy between the natural event and the soul of man, offered by the Ishmael who tells the story after the whole of it has been completed:

[1.] Look not too long in the face of fire, O man! Turn not thy back to the compass; accept the first hint of the hitching tiller; believe not the artificial fire, when its redness makes all things look ghastly. Tomorrow, in the natural sun, the skies will be bright; those who glared like devils in the forking flames, the morn will show in far other, at least gentler relief; the glorious, golden, glad sun, the only true lamp—all others but liars.

[2.] Nevertheless, the sun hides not Virginia's Dismal Swamp, nor Rome's accursed Campagna, nor wide Sahara, nor all the millions of miles of deserts and of griefs beneath the moon. The sun hides not the ocean, which is the dark side of the earth, and which is two-thirds of this earth. So, therefore, that mortal man who hath more of joy than sorrow in him, that mortal man cannot be true—not true, or undeveloped. With books the same. The truest of all men was the Man of Sorrows, and the truest of all books is Solomon's, and Ecclesiastes is the fine-hammered steel of woe. "All is vanity." ALL. This wilful world hath not got hold of unchristian Solomon's wisdom yet. But he who dodges hospitals and jails, and walks fast crossing graveyards, and would rather talk of operas than hell; calls Cowper, Young, Pascal, Rousseau, poor devils of sick men; and throughout a carefree lifetime swears by Rabelais as passing wise, and therefore jolly;—not that man is fitted to sit down on tombstones, and break the green damp mould with unfathomably wondrous Solomon.

[3.] But even Solomon, he says, "the man that wandereth out of the way of understanding shall remain" (i.e. even while living) "in the congregation of the dead." Give not thyself up then to fire, lest it invert thee, deaden thee; as for the time it did me. There is a wisdom that is woe; but there is a woe that is madness. And there is a Catskill eagle in some souls that can alike dive down into the blackest gorges, and soar out of them again and become invisible in the sunny spaces. And even if he forever flies within the gorge, that gorge is in the mountains; so that even in his lowest swoop, the mountain eagle is still higher than the other birds upon the plain, even though they soar.

The passage divides into three paragraphs which are more nearly three stanzas, and I have marked them accordingly. The subject of this, one of the richest meditations in all of Melville, is the different degrees of moral alertness—with variations on the realities present in the world and man, on the quality of moral illumination for the perceiver, on the states of being accompanying the various perceptions.

There occur (as Ishmael sees it) two dangerous alternative conditions. On the one hand: an empty innocence, a tenacious ignorance of evil, which, granted the tough nature of reality, must be either immaturity or spiritual cowardice. On the other: a sense of evil so inflexible, so adamant in its refusal to admit the not less reducible fact of existent good that it is perilously close to a love of evil, a queer pact with the devil. Each alternative is a path toward destruction; the second is the very embrace of the destroying power.

Now these two conditions have affinities with the contemporary moral visions of the party of Hope and the party of Memory. They could be grasped and expounded only by someone who had already by an effort of will and intelligence transcended them both. By the time he wrote *Moby-Dick*, Melville had dissociated himself in scorn from what he now regarded as the moral childishness of the hopeful.[4] But he was not blind to that hypnosis by evil which a bankrupt Cal-

4. Cf. Melville's annotations of his copies of Emerson's *Essays* (now in Houghton Library, Harvard). Checking one passage in *Spiritual Laws*, Melville added in the margin: "A perfectly good being, therefore, would see no evil—But what did Christ see? —He saw what made him weep." Checking Emerson's remark, "Trust men and they will be true to you," Melville commented: "God help the poor fellow who squares his life according to this." Emerson (in *The Poet*): "The evils of the world are such only to the evil eye"; and Melville: "What does the man mean? If Mr. Emerson travelling in Egypt should find a plague-spot come out on him—would he consider that an evil sight or not? And if evil, would his eye be evil because it seemed evil to his eye . . . ?" "Still," Melville added characteristically, in another place (opposite a passage in *Heroism*), "these essays are noble."

vinism had visited upon the nostalgic. He was beginning to share the good sense of Dante's Virgil, chiding Dante (in *Inferno*, XXX) for allowing himself to be momentarily transfixed by the spectacle of evil: "Il voler cio udir é una bassa voglia" (it is vulgar to linger in the fire-lit darkness, for the end of our journey is the center of light).

Melville, that is to say, had penetrated beyond both innocence and despair to some glimmering of a moral order which might explain and order them both, though his vision remained slender, as of that moment, and the center of light not yet known, but only believed in— and still ambiguously, at that. But, like the elder Henry James, Melville had moved toward moral insight as far as he had just because he had begun to look at experience dramatically. He had begun to discover its plot; and Melville understood the nature of plot, plot in general, better than anyone else in his generation. For Melville was a poet.

So "alternative" is a misleading word, in speaking of any characteristic passage in Melville. Indeed, one way to grasp this passage and Melville's achievement in general is to notice that Melville is *not* posing static alternatives but tracing a rhythmic progression in experience and matching the rhythm as best he can in language. This is the way of a Platonist, and not of a polemicist; much more, it is the way of a poet. We still tend, for all the good criticism of our time, to read a poem the way we watch a tennis-match: turning our heads and minds back and forth between what we presume to be unchanging opponents, as though a poem moved between fixed choices of attitude before plumping conclusively for one of them as the unequivocal winner. The best kind of poem is a process of generation—in which one attitude or metaphor, subjected to intense pressure, gives symbolic birth to the next, which reveals the color of its origin even as it gives way in turn by "dying into" its successor. Such a poem does not deal in dichotomies but in live sequences.

Here, then, in "The Try-Works," we have a series of displacements. Artificial light gives way to natural light, darkness to morning, and the imperative to the indicative. Then dawn and sunlight yield to darkness, to the moon and "the dark side of the earth"—to hell, to sickness, and to death. But hell and death are the source at last of a new and loftier life, new "sunny spaces" and new imperatives. Those sunny spaces are not the same bright skies of the opening stanza. The moral imagination which contemplates the sunny spaces in stanza 3 has been radically affected by the vision of hell and death at mid-point. The sunny spaces (tragic optimism) relate to the earlier morning skies (empty-headed cheerfulness) as does the Catskill eagle to "the other birds upon the plain"; it is the sky, as the eagle is a bird—but bird and sky have been raised to a higher power.

What Melville has done here is to accomplish what, in an ugly phrase translated from Nietszche, has been called "the transvaluation of values": something which Melville had to do in his poet's way, by what we perhaps can call the "transfiguration of figures." The figures are drawn from Melville's own cultural environment; their transfiguration here is a *précis* of Melville's development—and of this chapter.

The passage may be cited as Melville's guess about the design of experience. Like Hawthorne, Melville testified to a spiritual journey from sunlight through the fires of hell to a final serenity. But Hawthorne's guess was present to his mind before he started writing; the writing merely tested it. It was what remained to him of a shredding religious tradition, and it was a guess rather than a creed just because the tradition was in shreds. But for Melville the business of writing was not so much a test as a consummation. His guess was what he came out with only after his experience had drawn significance out of his account of it in 'anguage.

He had to come far, in order, by December, 1850, to make even the tentative guess contained in chapter 96 of *Moby-Dick*. We can follow him on his way by looking briefly at some of his experiences and a couple of his books prior to *Moby-Dick: Typee* and *Redburn*. With the "Try-Works" passage as a guide, we find *Typee* corresponding in mood to the morning spirit of stanza 1; and *Redburn* to the sense of sickness in stanza 2. During his apprentice years, Melville had lacked the well-rounded sense of life's potential that Hawthorne had had from the outset. He tended to hang on to each successive discovery with exaggerated intensity, as though it were the whole of the truth; and he released his grasp and clutched at the fresh perception only when he had acquired the means of a fresh articulation. The measure of achievement in *Moby-Dick* is the measure of great new resources greatly possessed.

III

Melville, who came of age in 1840 during the years when hopefulness was all the fashion, began his career as an unstable but energetic member of the forward-looking party. When he got around to reflecting on the American writer, he added his more robust accent to the hopeful program for literature: "This Vermont morning dew is as wet to my feet as Eden's dew to Adam's. . . . We want no American Goldsmiths; nay we want no American Miltons. . . . Let us boldly condemn all imitation." The accent was the product of personal experience; for Melville had long since contributed his robust symbolic gesture to that series of gestures by which the hopeful had signalized the driving motion from memory to hope. For Emerson, who could make so much out of so little, it had been enough to leave his Concord study and go tramping in mud puddles; Thoreau went farther, a few miles into the near-by woods to little Walden Pond. Melville's gesture was more sweeping and extravagant—he "jumped off" by crossing the Pacific and jumping ship to plunge into the interior of a primitive island. His action characterized a man whose imagination could expand into the mythic just because it was steadily nourished by the roughness of the actual. But as an act and as a kind of act, it assured the sequel: for in so all-engaging an assault upon life, Melville could scarcely avoid bumping into that part of it which was bitter, ugly, and destructive.

Melville and his friend Toby jumped ship in July, 1844. According to his account of the event two years later in *Typee*, the escape was made during a tremendous storm, and the first night was passed in a violence of wind and rain which left the narrator with "cold shiverings and a burning fever"—before the morning revealed "the beautiful scene" of the sunlit "Happy Valley." This suggests the transition accomplished more or less consciously in the book, even if only partially during the actual experience—a transition from the alarming night which begins "The Try-Works" meditation to the "natural sun" and the bright skies of "tomorrow," when "the morn will show in . . . gentler relief." The mood of *Typee* is pretty well warmed by "the golden, glorious, glad sun." Amid the wholly natural, preconventional life of the island paradise and during his Adam-and-Eve relation with Fayaway, Melville found a "continual happiness" and a surface beauty without blemish. "There seemed to be no cares, griefs, troubles, or vexation in all Typee." By contrast, civilization looked to Melville, from Typee, the way it would look to Thoreau, from his hut at Walden: a fantastic scene of self-imposed torments—"a thousand self-inflicted discomforts," as Melville said, with "a hundred evils in reserve."

Yet it was the very absence of cares and griefs and troubles that turned out to be unendurable. Melville stayed in fact less than a month in the Happy Valley; in *Typee*, he stayed over four months, for he was always able to invade and then enlarge ordinary units of time, he saw so much in any one moment; but he did depart at last, both in fact and in the book. In neither case was he altogether clear why such continual happiness was unacceptable. There was, to be sure, the occasional danger of being cooked and eaten; but Melville realized later that there had been a much greater danger of permanently arrested development. "That mortal man," Ishmael would say for him, "who hath more of joy than sorrow in him, that mortal man cannot be true —not true or undeveloped." All he could say at the time was that Polynesian life never advanced into the realm of spirit; its buoyancy, though extreme, came entirely from a "sense of mere physical existence." Melville's response was comparable to Thoreau's complaint that his neighbor, the French-Canadian backwoodsman, was an animal, a child. Life, in the Typee valley, was restricted to the visible spheres of love; it was Melville's restless ambition to penetrate to the invisible spheres, and it was his lot to find out that those were the spheres which were formed in fright.

So Melville returned to America. He never stopped "jumping off"; but after his return in 1844, the act was more purely symbolic and was coextensive with Melville's effort to become a writer. The act now consisted in dispatching hero after hero, Adam after Adam, in novel after novel—sending them forth like Whitman's child, full of hopeful expectancy, only to tell how, in every case, they fell among cannibals: Wellingborough Redburn, the lad called "White-Jacket," Pierre Glendinning, and Billy Budd.

In *Redburn* (1849), the Adamic coloration of the experience which most interested Melville became explicit. This has been remarked by Melville's best commentator, Newton Arvin, who observes that the boy-hero of the novel "sets out from his mother's house in a state of innocence like that before the fall"; and the voyage to Liverpool and back comprises for young Redburn "the initiation of innocence into evil." Here we are at the second stage of Ishmael's soliloquy: the exploration of the degree of sickness in the world, of hospitals and jails and graveyards, of deserts and griefs and "Virginia's Dismal Swamp." For Melville and Redburn the swamp is not a comforting assurance of nature's variety, as it was for Thoreau. Much of the physical and spiritual disease the young lad discovers is packed symbolically into the demonic figure of the sailor Jackson; and Jackson is introduced eating a bowl of mush that "looked for all the world like . . . the Dismal Swamp of Virginia." With the appearance of Jackson, the consciousness alive in the story passes from the opening mood of elementary cheerfulness to the injured tone at the novel's center.

But the emphasis in *Redburn* is perhaps less upon what happens to the boy himself than upon the wretchedness and depravity that are uncovered as existing independently of him in the world; Redburn emerges with, at most, a sort of jocular but puzzled ruefulness, like that of Major Molineux's disillusioned cousin in Hawthorne's story. The Liverpool through which Redburn wanders, growing ever more appalled at its stench of corruption, may well remind us of the plague- and crime-ridden Philadelphia of *Arthur Mervyn;* but Redburn is more the passive spectator than the ludicrous reformer. What Redburn beholds in Launcelot's-Hey, along the dock walls, and in "the booble alleys" of Liverpool merely adds to the cluster of scabrous impressions that began with the deceitful pawnshop-keeper in New York and continued with the drunken sailor who jumps overboard on Redburn's first nightwatch and the plague which breaks out among the passengers. All these impressions become concentrated and intensified for Redburn, in the "foul lees and dregs of a man" which were all that remained of the dying Jackson. It is Jackson who reveals to Redburn the power of the scabrous, the terrible power of mental superiority when it possesses a nerve of the diabolic. "He was the weakest man, bodily, of the crew"; but he was the crew's bully. His power operated through and not in spite of his wasted appearance; and the strength of his fascination for Redburn (who is aware, though only very dimly indeed, that Jackson in turn is covertly fascinated by him) suggests something not yet articulated about disease in the world at large. Yet, while Jackson is a wicked man, as Redburn tells himself in his Sunday-school language; there is a still deeper possibility—that "his wickedness seemed to spring from his woe."

This conjunction of sickness and power and wickedness and sorrow is the substance of *Redburn:* these and the impression they make upon the lad's character. But if there is something more astir in the novel, it derives from another dead figure: Redburn's father—not from his presence but from the acknowledgment of his absence. In Liverpool, taking with him a guidebook which his father had used to explore that very city "years and years ago," Redburn sets forth to follow his father through the town, "performing a filial pilgrimage." The sense of his father becomes so vivid that Redburn feels that, if he hurries, he will "overtak[e] him around the Town Hall . . . at the head of Castle Street." Both the hope and the guidebook are cheats; the guidebook is half a century out of date, and his father is not just around that corner or any other: "He had gone whither no son's search could find him in this world." This is the moment when Melville's hero realizes that he is an orphan; but since the realization comes together with the discovery of the amount of destructive unhealthiness in the world and in human nature, it has little of the hopeful joy of a liberation from family and history. It partakes rather of the tragic feeling of the lost son, or even, perhaps, of the son betrayed.

We ought to locate the moment chronologically not in 1839, when young Herman Melville actually did visit Liverpool, but ten years later, when he was investing that visit with meaning in the writing of *Redburn*. For in that book, two perceptions which would be the making of Melville as an artist hovered on the verge of fusion—the betrayal by the father and the corruption in nature. These were the elements which decisively shaped Melville's treatment of the hopeful legend: what we may cautiously call the "objective"—the knot of hostility in the very structure of created things; and the "subjective" —the bubbling-up of whatever Melville had suffered during those dreadful weeks in 1831 when his bankrupt father went mad and died, leaving behind (abandoning, deserting, as it must have seemed to the bewildered child) a lost, helpless, poverty-stricken family. These were the elements and the perceptions which took the form of a growing resentment in Melville: something which only just begins to get into the writing of *Redburn*, but which had, as Auden puts it, to "blow itself quite out" in the books that followed.

Moby-Dick begins where *Redburn* leaves off. The hero, all too absorbed in his contemplation of that "hopper of misfortune" to which Redburn alludes in his closing pages, is now "growing grim about the mouth." He has a "damp, drizzly November" in his soul; he pauses before coffin warehouses and falls into line in funeral processions. He wants to knock people's hats off and speculates about suicide. He has come so far from the saluting of the glad sun of morning that he feels most at home seated on a tombstone. No one should miss the fine, firm, knowing humor of these sentences in the first chapter of *Moby-Dick*. It is the firmest humor in the world: the humor which results from tragedy, and specifically from the "tragedy of mind" symbolically re-enacted in the story of *Moby-Dick*. But *Moby-Dick*, for all its humor, is, of course, a novel ablaze with anger. Yet it is the humor, or what the humor represents, that makes us fully aware of the scope of the anger.

What had been a mere rustle of resentment over a world false to the promises of hope had grown, by 1851, into a fury of disenchantment: Adam gone mad with disillusion. *Moby-Dick* manages to give very clear voice to that fury. If Melville could not yet overcome his anger, he was able to do something which a number of his critics would regard as better. He was able to hold his anger in balance, which may have been the only way to bring it alive and make it clear. Melville had discovered how to establish an attitude toward his own sense of outrage or, inversely, how to establish his outrage in relation to a comprehensive and in some ways traditional attitude. The relation expresses itself in *Moby-Dick* in the actual dramatic relation between frenzied Ahab and far-seeing Ishmael; and psychologizing critics might tell us that what happens in the novel is the "splitting-off" of a personality first introduced as Ishmael into fragments of itself—one still called Ishmael, others called Ahab and Starbuck and Pip and so on. But we can regard the achievement in terms of the materials of narrative. From this viewpoint, it may be argued that the success of *Moby-Dick* and the clarity of its anger are due to Melville's peculiar, yet skilful, exploitation of the legacy of European literature—and "the tradition" which that literature has made manifest.

The legacy was the greatest of Melville's resources as, in his own way and according to his own needs, he gradually came into possession of it. The anger in *Moby-Dick* becomes resonant in the tension it creates with the legacy and the tradition. And, conversely, it is the tradition which—in the choral voice of Ishmael and for what it is worth within the ironic frame of the novel—transvaluates the values implicit in the anger.

IV

For the author of *Moby-Dick*, the central strain in the European tradition was tragic. The tragic sensibility defined in the long quotation from the "Try-Works" is attributed to books as well as to men: "That mortal man who hath more of joy than sorrow in him, that mortal man cannot be true—not true or undeveloped. With books the same." There, plainly enough, is an antihopeful judgment, and almost the reverse of it can be read on many pages of Emerson and Thoreau. But there is a point beyond that, which has to do with the creative process itself; and we should recall the actual experience out of which Ishmael's meditation rises, for the enterprise of trying-out was an explicit trope for Melville of the act of creativity. He wrote Dana, while at work on *Moby-Dick*, that the novel would be "a strange sort of book . . . blubber is blubber you know; though you might get oil out of it, the poetry runs as hard as sap from a frozen maple-tree." And since trying-out was associated in the story with so hellish a scene and nightmarish an experience, it is hard to resist the inference that creativity for Melville was closely, dangerously, associated with the monstrous vision of evil. You have to go through hell, he suggests, either to get the oil or to write the book.

Melville, that is to say, belongs to the company of gifted romantics from Blake and Baudelaire to Thomas Mann, who have supposed that art is somehow the flower of evil and that the power through which the shaping imagination is raised to greatness may also be a power which destroys the artist; for it is the strength derived from the knowledge of evil—not the detached study, but perhaps a very descent into the abyss. At some stage or other, Melville felt, art had to keep an appointment with wickedness. He believed with Hawthorne that, in order to achieve moral maturity, the individual had to engage evil and suffer the consequences; and he added the conviction that, in order to compose a mature work of literature, the artist had to enter without flinching into the "spheres of fright." For Melville, the two experiences happened not to be separable.

But how, having looked into the fire, was the artist to articulate his vision of evil in language? Still another clue is provided by the "Try-Works." It can scarcely be a coincidence that, after the slices of blubber (the source of oil) have been pointedly referred to as "Bible leaves," the insight gained from the spectacle is conveyed by Ishmael in a cluster of biblical references. The "Bible leaves" are passed through the furnaces, and oil is the result; similarly, Melville hints, the formed and incrusted language of the past must be "tried-out" in the transforming heat of the imagination, and the result is the shaped perception which can light up the work of art.

The transforming process was crucial, for Melville never simply echoed the words of the great books of the past; he subjected them to tremendous pressure and forced them to yield remarkable new revelations. His characterizing "relation to tradition" was extremely ambiguous: it was no more the willing enslavement exemplified by the nostalgic than it was the blithe patriotic indifference manifested by the hopeful. I take his reading and his treatment of the *Odyssey* of Homer as a major illustration of Melville's "trying-out" of a traditional poem.

Melville's Homer, like Keats's, was the Homer of George Chapman. He acquired the Chapman translations in 1858 and preferred them at once to the translations by Pope, which he probably read (and read carefully) as early as 1848.[5] What impresses us at once as

5. Cf. Merton M. Sealts, Jr., "Melville's Reading: A Check-List of Books Owned and Borrowed," *Harvard Library Bulletin*, Vol. III, No. 2 (spring, 1949), pp. 268 ff. I quote from a letter Mr. Sealts kindly wrote to me, February 21, 1949: "On 19 March 1848 HM was charged with '1 Classical Library, 37 v. 12.23.' . . . Pope's Homer constitutes three of the volumes." Melville purchased the complete works of Pope at some time after 1856. Mr. Sealts concludes: "He may have known [Pope's Homer] before

we follow his check-marks, underlinings, and marginal comments through the poems is this: that Melville was a creative reader; he was the poet as reader who became the reader as poet. His markings, rarely casual or isolated, fall usually upon essential threads and force the poems to yield the figure within them. But it is Melville's figure, and not always the figure we are accustomed to discover ourselves.

His responsive reader's effect upon the *Iliad* is, to be sure, less conspicuous than its effect upon the *Odyssey*. The *Iliad*, under Melville's inspection, emerges as the somber portrait of a world at war, of sorrowing men caught up in vast forces and moving without hope to the violent death which awaits them, under the rule of implacable divinities. This is perhaps the *Iliad* we too are disposed to see; though it was not the *Iliad* of Melville's contemporary, Emerson, whose hopeful reading showed him only the "firm and cheerful temper" of a Homer who lay in the sunshine. But Melville read the *Odyssey* on a more symbolic level; his markings lead it to take the form of a tragic *Bildungsroman*, with the relation between the characters and the sequence of events standing for growth of insight into the heart of reality. There is evidence of Melville's immense enjoyment of the adventures themselves; but he was primarily interested in meaning.

The meaning Melville found borrows force from the unusual emphasis his markings laid upon the griefs and hardships of Odysseus and the generalizations about the evil lot of mankind, to the point where a rich and spacious poem looks surprisingly gloomier than we remembered it. Melville seized upon the recurring descriptions of Odysseus and his dwindling crew sailing on, stricken at heart after some frightful encounter; and he made much of the hero's artful lament to Nausicäa that he was the victim of "a cruel habit of calamity" (vi, 257). He marked the disclaimer of Telemachus:

> Not by any means
> If Hope should prompt me or *blind confidence*
> (*The God of fools*) or ever deity
> Should will it, for 'tis past my destiny.
> [iii. 309—Melville's italics.]

And the reaction of Telemachus to the dishonor shown his father:

> Never more let any sceptre-bearing man
> Benevolent, or mild, or human be,
> Nor in his mind form acts of piety,
> But ever feed on blood [ii. 348].

Moby-Dick or even as early as his days at the Albany Academy, though that last is pure speculation. He *almost* bought a Chapman's Homer in London" in 1849.

The gods are no more benevolent than they had been in Melville's *Iliad*. There they had comprised a remote and hostile race, indifferent to man and interfering in his affairs only to blast his tenuous hopes; here Melville obtrudes Nestor's observation that "I know God studied misery to hurl against us" (iii). By focusing attention on these lines and many more like them, Melville forced the *Odyssey* to move perceptibly, to shift and re-form; he exposed within it a vision of terror and evil which casts a deep shadow over the beauty and steady assurance the poem could otherwise be seen to reflect.

That vision is the frame for the educational process Melville traces for us. The process begins with the departure of Telemachus for sandy Pylos and the admonitions of his nurse and his mother, both of which are strongly checked:

> It fits not you so young
> To suffer so much by the aged seas
> And err in such a wayless wilderness [ii. 545].

> Why left my son his mother? Why refused
> His wit the solid shore to try the seas
> And put in ships the trust of his distress
> That are at sea to man unbridled horse,
> And run past rule? [iv. 492.]

The echoes of Redburn and of Melville's personal life and relation to his mother are clear. Going to sea, both in deed and in symbol, was always Melville's way of fronting what Thoreau called "the essential facts of life"; and what must be stressed is that the venture was so much the more harrowing for Melville because malice and evil were central among the facts to be fronted. As he read on in the *Odyssey*, Melville ran a line alongside Proteus' warning to Menelaus, indicative of the dangerous nature of the venture:

> Cease
> To ask so far. It fits not to be
> So cunning in thine own calamity.
> Nor seek to learn what learned thou shouldst forget.
> Men's knowledges have proper limits set
> And should not prease into the mind of God [iv. 657].

Melville's conviction about the peril did not prevent his own heroes from making the plunge nevertheless and "preasing" with all their might into the mind of God: into whatever it was which lay behind the appearances of things; and so they all "suffered so much by the aged seas." It is with the suffering and the lies and the silence of the much-buffeted Odysseus that Melville's pencilings of the *Odyssey* come to an end.

Having noticed Homer's observation (vi. 198) that "the hard pass [Odysseus] had at sea stuck by him," and, having digested the obvious fabrications with which Odysseus regaled the court of Antinöus, Melville greeted the wanderer's decision, upon arriving at last in Ithaca, with one of his heaviest markings, three emphatic lines in the margin:

> He bestowed
> A veil on truth; for evermore did wind
> About his bosom a most crafty mind [xiii. 370].

That scene, in which the slippery explanations of Odysseus are affectionately shown up by Athena, can be read as high comedy. If Melville did not read it so, and if this moment is one of the last he would underscore in the poem, it was not only because he felt as Lear's Fool felt (in a passage he checked elsewhere) that "Truth's a dog must to kennel." To suppose so would be to remember the markings while forgetting the poem. And I want to suggest that the markings and the poem together make a curious tension which is representative both of Melville's relation to tradition and of the operation of that relation in the best of his fiction.

Melville had perhaps the most strenuous doubts of his generation about the possibility of uttering the truth, and in his later years he was greatly taken by Arnold's allusion to the "power and beauty in the well-kept secret of one's self and one's thoughts." Here we find him, perhaps, attributing such beauty to the secretive Odysseus in Ithaca. But these doubts were embraced by a larger doubt which had to do with the nature of the truth to be uttered; and Melville was increasingly sure that truth was double—that it was dialectical and contained, so far as any poet could utter it, in a tension. In his reading of the *Odyssey*, Melville inserted a tension into the poem: the tension between his own tragic and truncated design—the departure, the journey of inquiry, the suffering, the secretiveness—and the grand pattern which the poem nonetheless maintains of homecoming, reunion, and resounding victory.

Melville's reading reinforces the sense we have of how any formal and formulated myth functions in *Moby-Dick* and afterward. What I have said about the *Odyssey* myth can be matched by his response to the Christian myth (if that is the right phrase for it), or to the tragedies of Aeschylus or Shakespeare. Bits and pieces or the whole of these myths are introduced into the narrative. But they are not precisely the model echoed in the central action, re-enacted by the main event.

They are the known elements by a sort of bold breaching of which the incident or the character or the phrase or the whole action must be understood. Yet the mythic elements are not negated either. They serve to comment contrapuntally on the action and the hero, which, of course, comment in turn upon them: and this is how the figures on both sides become transfigured.

The process is not always radiant in Melville, for the traditional materials appear raggedly, they are lumpy and not altogether digested; there is hardly a doctrinaire theory behind their treatment. A much clearer example in recent fiction is the functioning of *The Divine Comedy* in Thomas Mann's *The Magic Mountain*. When, for instance, Hans Castorp's second "guide," Naphta, challenges the young man's first "guide," Settembrini, to a duel and then kills himself, we are meant to hear the almost endless discordant vibrations set up by the contrast between this event and the relation, in the *Comedy*, of Dante's guides—Virgil (whom Settembrini cherishes and resembles) and Beatrice (like Naphta, a theologian). The relation between Virgil and Beatrice is perfectly harmonious; it enacts, indeed, the process toward perfection; it dramatizes the formula of St. Thomas that grace does not destroy nature but perfects it. The harmonious hum of the *Comedy* behind the pistol-shots of *The Magic Mountain* establishes the tension: a tension of symbolic relationships, which is a tension of worlds; and the world of Mann's novel announces itself in its ironic contrast to Dante's.

Nothing so crafty or so conscious may be found in the fiction of Melville; yet the achievement is comparable. And even the lumpiness of the traditional elements included is significant: significant, anyhow, that his relation to the tradition was American. For the American writer has never (if he is honest and American) been able to pretend an authentic initial communion with the European past; and especially not if he begins, as Melville did, imbued with the antitraditional principles of the party of Hope. He can know a great deal, even everything, about that past; he can go after it, which is just the demonstration that he is not in communion with it. And if he establishes a communion, it is one of a quite different order from that which most European writers—until 1939, at least—possessed as their birthright. The American kind of communion will usually be a sort of tussle, and the best of our writers (like Melville) can convert the tussle into drama. At the same time, since the American writer is outside the organic world of European literature to start with, there is no limit to how much of the world he can draw upon. He has the Protestant's contempt for the long line of commentary and influence; he can go directly to the source and find it anywhere. Nothing is his by right; and so nothing constrains him; and nothing, ultimately, is denied him. Such has been and such must continue to be the actual relation between the American writer and the European tradition: a queer and vigilant relation, at once hospitable and hostile, at once unlimited and uneasy.[6]

V

A comparison between the description of Jackson in *Redburn* and our first glimpse of Ahab in *Moby-Dick* may further illustrate Melville's practice. Here is Jackson: "Nothing was left of this Jackson but the foul lees and dregs of a man; he was thin as a shadow; nothing but skin and bones; and sometimes used to complain that it hurt him to sit on the hard chests." A man who could write a sentence like that might not be thought to need any further resources. There had been no sentence in previous American fiction to match its deceptive cadence, its linking of perfectly common language with the shock of almost literally felt visual detail. These words *stick* to their subject. But then here is Ahab:

> He looked like a man cut away from the stake, when the fire has overrunningly wasted all the limbs without consuming them, or taking away one particle from their compacted aged robustness. . . . His bone-leg steadied in that hole; one arm elevated, and holding by a shroud; Captain Ahab stood erect, looking straight out beyond the ship's ever-pitching prow. There was an infinity of firmest fortitude, a determinate, unsurrenderable wilfulness, in the fixed and fearless, forward dedication of that glance. Not a word he spoke; nor did his officers say aught to him; though by all their minutest gestures and expressions, they plainly showed the uneasy, if not painful consciousness, of being under a troubled master-eye. And not only that, but moody stricken Ahab stood before them with a crucifixion in his face; in all the nameless regal overbearing dignity of some mighty woe.

The visual image is not less sharp; but it is incomparably larger, indeed it is almost outsize—and chiefly because Ahab is animated within a density of suggestive and echoing language that carries us into the outsize world of heroic legend, without wholly detaching us from the hard wood of the quarter-deck. But the substance of that heroic dimension is a fusion of violently contradictory "visions"—the vision vitalized by anger and vengeance and pride and wilfulness, on the one

6. Cf. the discussion of "communion" in chap. 9, and especially in the closing pages of that chapter. "Communion"—or the attempt to achieve it—is, I suggest there, a link between the various members of what I call "the third party": the elder James, Bushnell, Hawthorne, Melville, Parkman, etc. Cf. also the mention on p. 160 of the American loss of "communion with history."

hand, and the vision of Christian-cum-Greek tragic acceptance, on the other.

It is in the interplay, the so to speak open-ended dialectic, of the visions that Melville's "relation to tradition" is to be found and where his expanded resources reveal themselves. Ahab's heroic pride, his wilfulness, his defiance of God and his destruction of the world make sense within our imaginative recollection (constantly prodded throughout the novel) of Christian heroism—meekness, submission, obedience, and the salvation of mankind. Annihilation at sea makes sense within our stimulated recollection of the homecoming myth, the *Odyssey*. *Moby-Dick*'s sustained mood of impending disaster sharpens itself against the Homeric echo of impending triumph. The cosmic anger of Ahab at betrayal, by God, by the father, is correlative to Melville's anger at the devastating betrayal by experience of the promises of hope. All this rage assumes its full dimension because it is established in opposition to the traditionally comprehensive acceptance voiced by Father Mapple and by Ishmael.

Moby-Dick is an elaborate pattern of countercommentaries, the supreme instance of the dialectical novel—a novel of tension without resolution. Ishmael's meditation, which transfigures the anger and sees beyond the sickness and the evil, is only one major voice in the dramatic conversation; and not until *Billy Budd* does this voice become transcendent and victorious. In *Moby-Dick*, Melville adopted a unique and off-beat traditionalism—a steadily ambiguous re-rendering of the old forms and fables once unequivocally rejected by the hopeful —in order to recount the total blasting of the vision of innocence. He went beyond a spurious artistic originality to give narrative birth to the conflict with evil: that evil against which a spurious and illusory innocence must shatter itself. In doing so, he not only achieved a sounder originality but moved a great step toward perceiving a more durable innocence. In *Pierre*, the following year, Melville faltered and went back once more over the old dreary ground of disillusion; but in *Billy Budd*, he was to come home.

VI

The new Adam . . . is the Lord from heaven [St. Paul, I Cor. 45–47].

At least one of Melville's critics has found Homer's *Odyssey* a broad metaphor useful not only for gauging Melville's novels but also for describing his life. Toward the end of that life, W. H. Auden says in his poem "Herman Melville":

> he sailed into an extraordinary mildness,
> And anchored in his home and reached his wife
> And rode within the harbour of her hand,
> And went across each morning to an office
> As though his occupation were another island.
>
> Goodness existed: that was the new knowledge
> His terror had to blow itself quite out
> To let him see it; but it was the gale had blown him
> Past the Cape Horn of sensible success
> Which cries: "This rock is Eden. Shipwreck here."

Mr. Auden's poem, which outlines Melville's life perhaps a shade too tidily by means of the Homeric allusions, has to do with the final tranquillity and the firm concluding Christian acquiescence out of which—according to Mr. Auden—Melville composed *Billy Budd*.

> . . . now he cried in exultation and surrender
> "The Godhead is broken like bread. We are the pieces."
> And sat down at his desk and wrote a story.

Melville's cry about "the Godhead" was in fact uttered in 1851, in the letter responding to Hawthorne's praise of *Moby-Dick*, some forty years before Melville sat down at his desk in New York and wrote Billy's story. But *Billy Budd* is, of course, unmistakably the product of aged serenity; its author has unmistakably got beyond his anger or discovered the key to it; and it would be pointless to deny that it is a testament of acceptance, as Mr. Watson has said, or a "Nunc Dimittis," as Mr. Arvin proposes. It is woeful, but wisely, no longer madly. Its hero is sacrificially hanged at sea, but its author has come home, like Odysseus.

In Melville's last work, the New World's representative hero and his representative adventure receive a kind of sanctification. Mr. R. P. Blackmur has said of the last three novels of Henry James that they approach the condition of poetry, which Mr. Blackmur explains as the exemplification in language of the soul in action—"the inner life of the soul at the height of its struggle, for good or evil, with the outer world which it must deny, or renounce, or accept." This, precisely, is what *Billy Budd* asks us to say about it; *Billy Budd* helps us to see that the action so described is one grounded in the pressures and counterpressures not of any world but of the New World. It is the action of the soul in general as shaped under a New World perspective. Melville's achievement was double: he brought myth into contemporary life, and he elevated that life into myth—at once transcending and reaffirming the sense of life indicated by the party of Hope.

The American Adam

Compare, for example, the personality and the career of the Handsome Sailor with the analysis of historic American Adamism offered by Horace Bushnell in 1858. Billy is innocence personified—"To be nothing more than innocent!" Claggart exclaims, in malice and tears. He can neither read nor write, though he can sing like an angel. He springs from nowhere; he returns a cheerful "No, sir," to the officer's question, "Do you know anything about your beginning?" "His entire family was practically invested in himself." He fulfils every hopeful requirement; no historic process or influence intrudes between him and the very dawn of time; his defining qualities seem to be "exceptionally transmitted from a period prior to Cain's city and citified man."

So it can be said of him that he "was little more than an upright barbarian, much such as Adam presumably might have been ere the urbane Serpent wriggled himself into his company," and that "in the nude [he] might have posed for a statue of Adam before the Fall." This is just the personality that Bushnell saw his culture fostering and which he deplored. Even Billy's stammer and his illiteracy are integral to the portrait: they are the evidence of that "condition privative," they constitute that "necessary defect of knowledge and consequent weakness" which Bushnell assigned to any "free person or . . . power considered as having just begun to be." The defect and the weakness, under Claggart's goading, precipitate the disaster; and Billy falls, as the mythological Adam had fallen, and as Bushnell foresaw that any Adamic American would fall. The myth enters into the life and reenacts itself: *but not at the expense of the life.* Bushnell invoked the myth in order to chastise the tendencies of life in his day. But if Melville celebrates the fall, he also celebrates the one who fell; and the qualities and attitudes which insure the tragedy are reaffirmed in their indestructible worth even in the moment of defeat. Melville exposed anew the danger of innocence and its inevitable tragedy; but in the tragedy he rediscovered a heightened value in the innocence.

Melville's achievement, as in *Moby-Dick*, was an artistic achievement, and it may be measured by the failure of *Pierre*, more than three decades earlier. For the action fumbled with in *Pierre* is essentially the same as that of *Billy Budd*. From the moment on the novel's first page when we are introduced to a "green and golden World" and see young Pierre on a "morning in June . . . issuing from the embowr'd . . . home of his fathers . . . dewily refreshed and spiritualized by sleep," we know where we are and what and whom we have to deal with. The

148

very language contains strong verbal echoes of Whitman's most explicit Adamic verse:

> As Adam, early in the morning,
> Walking forth from the bower refresh'd with sleep. . . .

The story of Pierre Glendinning consists in the explosion of what Dr. Murray has called "this myth of paradise"—an explosion resulting from an unpreparedness for the subsequent myth of the Fall; and in the explosion both the book and its hero are blown to pieces. It is not the hero who is at fault; he is not obliged to be prepared, his condition forbids it. But we have the impression that the hero's inventor was unprepared: he is not less shocked than Pierre when he sees what he says. The symbolic distance accomplished in *Moby-Dick* narrows fatally in *Pierre;* and if ever there was a case of symbolic suicide in literature, it is Melville's in the indiscriminate destruction in the concluding pages of *Pierre*. The myth which had been an ambiguous source of strength in *Moby-Dick* has now overwhelmed the life. And so in *Clarel,* Melville's next extensive piece of writing, we are not surprised to find an imagination winding its way through a maze of wasteland imagery, quite explicitly lamenting the bewildering and painful loss of Eden.

The recovery in *Billy Budd* is astonishing. The entire story moves firmly in the direction of a transcendent cheerfulness: transcendent, and so neither bumptious nor noisy; a serene and radiant gladness. The climax is prepared with considerable artistry by a series of devices which, though handled somewhat stiffly by a rusty creative talent, do their work nonetheless. The intent of all of them is to bring into being and to identify the hero and his role and then to institute the magical process of transfiguration. Billy appears as another Adam: thrust (like Redburn and Pierre) into a world for which his purity altogether unfits him. His one ally, the Danish sailor who is the prophetic figure in the story, eyes Billy with "an expression of speculative query as to what might eventually befall a nature like that, dropped into a world not without some mantraps and against whose subtleties simple courage lacking experience and address and without any touch of defensive ugliness is of little avail; and where such innocence as man is capable of does yet in a moral emergency not always sharpen the faculties or enlighten the will."[7]

---

7. *Melville's Billy Budd*, p. 177. Mr. Freeman, the editor, observes in a footnote that Melville wrote "an expression of speculative *foresight*," then changed the final word to "query." It is instructive to watch, with Mr. Freeman's scholarly aid, as Melville subdues his more explicitly ritualistic language to the more realistic and dramatic.

The Dansker carries the burden of awareness within the *novella*—awareness that "the matter of Adam" is being tested again; and the atmosphere grows thick with echoes of *Paradise Lost*. But all the time, other energies are linguistically at work. Melville sets swirling around his hero other allusions which relate Billy by inference to other beings: splendid animals, Catholic priests, royalty, the gods—Apollo, Hercules, Hyperion. It is the destiny of these figures to suffer transfiguration, to die into their sacrificial counterparts—the sacrificial bull, the "condemned Vestal priestesses," the slain monarch, and the dying god. This is the process by which Adam changes into the "new Adam" of St. Paul—"the Lord from heaven." The value of the American Adam is thereby, at last, transvalued.

The process is both complicated and enhanced by the ironically entitled "digression" on Lord Nelson. The story of the common sailor is suddenly stretched into great drama by a glimpse of the "heroic personality" of "the greatest sailor since the world began." Nelson, too, is killed at sea; and Melville anticipates the quality of Billy's death by investing Nelson, at the moment of *his* "most glorious death," with "a priestly motive," which led him to adorn himself as "for the altar and the sacrifice." The classical drama of the heroic nobleman points up the little adventure of the stammering and illiterate orphan; and Melville gets back to that adventure by remarking that profoundest passion does not need "a palatial stage" but may be enacted "down among the groundlings."

Accused by Claggart of mutiny and thereupon striking and killing his accuser, Billy Budd falls like Adam, tempted (through Eve) by the serpent; it is observed that the lifeless sergeant-at-arms resembles "a dead snake." In the court-martial and conviction of Billy which follow, the institutionalized world has its familiar way with the defenseless hero. But where the Hawthorne version came to its end in the imprisonment of Donatello, a new dimension of meaning and emotion is introduced in *Billy Budd*, and the story moves toward ecstasy. The sense of divine commandment is indicated in a linking of Billy with Isaac; and the ship's deck—where Billy lies handcuffed and at peace through the vigil of his death—is associated with a cathedral. The pitch of exaltation is reached at the instant of the hanging.

"The last signal . . . was given. At the same moment it chanced that the vapory fleece hanging low in the East, was shot through with a soft glory as of the fleece of the Lamb of God seen in mystical vision, and simultaneously therewith, watched by the wedged masses of upturned faces, Billy ascended; and, ascending, took the full rose of the dawn."

After such a sentence, which is wholly saved from sentimentality by the breath-taking detail of the "wedged masses," it must be regretted that Melville thought it necessary to tell us that, for the sailors who witness the sacrificial death, a chip of the spar from which Billy was hanged "was as a piece of the Cross." It is enough that Captain Vere, dying himself a little time later, murmurs "Billy Budd, Billy Budd" at the last—in agony of spirit, but also in a kind of prayer. And it is enough that the manner of Billy's death transforms the sailors' mutinous anger into acceptance and understanding and that, for them, Billy is the subject of song and fable thereafter.

Billy is the type of scapegoat hero, by whose sacrifice the sins of his world are taken away: in this case, the world of the H.M.S. "Indomitable" and the British navy, a world threatened by a mutiny which could destroy it. Melville brought to bear upon such a hero and his traditional fate an imagination of mythic capabilities: I mean an imagination able to detect the intersection of divine, supernatural power and human experience; an imagination which could suggest the theology of life without betraying the limits of literature. Hawthorne, for example, had only very faint traces of such an imagination; his fiction never (unless in *The Scarlet Letter*) rose beyond the unequivocally humanistic level of insight and expression. He realized that the "pristine virtues" would inevitably encompass their possessor's destruction; and for him the proper denouement was the acquisition through suffering of different and tougher virtues. His version of the fortunate fall found the fortune in the faller; and it suggested an acceptance of the world and its authority. In the doctrine of *felix culpa*, the Fall was regarded as fortunate not because of its effect upon Adam the sinner but because of its effect upon God the redeemer; and the world was to be transformed thereafter. Melville's achievement was to recover the higher plane of insight, without intruding God on a machine: by making the culprit himself the redeemer.

It is this, I suggest, which accounts for something that might otherwise bother us in the *novella*: the apparent absence of impressive change—not in the world but in the character of Billy Budd. We expect our tragic heroes to change and to reveal (like Donatello) a dimensionally increased understanding of man's ways or of God's ways to man. Billy is as innocent, as guileless, as trusting, as *loving*, when he hangs from the yardarm as when he is taken off the "Rights of Man." What seems like failure, in this respect and on Melville's part, is exactly the heart of the accomplishment. For the change effected in the story has to do with the *reader*, as representative of the onlooking world: with the perception forced on him of the indestructible and in some sense the absolute value of "the pristine virtues." The perception is aroused by exposing the Christlike nature of innocence and love, which is to raise those qualities to a higher power—to their highest power. Humanly speaking, those qualities are fatal; but they alone can save the world.

So, in *Billy Budd*, Melville's own cycle of experience and commitment, which began with the hopeful dawn and "the glorious, glad, golden sun," returns again to the dawn—but a dawn transfigured, "seen in mystical vision." Melville salvaged the legend of hope both for life and for literature: by repudiating it in order to restore it in an apotheosis of its hero. There will be salvation yet, the story hints, from that treacherous dream.

VII

Melville had reason, then, to "bless" the story of "the Good Being hung and gone to glory": Billy's story was perfectly designed not only to carry that archetypal action with which the American legend-life had so long been concerned, but to transform the archetypal agent from a mere helpless innocent into a figure of redemption, a Good Being. But the story of that story did not, of course, end with *Billy Budd*; and I shall suggest in my Epilogue that it has, happily, not ended yet. "The matter of Adam," however rearranged or even inverted, continues to supply the motivating force in the composition of our liveliest and most durable fiction. I suspect, indeed, that the future of American fiction depends in some real part upon the durability of the image of the hero as Adam.

Within that narrow world where literary example is genuinely influential, the durability of the Adamic narrative image owes as much to the achievement of Henry James as to that of Melville and Hawthorne. *Billy Budd* was finished in 1891 and was not discovered and published until 1924; but, for all that, it was a story of the pre–Civil War generation, and W. H. Auden is imaginatively (if not historically) correct to relate it to the Melville of 1851. More than a decade before Melville began on his last work, Henry James was introducing the first of the very long series of innocent and metaphorically newborn heroes and heroines. Those qualities, actualized by James with every conceivable variety of ethical weight, defined his protagonists in novel after novel. An exhaustive list of James's innocents would approach a catalogue of his major writings in fiction: Christopher Newman in *The American;* Daisy Miller; Isabel Archer; Hyacinth Robinson in *The Princess Casamassima;* Miles and Flora in *The Turn of the Screw;* Lambert Strether in *The Ambassadors;* Milly Theale in *The Wings of the Dove;* Maggie and Adam Verver in *The Golden Bowl;* Ralph Pendril in the unfinished *Sense of the Past.* These are only among the more prominent and memorable names on the list.

The dialectic of innocence and experience—usually, but not always, dramatized as the American and Europe—was so obsessive and constant a theme for Henry James that one is tempted to say it was not, finally, a theme at all: but rather the special and extraordinarily sensitive instrument by which James gauged the moral weather of the life he was imitating. It was part of his technique as well as his content. An account of "innocence" in the fiction of Henry James, therefore, would be much the same as a book about James's fiction in general; it would have to be a book at least as long as this one.

But although James can be rewardingly examined in many different perspectives, one of the surest approaches to his work is that of the Adamic mythology I have been tracing. He saw himself in relation to French, Russian, and English novelists; but the form which life assumed in James's fiction reflected the peculiar American rhythm of the Adamic experience: the birth of the innocent, the foray into the unknown world, the collision with that world, "the fortunate fall," the wisdom and the maturity which suffering produced. The longer James lived abroad, the closer he moved toward a classic representation of the native anecdote. His initial treatment was realistic, in the Gallic manner; but his last novels shared the romantic, melodramatic, and mythic orientations of Cooper and Hawthorne and Melville. In *The Portrait of a Lady*, James took care to identify the social, domestic, and economic factors which led to Isabel Archer's entrance into the damaging world. In *The Wings of the Dove*, realities lie in the background; in the foreground, James enacts a singular combination of fairy tale and horror story. And the more James rehearsed the story, the more ambiguity he introduced into it. The later fiction reached sustained heights of narrative equivocation, and it is no longer possible to say that innocence is being either celebrated or exposed in its weakness; our allegiance is played with too cunningly, the wheel revolves too swiftly.

The final turn occurs in *The Golden Bowl*. In James's last completed novel, as in those of Hawthorne and Melville, the Adamic metaphor becomes explicit and central. Familiar qualities reverberate in the protagonist's name: Adam Verver, a linking of the first member of the human race with a two-syllable suggestion of greenness or freshness. But those familiar elements have taken on a potency not much less than sinister (something foreshadowed in the demonic innocents of *The Turn of the Screw*). The Prince and Charlotte Stant, representatives of "the world," are notably foreshortened; it is their destiny to be brought to heel, even crippled—where formerly the worldly Osmond had tamed the innocence of Isabel Archer. *The Golden Bowl* is a startling inversion of the Adamic tradition; it is the world, this time, which is struck down by aggressive innocence. For James saw very deeply—and he was the first American writer to do so—that innocence could be cruel as well as vulnerable; that the condition prior to conscience might have insidious undertones of the amoral as well as the beguiling naïveté of the premoral. In the mythology which he inherited, as an American artist, James detected paradoxes and tensions only hinted at by his American master, Hawthorne, and virtually unsuspected even by the most skeptical of Hawthorne's contemporaries.

There should be no doubt, however, that the Adamic mythology was James's first and most important inheritance from his own culture. He got some of it from Hawthorne; and what he got he was able to organize and contemplate in his little book on Hawthorne in 1879. He must have got some of it, too, from his father, whose best statement of the philosophical drama of individual experience—*Society the Redeemed Form of Man*—was likewise published in 1879. But he got most of it, one is forced to conclude, where everyone else seemed to be getting it: in the impalpable atmosphere of the time. The myth of the American Adam was simply a formula for the way life felt to alert and sensitive Americans during the second and third quarters of the nineteenth century; it could hardly have been missed by the younger Henry James.

It has been argued by Professor Quentin Anderson that the novels of Henry James, especially the final trio, comprised a very close working-out in narrative terms of the Swedenborg-directed philosophy of his father.[8] The parallels are suggestively close, as I myself have attempted to show. But the father's philosophy, as I have also suggested, was itself a reflection of the intellectual activity and the cluster of

8. In *Scrutiny*, September and December, 1947; and in *Kenyon Review*, autumn, 1946. Cf. a rebuttal by F. R. Leavis in *The Common Pursuit* (New York, 1952) and an elaboration by Francis Fergusson in *Sewanee Review*, winter, 1955. Professor Anderson has completed a full-length treatment of his subject—the relation between the two Henry Jameses—in a forthcoming book, appropriately titled *The American Henry James*.

moral attitudes of his generation. It was the elder James's way of participating in the cultural dialogue he heard going on around him; like Hawthorne, whom he loved, and like Horace Bushnell, whom he never knew at all, James tried to explain to his hopeful contemporaries the need and the value of sounding the "profoundest tragic depths." But his explanation did not amount to a system; it was a sort of huge and almost inarticulate growl of the spirit. His son William, trained in logic and metaphysics, had difficulty in piecing it together; it is hard to imagine the younger Henry even trying to. The phrase has become stale through repetition, but Eliot's remark still has truth in it: that Henry James (the son) had a mind so fine that no idea could violate it.

What should be added is that James had an imagination so vigorous that no idea could fail to be violated *by* it. James's fiction was a series of expert violations of the Adamic idea. And that idea with all its ramifications was what everything in his American background—including the table talk of his father—connived to give him.

The Golden Bowl, James's most thorough rendering and most remarkable transformation of the American story, achieved a kind of ultimacy in the direction it pursued. But there are other directions, and they are being pursued today. I come back to that in the Epilogue. Meanwhile, I move to areas other than fiction: to history and theology, where the themes which gave rise to the American genre of fiction were providing comparable challenges to inquiry and stimuli to insight. To hear those echoes and interpret them is to understand how oddly homogeneous was the cultural conversation of the day. The atmosphere was strange, but it was distributed evenly.

III

The Past and the Perfect

A people without history
Is not redeemed from time, for history is a pattern
Of timeless moments.

T. S. Eliot, *Little Gidding*

III

The Past and the Future

8

The Function of History
Bancroft and Parkman

Of all pursuits that require analysis, history . . . stands first.

GEORGE BANCROFT (1854)

THE age of hope surprised even itself by a lively and increasing
curiosity about the historical past it had so roundly repudiated.
When Emerson suggested, in an essay called *History*, that some in-
struction might, after all, be drawn from the study of former times and
events, the idea was received uneasily (by the *Democratic Review* in
1842) as "almost a paradox." "Probably no other civilised nation," it
was observed, "has at any period . . . so completely thrown off its allegiance to the past as the American. The whole essay of our national
life and legislation has been a prolonged protest against the dominion
of antiquity in every form whatsoever." The protest continued in
undiminished intensity; but, as the years went by, it became evident,
as the *Literary World* in 1849 pointed out with considerable surprise,
that "the movement on the part of American scholars and writers has
of late been in a marked manner in the direction of history." The
forward-looking age was, indeed, a great age for the study and the
writing of history; for the compiling of documents and records and
the founding of historical societies to preserve them; and as against
Tocqueville's assertion that Americans never kept records, it was possible for one reviewer to grumble with reason that the opposite was
almost alarmingly the case.

This paradox—the dedicated absorption with history at a moment
when it was being claimed that a new history had just begun—may be
resolved by noticing some of the subjects which occupied the attention
of the historians and, perhaps more important, the informing tone in
which the historical materials were presented. In no other area of dis-

course was the interchange of ideas so distinct. It was a conversation (carried on by means of historical treatises) about the second of the two ideas which went into the moral profile of the American as a new Adam: about "newness"—about the status of past time and the relation of the past to the present. In this conversation, the chief speakers were Prescott, Bancroft, and Parkman.

I

Chronologically and logically, one must begin with William Prescott (1796–1859), the author, among other works, of those two splendid historical narratives, *The Conquest of Mexico* and *The Conquest of Peru*. Prescott, who was the very embodiment of learned nostalgia, understood the function of the historian to be the scrupulous setting-off of the past from the present; the investigation of the past in its intact, reassuring pastness; and the perception of it as remote, invulnerable, and (therefore) radiant with truth. It was his aim, he said in the Introduction to *The Conquest of Mexico* in 1843, "to surround [the reader] with the spirit of the times, and . . . to make him . . . a contemporary of the sixteenth century." The very "distance of the present age from the period of the narrative" bespoke the truth of his work and made that truth visible.

Prescott was the most notable and impressive of those who responded to the forward-looking enthusiasms of the age by looking backward with compensatory vigor. He detected and deplored the current habit of "innovations" in speech and in opinion, and he warned against the excesses of an overly "inventive population." He resented the ambition of the day to new-name the elements of the world, like Adam in the garden; and he managed, in opposition, to make himself and his reader the members of another, more settled century. In doing so, he illustrated the later insight of Nikolai Berdyaev in *The Meaning of History:* that historical research is apt to flourish not during periods when the human mind exercises itself in a deep, organic communion with actual, concrete history but precisely during periods when the mind has been jolted out of such communion, when it is sufficiently detached from the continuing flow of history to reflect self-watchfully upon it. The American mind had been so jolted at some time between the waning of the Colonial age and the second quarter of the nineteenth century; and it had, as a consequence, become aware of the temporal order and of distinctions within it of past and present. The pervasive "protest against the dominion of antiquity in every form whatsoever" quickly produced a consciousness of antiquity as antiquity. As the present was cut away from the past, so the past appeared unexpectedly as an isolated, authentic object of inquiry; and persons made unhappy by the clamor of prophesying took to examining the records. Lowell had urged upon his countrymen the supremely hopeful formula: "Forget Europe wholly." Prescott came up with exactly the contrary advice.

We should, perhaps, distinguish here between the nonhistorical and the antihistorical mentality; Prescott began in a reaction to the latter. The antihistorical mind expressed itself in imperious negatives; it announced on all occasions its contempt for any idea which, as Hawthorne's Coverdale put it in *The Blithedale Romance*, "had not come into vogue since yesterday morning." And on deeper levels the antihistorical spirit wrestled with the facts of history in order to escape from the burden they had hitherto imposed. But to the nonhistorical view of Emerson and Thoreau and Whitman, no temporal distinctions were admitted, as none were sought. "What is near to the heart of this generation is fair and bright still," wrote Thoreau; all good men, good deeds, and good sayings exuded a simultaneous glow, when the accidents of their historical clothing had been removed. History dissolved under such a glance; under Prescott's it froze.

The assault upon history corresponded to the noise of denial and protest that Emerson had reported hearing in other phases of the culture. But while it produced, in contrast, the consecration of the past by a writer like Prescott, it also led to a new mode of historical writing, a studied demonstration in historical terms of the validity of the hopeful legend, the legend of the second chance. More than anyone else, George Bancroft typified this second chapter in the recurring cultural story of the generation.

II

George Bancroft of Massachusetts (1800–1891) was a robust and yet unstable figure, the most politically active among the hopeful party, a writer of gusto, and a man who managed just to miss greatness in several fields. He studied under Hegel in Berlin and Heeren in Göttingen;[1] he was minister to London under Polk and to Berlin under Johnson and Grant; he was Secretary of the Navy for one year (1845–46) and founded the Naval Academy at Annapolis. He had a talent at

1. Bancroft to his former teacher, Edward Everett, from Berlin, December, 1820: "I took a philosophical course with Hegel. But I thought it lost time to listen to his display of unintelligible words" (*The Life and Letters of George Bancroft*, ed. M. A. De Wolfe Howe [New York, 1908], I, 92).

once for an almost Lincolnian political prescience and for self-seeking compromise. His diplomatic and political career does not really concern us here; but both the powers and the instability which that career revealed must be mentioned. It is as a historian that Bancroft comes into this story; but there is a sense in which his notion about history was a response to his feeling of instability—in himself, in the world. For Bancroft turned to history as the body of knowledge which could make sense out of an experience characterized by incessant change. And, as shaped under his powers and as animated by his gusto, history became for Bancroft a myth which revealed the purpose behind the change: an explanation of the very essence of the New World. The New World became the crown, the key, and the consummation of a universal historical process.

The chorus of denial and protest against nearly all inherited institutions, forms of thought, habits of mind, and paths of conduct created —among all but the inveterately hopeful—a feeling of almost cosmic unsettledness. Movement and change, dissolution and disappearance, seemed virtually to characterize reality. In essays and articles, in stories and poems which attempted to catch the life of the times, the imagery of flowing abounded, intermingled with imagery of burning, of storms and hurricanes, of high winds sweeping all before them. "It was impossible," Coverdale recalled, speaking of the community at Blithedale (the fictionalized Brook Farm of West Roxbury), "not to imbibe the idea that everything in nature and human existence was fluid or fast becoming so; that the crust of the earth in many places was broken, and its whole surface portentously upheaving."

For those incapable of perceiving (as Emerson perceived) the few, simple, eternal principles of truth and goodness shining steadily through the chaotic surfaces of experiences, the facts of human history and the discipline of the historical method came to the rescue, restoring order and disclosing meaning. For human history, when enough was known of it, yielded up its governing law: the law of progress. In an essay in the *Democratic Review*, very possibly written by George Bancroft, the evidence of endless mutability was rehearsed, in a way to lead to the rhetorical questions and answers: "Is this, then, indeed a chaos? Is it no more than a lawless tumult? . . . Far from it. . . . On all is written the great law of Progress. . . . The course of the whole race is onwards. Every age takes some step in advance of its predecessors."

In an oration before the New York Historical Society in 1854, Bancroft was more succinct, more assured. "Everything is in motion, and for the better," he announced. "The last system of philosophy is always the best. . . . The last political state of the world likewise is ever more excellent than the old." Chaos was redeemed by progress. And progress was the lesson of history. It was a secular version of faith in search of reason: progress was the faith; history supplied the reason. So it was that Bancroft could lay it down confidently that "of all pursuits that require analysis, history . . . stands first." Among history's competitors, philosophy was not equipped to follow motions; and the natural sciences knew nothing about the better.

The kind of history which substantiated the progressive faith was brought over and adapted from various European speculators and called "universal history." These vast, metaphysical musings on the whole course of the human drama had stirred many European minds since the third quarter of the eighteenth century, as a response to the radical changes effected by the Revolution and its consequences. The response corresponded to that of St. Augustine, fourteen hundred years before, when in the light of comparable dislocations, he had sought for the historical substantiation of the Christian faith and had composed *The City of God*. In America in the 1840's and 1850's the charting of universal history became something like a fashionable game; commentators in books and periodicals vied with one another in labeling and plotting the several grand stages of the human story—the grandest, in all cases, being the present stage, which was also the final one.

The distinction of George Bancroft's use of imported doctrine may be indicated in a comparison with Richard Hildreth, a contemporary and colleague, who, like Bancroft, was a former pupil of Edward Everett at Harvard. Hildreth (1807–65) bore a relation to Bancroft not unlike the relation of Dr. Holmes to Walt Whitman. Hildreth, that is, detected (like Holmes) a slow, uneven "rise" of the human society; and Bancroft testified (like Whitman) to a triumphant new beginning. Hildreth, a legalist and a Boston editor, was not impressed by claims of human or institutional perfectibility; he wasted little time in mulling over the operation of large principles; and he had a cold dislike of what he called "mystical ideas." But he agreed that the history of mankind did, for the studious, show a development toward the better: a better measured in terms of "the municipal spirit—in other words of democracy." The subject was explored in Hildreth's *Theory of Politics* (1853), where—in the course of explaining and commending the new discipline of universal history—he contended that civilization had passed through a series of progressively superior stages, distinguishable in terms of the focus of political power. One power structure had given way to the next: the priests to the nobles, the nobles to the absolute monarchs, they to the burghers—and finally, in the American democracy, the burghers gave way, as the embodiments of power, to the workingmen of the entire society.

So far, Richard Hildreth, a man who had more affinities with Jeremy Bentham (whose hard-headed theories he admired) than, say, with Emerson. But Bancroft, reflecting poetically on the course of history, thought he found a difference not merely of degree but of kind in the American experience. Liberty, rather than power, was Bancroft's major term of analysis. In this respect, he followed his teacher, Everett, who had declared in 1828 that "history, as it has often been written, is the genealogy of princes. . . . But the history of Liberty . . . is the real history of man." Liberty and slavery played out their long dialectic in Bancroft's historical essays as the cities of God and of Man had done in the masterwork of St. Augustine. The American Revolution was the true and long-prepared-for birth of freedom, the ultimate clue to human history: as once the birth of God as man had been thought to be. The Revolution ushered in the fourth and final stage of history. The first stage had extended from the beginning of the world to the age of Socrates; the second from Athens to the start of Christianity. "The third extends from the promulgation of the glad tidings of the Gospel by the Saviour to the American Revolution, which events may be deemed the two most important in the history of mankind. With the latter commences a new and more glorious era, of which the one immediately preceding it may be considered as little more than formative."

The historic struggle which led to that new and more glorious era—that era for which the Christian centuries had been but a prologue—was the subject of Bancroft's *History of the United States*, a work of ten volumes written between 1834 and 1876. Like Hildreth (who had composed a six-volume *History of the United States* between 1849 and 1852, a more accurate and considerably duller achievement), Bancroft chose to document the last, the American, stage of universal history. What he provided, in fact, was less a history than a myth of origins, a narrative representation of the essential glory of the new era. Bancroft was right to call his *History* "an epic of liberty." For if undependable as history, it is recognizable as epic myth. It is thematic, not inclusive; its language is incantatory; it is not an account but a celebration of its subject: how Providence, as Bancroft said in the Introduction, "conducted the country to its present happiness and glory." As the massive story unfolds through the opening volumes, it becomes clear that what Bancroft had envisaged was not an irresistible and irreversible rise of man, but rather a death and a rebirth—the final disastrous fumbling of man's chance in the Old World and the seizing and the triumphant exploitation of man's second chance in the New.

The story begins amid the intricate political and spiritual corruptions which fatally darkened the world of late medieval and Renaissance Europe. It traces the departure of those few hardy souls able to escape the collapsing citadels, watches their perilous landing on the new continent, and recounts the long series of crises out of which the new society was finally born. Defeat, escape, travel, landings, war, victory, rebirth: it is one of the great epic patterns. If there is not a single hero, there is at least a single kind of heroism—incarnated variously in persons like Winthrop, Bradford, Roger Williams, Anne Hutchinson (in the first generation), and those in later decades who emulated their combative love of liberty. "The citizens of the United States," Bancroft intoned, "should . . . cherish . . . the men who, as they first trod the soil of the New World, scattered the seminal principles of republican freedom and national independence." And so the story goes forward, through endless dangers, forays, intrigues, and rebellions, until, with the battles of the Revolution, the final crisis is passed, and the new history begins. Bancroft's *History* functioned as a positive demonstration that the New World was the victorious climax of the long and painful effort to start afresh.

III

Bancroft was occupied primarily with newness, the new birth of freedom. But if, alongside Bancroft's histories, we place those of Francis Parkman covering the same American centuries, we perceive at once that—by contrast—Bancroft's historical temperament was undeviatingly innocent. He was innocently cheerful about human nature generally and about the men who opened up the new life in the New World. "Happiness and glory" were the end-products of their activities, according to Bancroft. For Parkman the American story was, if anything, the story of a loss, rather than a gain. It was the loss of a world in which the possibility of tragedy was central. And for Parkman tragedy revealed and tested the authentic greatness of the human spirit.

Parkman (1823–93) was the greatest of the nineteenth-century historians, as Melville was the greatest of the novelists. Like Melville, Parkman was stimulated by the age's most pronounced aspirations, and, like him, Parkman probed those aspirations to discover and dramatize the reality of suffering and tragedy lying beneath them. Behind his scholarly devotion to the established facts, we can plainly hear the poet commenting on current tendencies. Without those tendencies, Parkman might have been no less devoted to historic truth; but the nature of his comment would have been altogether different. Parkman's comment was most emphatic about the claims of present glory, as uttered by Bancroft, and on the image of the benign forest and its taintless inhabitants, as narrated by Cooper.

Parkman took as his historical subject what had been Cooper's fictional subject: the American forest. At an early age, as he said later, his plans crystallized in the idea of writing the story of "the war that ended in the conquest of Canada—for here as it seemed to me the forest drama was more stirring and the forest stage more thronged with appropriate actors than in any other passage in our history." He enlarged his plan eventually "to include the whole course of the American conflict between France and England, or, in other words, the history of the American forest; for this is the light in which I regarded it." But both the forest and the drama which Parkman went on to explore were substantially and suggestively different from those of Cooper—or indeed of the novelist Bird, or even of Hawthorne. Parkman's attitude to the forest revealed his attitude to history; and his attitude to history helped shape his image of the forest.

Parkman brought to his subject a prose style not easily matched in the entire course of American literature for precision and energy and hard grace. He was the Melville of the historians—incomparably the best writer among them; and about his style the only complaint is that it was almost overpoweringly masculine. Parkman's masculinity of spirit (a key aspect) was very likely an overcompensation for his life-long feebleness of body; for Parkman, as for Brockden Brown, life was a continuous dull ache—but Parkman did not dramatize the ache, he fought it down; and what he dramatized was the zest of the fighting. Parkman was a dramatizer to the core: but not a self-dramatizer. He brought to his subject not only style, but a histrionic sensibility of the first order. When he was barely coming of age, in Rome during his grand tour, he recorded in his journal about a Roman priest: at the announcement of his (Parkman's) Unitarian background the priest "rolled up his blood-shot eyes in their black sockets, and stretched his skinny neck out of his cowl, like a turtle basking on a stone in summer." And he sympathized dramatically, though not doctrinally, with the histrionic sensibility of the priests themselves on Good Friday.

The Function of History: Bancroft and Parkman

"All the priests looked wretched and disconsolate, as if afflicted with some awful disaster. 'He is not up yet,' whispered Mancinelli to me, in explanation of the dismal appearance of things."

These literary gifts made it possible for Parkman as a historian to be a novelist of distinction. As a novelist, he was nothing at all; *Vassall Morton* (1856), his only novel, was a flat failure, all surface and no depth, and the surface a dry collection of conventional phrases and postures. What Parkman was quite unable to do in his effort to convert autobiography into fiction was just what he did do in his effort to bring together the extant records of the French and English in North America. He saw the form and contours of the story in them. It is Parkman who illustrates better than any of his colleagues the phrase "literary historian," which does not mean a historian with a talent for turning an occasional pleasing trope to decorate the collected facts. The literary historian—Parkman, par excellence—was the historian who saw the body of his subject while still it lay scattered in unorganized source materials; who re-created the body by reanimating the form it required.

But though Parkman may be usefully compared with Melville, in respect of stature and relationship, he was never at any time—as Melville was, at least partially—a member of the party of Hope. The New England political idealists who crowded that party were dismissed by Parkman, in a revealing epithet, as "she-philosophers"; Brisbane and Dana were "windy"; and a reformer he saw listening to their discourses was pictured as looking "much more like a lunatic or beast than a man." In Malta, at the age of twenty, he commended the "wholesome system of coercion" he found there; he much admired the Maltese treatment of criminals—the treatment of "manfully kicking the offender into the gutter." "I seem, thank heaven," he reflected, "to be carried about half a century backward in time." Here clearly marked is the unequivocal accent of the staunch adherent to the party of Memory. And yet the motivations for Parkman's peculiar brand of nostalgia—motivations hinted at by his language: "man," "manfully," "she-philosophers," with the gestures those words unmistakably carry—led him to certain initial attitudes curiously close to those of the hopeful.

They led him, anyhow, to the American forest: literally and physically into it, and to a tremendous love for it. He said of himself, in the third person, that from his adolescent years onward "his thoughts were always in the forest, whose feature possessed his waking and sleeping dreams filling him with vague cravings impossible to satisfy."

When he was eighteen, he went up into the White Mountains, in order "to have a taste of the half-savage kind of life necessary to be led, and to see the wilderness where it was as yet uninvaded by the hand of man." Henry David Thoreau, tearing a woodchuck apart with his fingers and eating it raw, hovers close to that passage, and provides a conclusion for it: "I love the wild not less than the good." It may perhaps be said of Parkman that for him the wild was itself the good: or at least the realm of the good. His contempt for "civilisation" rivaled that expressed by Thoreau in the opening chapter of *Walden;* but the two men arrived at their contempt from suggestively diverse starting points. Parkman's attitude betrays itself in the brief survey he gave, toward the end of his life, of the changes which had occurred in the land beyond the frontier:

> The buffalo is gone, and of all of his millions nothing is left but bones. Tame cattle and fences of barbed wire have supplanted his vast herds and boundless grazing grounds. The wild Indian is turned into an ugly caricature of his conqueror; and that which made him romantic, terrible and hateful, is in large measure scourged out of him. The slow cavalcade of horsemen armed to the teeth have disappeared before parlor cars and the effeminate comforts of modern travel.

The oppositions established there tell us a good deal. "Tame" is opposed to "wild," and "fences" to "boundless": thus far Parkman seems to echo both Thoreau and Cooper. But the basis of the oppositions is shown in the controlling contrast between "terrible," "hateful," and "armed," on the one hand, and "effeminate" and "comforts," on the other. Parkman arrived at his dedication to the unfenced, the wild, and the boundless not out of a dream of innocence and novelty in a *vita nuova* but out of a hard, uncompromising, impatient, and severely masculine ideal of life. Parkman's ideal led him to condemn the allegedly civilized as thoroughly as did Thoreau, and to project, like the hopeful generally, the vision of a state of nature. But Parkman's state of nature was Hobbesian, with the difference that Parkman only regretted its disappearance. His state of nature was a world of violence and total, unending war; a world in which only the fittest survived—only those with the most unconquerable will; a world realizing in outline and content the life worth living, and demanding at every moment the only human virtues worth having.

This is the world which comes into being in Parkman's histories: the world of the American forest from Canada to the mouth of the Mississippi and from the sixteenth century onward.[2] It is perhaps a minor

2. After *The Oregon Trail* in 1849, Parkman published *History of the Conspiracy of Pontiac* in 1851; both books, chronologically, are epilogues to the series which then

paradox that the historian who felt antipathy for the premises of hope should come closer in his history to the image of an American Eden than did that very type of hopeful historian, George Bancroft. But the paradox diminishes as we begin to perceive the quality of experience in Parkman's world. One of Parkman's major devices for explaining the forest was to distinguish its reality, as he saw it, from the peaceful image of the hopeful. "Should anyone of my readers ever be impelled to visit the prairies [he said in *The Oregon Trail*] . . . I can assure him that he need not think to enter at once upon the paradise of his imagination." He concedes that there is a stretch of country which "will answer tolerably well to . . . preconceived ideas of the prairie; for this it is from which picturesque tourists, painters, poets and novelists who have seldom penetrated further, have derived their conceptions of the whole region." "But let him," he concludes, "be as enthusiastic as he may, he will find enough to damp his ardor. His wagons will stick in the mud; his horses will break loose; harness will give way; and axletrees prove unsound." The discomforts and the dangers, Parkman felt, were there primarily to make the foolish turn back, with their burden of illusion. For a man, the discomforts were the prerequisites of enjoyment: life advanced only through challenging encounters.

The native representative of that harsh and deceptive world was the American Indian: the person whom the Jesuits had come to convert two centuries earlier. But the inhabitant was like his environment; and he was not, Parkman is careful to point out, the Chingachgook of Cooper, the brave and innocent personality untroubled by time. "The mind of the savage was by no means that beautiful blank which some have represented it." Neither blank nor entirely beautiful, but packed with fierce legacies of attitude and aspiration—the treacherous and the deadly mingling freely with the loyal and the courtly. The actor suited his setting; and Parkman devoted nearly a hundred introductory pages of *The Jesuits in North America* to sketching the actor's qualities, habits, and instincts. The sketch and the narrative which followed it show the Indian and his forest to be closer to Bird's than to Cooper's. But though Parkman, like Bird (to whom Parkman refers with respect), sets up his image by a critique of Cooper, he exhibits no

---

followed. Parkman's next five historical volumes move forward in time, their order of appearance matching the order of events: *Pioneers of France in the New World* (1865), *The Jesuits in North America* (1867), *The Discovery of the Great West* (1869), *The Old Regime in Canada* (1874), and *Count Frontenac and New France under Louis XIV* (1877). It is in these volumes that a world "comes into being." The saga of *Montcalm and Wolfe*, published in 1884, dealt with events occurring later in time than those of Parkman's final volume, *A Half-Century of Conflict* (1892).

trace of the angry and bewildered disenchantment of Nick of the Woods—for Parkman had never entertained the dangerous illusion to begin with. He reveled in just those realities which shocked Nathan Slaughter to the edge of madness.

The whole of Parkman's history, the seven volumes of *France and England in North America* (1851–92), comprises an account of a series of great assaults upon the forest and its inhabitants: the assault of the spirit, by the Jesuit missionaries; the assault of the will, by soldier-adventurers like La Salle; and the assault of craft and political ambition. It includes also the occasional counteraction by the inhabitants themselves, chiefly the conspiracy of Pontiac, the Iroquois leader. Parkman remains today the major source for our knowledge about those events; and his reputation as a historian is undoubtedly deserved. The reputation is also somewhat misleading, for it rests in part upon the notion that Parkman was an impartial spectator, that he was "scientifically" detached from his subject. It is true enough that Parkman does not seem to be supporting any one of the participants, though he pays lip service to the eventual triumph of liberty; and as he tells of that triumph, he appears to favor neither the French nor the English, neither the Jesuits nor the Indians, neither Montcalm nor Wolfe. The fact is, nonetheless, that Parkman had no difficulty in being dispassionate about the outcome, because the outcome was not what interested him personally. What interested him was the struggle, not its resolution; the quality and power of the assaults, not their conclusion. What interested him was struggle in general—as the condition of life. It was the condition which was supreme in the world with which his histories were concerned.

As a minor instance of his mode of involvement, we can notice his treatment of the duel between the Jesuit priest, Le Jeune, and an Algonquin medicine man. "From the antagonism of their respective professions, the sorcerer hated the priest, who lost no opportunity of denouncing his incantations, and who ridiculed his perpetual singing and drumming as puerility and folly. The former . . . used every device to retort ridicule upon his rival. . . . So sorely was [the missionary] harassed, that, lest he should exasperate his tormentor, he sometimes passed whole days without uttering a word." Passages like that are reminiscent of other debates: the debates, for example, between Dr. Holmes's medicine men—his psychologizing doctors—and the ministers they so effortlessly overcome. Parkman, alert to the displacement of traditional religious positions in his own generation, handles the tug-of-war between priest and sorcerer with a chilly humor, displaying what there was in them of the ancient battle of rival magicians, hinting at their generalized symbolic significance. He enjoyed the duel and admired each of the duelers only in so far as each showed competence for the act engaged in.

As the unfenced, boundless world sheds its cozy, Edenesque qualities and assumes the character of the war-torn state of nature, so Parkman's representative hero becomes—not the innocent, time-free Adam, the brave and modest Hawkeye, but the man of will, practical forcefulness, and unrelenting pride. Of all the particular heroes in his long story—and there are many from various nations and tribes—the one who stands out is René-Robert Cavelier, Sieur de la Salle: La Salle (1643–87), who brought the Great Lakes region and its Indian tribes under the control of France, and who presented to France the "stupendous accession" he himself named Louisiana—stretching "from the Alleghenies to the Rocky Mountains; from the Rio Grande and the Gulf to the farthest springs of the Missouri." La Salle moves through Parkman's volume like a French Ahab, en route by way of tremendous leadership and extraordinary accomplishments to a resonantly tragic destiny: for La Salle's pride and power and the intolerable exertions he demanded of less dedicated men brought about his downfall and death, and in the end he was assassinated by one of his own soldiers. Parkman's concluding estimate of La Salle deserves full quotation:

He belonged not to the age of the knight-errant and the saint, but to the modern world of practical study and practical action. He was the hero not of a principle nor of a faith, but simply of a fixed idea and a determined purpose. As often happens with concentrated and energetic natures, his purpose was to him a passion and an inspiration. . . .

Serious in all things, incapable of the lighter pleasure, incapable of repose, finding no joy but in the pursuit of great designs, too shy for society and too reserved for popularity, often unsympathetic and always seeming so, smothering emotions which he could not utter, schooled to universal distrust, stern to his followers and pitiless to himself, bearing the brunt of every hardship and every danger, demanding of others an equal constancy joined to an implicit deference, heeding no counsel but his own, attempting the impossible and grasping at what was too vast to hold,—he contained in his own complex and painful nature the chief springs of his triumphs, his failures, and his death.

It is easy to reckon up his defects, but it is not easy to hide from sight the Roman virtues that redeemed them. Beset by a throng of enemies, he stands, like the King of Israel, head and shoulders above them all. He was a tower of adamant, against whose impregnable front hardship and danger, the rage of man and of the elements, the southern sun, the northern blast, fatigue, famine, disease, delay, disappointment, and deferred hope emptied their quivers in vain. That very pride which, Coriolanus-like, declared itself most sternly in the thickest press of foes, has in it something to challenge admiration. Never, under the impenetrable mail of paladin or crusader, beat a heart of more intrepid mettle than within the stoic panoply that armed the breast of La Salle.

All of Parkman is in those lines: all of his world and the push and pressure of the life within it; his image of heroism; and the reverberating relation between that kind of hero and that kind of world; and, finally, the poetic principle (the principle of tragic poetic drama) by which he brought the world and its hero into being.

There are other heroes for Parkman—all those, Jesuits or Indians, as well as French or English, who shared, according to their natures, the great virtues of La Salle: the fixed determination, the unflinching, forward-thrusting courage, the pride either of person or of purpose or of sacred mission, virtues appropriate to their untamed world. Pontiac, the Iroquois, stands close behind La Salle and, like him, won for himself a tragic climax of assassination by a member of his own race; behind Pontiac, there are the almost unbelievably durable Jesuit priests, continuing, mutilated and reviled, upon their business of conversion. Parkman's scorn is reserved for the faltering and the cowardly and the undedicated; and his harshest criticism is directed toward those who are unable to engage in the struggle which is life. There is regret and exasperation in Parkman's summary of the causes for the eventual destruction of the Indian tribes (even though that destruction led to the triumph of the British and of "liberty"):

> Could they have read their destiny and curbed their mad ambition, they might have leagued themselves, with four great communities of kindred lineage, to resist the encroachments of civilisation and oppose a barrier of fire to the spread of the young colonies of the east. But their organisation and their intelligence were merely the instruments of a blind frenzy, which impelled them to destroy those whom they might have made their allies in a common interest.

Resisting "the encroachments of civilisation" would have been, Parkman appears to suggest, a noble and saving action. He looked back upon the world of the forest, the world of La Salle and Le Jeune and Pontiac, not with wistfulness, not with nostalgia, but with intense, full-hearted admiration. The passing of this world was no doubt a victory for freedom, but not for any freedom Parkman could honestly respond to. He did not regret that the colonials won; he regretted that anybody had won. Whether his image of the forest was an accurate image of the world as it had been, it was clearly not an image of the world as it was; perhaps it was an image of the world as it ought to be. Parkman replaced the contemporary dream of a new Adam by his own curiously dense and dangerous Eden, where life refreshed itself by constant exposure to annihilation.

But without that contemporary dream, Parkman's tough, ironic, masculine ideal might scarcely have been articulated; for it was voiced contrapuntally, as a detailed, critical gloss upon the dream. Through history, Parkman got in touch with what he took to be the nourishing reality behind the current illusion; and history functioned as a measure of the soft inadequacies of his own age, a comfort to the temperament wearied by the comforts of civilization.

9

The Real Presence: Parker
and Brownson

[Theodore Parker] was mad at religion ... and he
wished to turn men in utter nakedness out into this bleak
and wintry world to rely on themselves alone, and to support themselves as best they might from their own native
resources.

ORESTES BROWNSON (1857)

THE historical discussion, a century ago, blurred into the theological, as certain of the more traditional theologians chose to defend
their own cherished doctrines by attacking the moral assumptions and
the metaphysical presumptuousness implicit in the historical writings
of George Bancroft. Those somewhat nervous rebuttals may serve as
a prologue to inspecting the contemporary theological version of the
Adamic dream, as well as the theological animadversion it instantly
aroused. But, first, mention must be made of the special complexities in
talking about theology at all, as it manifested itself in the age of hope.

In the history of earlier cultures, the theological aspect might well
be the crowning aspect, the natural climax of the history in question,
the final chapter and the end in view. This would be the case in any
period when theology was regarded as the queen of the sciences and
the source of their governing principles. In any period persons of a
certain caste of mind may attempt to follow the medieval method
announced in the title of St. Bonaventura's famous treatise, and reduce all the arts to theology. But in the nineteenth century, the movement ran sharply in the other direction: toward a reduction of theology to one of the arts, or toward a diffusion of it among them all. Theology in that age was thus a singularly Protean affair; it existed and
exercised its influence everywhere and nowhere; intellectual history
scarcely knows where to have it. For if, by theology, we mean the notions held—and rendered more or less articulate and orderly—about
the relation between God and man; and if, by religion, we mean a radi-

The Real Presence: Parker and Brownson

ance of conscience inciting actions with respect to that ultimate relation: then we are faced with a paradox. A century ago, matters (of literary endeavor, of historical perspective, of morals) brought forward with nothing like doctrinal theological definition were nonetheless propelled with something very like a religious force.

In a sense, the entire program of the party of Hope was religious in temper. It represented a concerted effort to renew immediate contact with the root source and begetter of things, cutting back through all the conditioning legacies which had long formed the context within which the ultimate relation was to be established. The repudiation of tradition in all its phases was a first step toward getting back—as Lowell acutely noticed—to "the original and eternal life out of which all tradition takes its rise." It revealed the perennial Protestant impulse toward unmediated communication with divinity. The legend of the second chance, the association of the American with the figure of Adam, were in this regard altogether the product of a simplified and sunny theology. But the legend issued customarily in practices of an essentially nontheological nature.

"The Church, or religious party," Emerson remarked in 1844, with his uncanny seismographic accuracy, was "falling away from the Church nominal, and . . . appearing in temperance and nonresistance societies; in movements of abolitionists and of socialists; and in very significant assemblies . . . composed of ultraists, of seekers, of all the soul of the soldiery of dissent."[1] The "soldiery" included all the persons I have collected under Emerson's phrase, the party of Hope. Their major accomplishment, perhaps, was to transfer religious ardor to the realm of human relations: so that the ancient theological virtue of hope (which rested on faith in God) was transformed into the human quality of hopefulness (which rested on faith in the heroic American). For the most part, the theology of the hopeful was coextensive with their feeling about the possibilities of life for the new man in the New World.

There remained a few persons, however, still determined to perform the classical functions of theology. What these men had to confront was not only the current Adamic dismissal of sin and history but also the cheerful religious air which accompanied the act of dismissal. In order to combat the pretensions of innocence, theologians of an older persuasion found it necessary, first of all, to re-establish what they took to be the true nature of theology itself. For the central issues, in

1. Cf. the early chapters of Daniel Aaron's *Men of Good Hope* (New York, 1951). Professor Aaron emphasizes the value of what he calls the "religious baggage" of the mid-century reformers, in contrast with the opportunistic juggling of their successors in the twentieth century.

their minds, could be resolved only in theological terms: in terms, that is, of the relation between man and God.

The historian George Bancroft was a particular target of the theologians, as historicism in general was their special enemy. Orestes Brownson, for example, reviewing the first four volumes of Bancroft's *History*, accused Bancroft of confounding history and theology almost beyond the possibilities of disentanglement. Brownson by this time (1852) was a Roman Catholic busy with the task of fitting the expanding jumble of American culture within the orderly schemes of the Roman church: a preposterous, though honorable, enterprise. To that end, Brownson was anxious to press anew the traditional scholastic distinctions; and he condemned Bancroft for muddling the disciplines, for using history rather than writing it—using "history for the purpose of setting forth his speculative theories on God, man and society," a singularly effective and insidious device for "destroying all true intellectual and moral life." In Brownson's eyes, Bancroft offered bad history in order to conceal a spurious theology.

Meanwhile, Taylor Lewis, an irascible professor of Old Testament at Union College—a man who showed up fairly often in the periodicals of the fifties expressing his nostalgic distaste for the drift of religious thought—urged against Bancroft and his colleagues a like distinction in the area of observed human experience. Lumping together Emerson, Parker, Fourier, and Horace Greeley along with Bancroft in a shared mystique, Lewis saw all of them as systematically breaking the distinction—not only between theology and history, but more fundamentally between the finite and the infinite—between man and God. In their view, Lewis reported vexatiously, God himself was a historical phenomenon; history encompassed everything; and any intrusion of a divine or supra-historical being in the flow of temporal events was categorically denied. "The very instinct by which we pray proves the possibility of Divine interposition," Lewis argued; but he acknowledged that the need for prayer had been implicitly abolished by the hopeful. What was there to pray for?

Perhaps the most illuminating of the rebuttals to Bancroft was made by one Caleb Sprague Henry, an Episcopal clergyman of New York, an alert and forward-looking scholar, and a "Christian transcendentalist." In his "Remarks on Mr. Bancroft's Oration of Human Progress" (1855), Henry's normally charitable soul was enflamed to the point of calling the doctrine carried in that oration "pernicious rigmarole"—because "it is calculated to make men 'accept the present state of the world' in a way that we regard as detrimental to true progress."[2] True progress, Henry insisted (as the elder James and Horace Bushnell were simultaneously insisting), "begins in a sense of the need for reformation. It begins . . . with repentance, and that begins in the sense of sinfulness and evil." Henry's antinostalgic motivation is clear from his emphasis on the optimistic character of the recognition of evil: "the promise is hopeful in proportion as the sense of sin is pervading and deep."

Henry was more concerned with the hope than with the sin; but he felt that that hope would remain smothered so long as the contemporary indifference to or hatred of the past persisted. "The old historical life of humanity," he urged, "must not be regarded as standing in no relations, much less relations purely hostile, to the life of the present"; for "the spirit of true progress"—just as it began in the sense of sin—"is an organising not a destroying spirit." And with an exceptional sharpness of insight that carried him a crucial step forward into the area of theology proper, Henry touched the nerve-center of the entire problem: the intimate connection (as he believed) between the sense of sin and the real value of "the old historical life of humanity." What gave that historical life its *life*, Henry proposed, was the active presence within it of the supra-historical. From the latter there could be no break: not, at least, without moral diaster. History so considered was primarily the history of "an historical institution" which embodied "*supernatural* divine efficacies." History so understood was thus the channel of grace. The past was the vessel of the perfect and the means by which imperfection restored itself in communion with the perfect. The human spirit, contemplating divine perfection, could not but perceive its own relative sinfulness, and so be stirred to the course of true progress. It was, Henry thought, to sustain that progress that the "divine efficacies" were present in history. A hostility to the past was therefore a form of moral self-enslavement.

What Henry wrote sparingly—in articles and letters to the press—Orestes Brownson was at the same time writing very large. But Brownson is not to be separated from his friend, the hopeful theologian Theodore Parker. The issue between the two men had a kind of clean finality. Both men agreed that the question of tradition was bound up with the question of human nature and its resources and

2. This quotation and the major part of Henry's most relevant comments are contained in a volume of essays and articles called *Considerations on Some of the Elements and Conditions of Social Welfare and Human Progress* (New York, 1861). The phrase "Christian transcendentalist" is borrowed from Ronald V. Wells, *Three Christian Transcendentalists* (New York, 1943), a book which includes studies of James Marsh and Frederick Hedge as well as Henry.

that the problem was ultimately theological. But Parker, confident about humanity, saw theology exploding the value of tradition. And Brownson, aroused by that verdict, went on to the belief and the attempted demonstration that tradition was the supreme resource of imperfect mankind.

II

Theodore Parker of Massachusetts (1810–60) had a powerfully defined personality; and in seeking to identify him, one is drawn—as his friends were—to a host of analogies from the age of the Renaissance, the time when personality first came into its own. "Our Savonarola," Emerson called him, alluding no doubt to Parker's zeal and rhetorical skill rather than to his beliefs. For Parker was also a kind of Rabelais, or Savonarola *revolté:* a man of enormous learning, which he fairly hurled in all directions in support of the most trivial point; a man drunk on *la dive bouteille* of the accumulated knowledge of innumerable traditions, in none of which was he enlisted; a man of passion and temper, of boisterous humor and large appetites. He was an American Rabelais, surprisingly engaged in the mission of an American Luther; for through all the ringing declarations of man's natural and unlimited potentialities, we hear the violently earnest, ruggedly intractable voice of Martin Luther—insisting again on the individual's direct and personal communication with his God.

Contemplating the vastness of his erudition—he was said to have owned the largest library of its kind in New England, while his editors point in some consternation to allusions in his writings to nearly as many volumes more—it is astonishing how little he finally had to say. A small mouse of a doctrine emerged after all the convulsions of labor by a whole mountain range of information. On the theological side, his entire intellectual progress was reductive. His learning was exploited in the way of refutation and denial. His theology was a singular application of Thoreau's injunction to simplify, simplify, simplify. His theology was in fact Adamic; the very first and the very least that could or need be said about his primary relation, by the free individual spirit standing flush with the universe at the dawn of time. Parker's great and simple ambition was just that: to persuade all individuals that they were as freshly created and as close to their creator—"now [in his own words] as in the days of Adam."

He arrived at his religious doctrine, in the manner of his age and party, by gradually shedding the cultural inheritance. The Calvinist creed he found it unnecessary to reject; he had only to hate it. His parents had rejected it for him: his father (a Lexington, Massachusetts, farmer of some indiscriminate learning) on rational grounds; his mother, because it seemed monstrous. His progress at first was slow, almost sluggish. In 1831, he could confess to having "derived much advantage" from a six-day meeting conducted by that unrelenting Presbyterian, Lyman Beecher, though Parker added that Beecher had, perhaps, offered "too harsh a remedy for gentle souls." At the Divinity School in Cambridge (1834–36), his meditations, so far as they are recorded, were conventional enough. Doctrine scarcely interested him, as he dutifully copied into his notebook inert and moralistic advices on personal conduct. It was not Cambridge which awoke him but the stimulating agitations he encountered after his ordination in 1837 and his first appointment, to West Roxbury: agitations which, sparked by the first orations and addresses of Emerson, were the birth pangs of the intellectual party which would symbolize the age. Parker soon was adding his comments to conversations in Boston between Dr. Channing, George Ripley (Parker's best friend), Bronson Alcott, Frederick Hedge, Wendell Phillips, and others no less hopefully minded. The agitations and the talk, combined with Parker's almost unbelievable capacity for reading, suddenly appeared to shoot the man forward—to get him out, in a single burst of energy, from the old fuzzy round of Unitarian speculation. By November, 1838—only a couple of years after leaving Cambridge—Parker was writing to a friend with much authority that the Christian miracles "relate to the history, but not to the doctrines of Christianity. Prove to me that they never took place, that there never was a Paul or a John or a Jesus, and I will still prove that Christianity is true; it was true before Christ; for it is older than the creation." He had come almost at one bound to the position he would never thereafter abandon.

For Parker's identifying position—the core and, indeed, very nearly the whole of his hopeful theology—was the absolute separation of history and religion. He was not merely willing, more and more publicly, to discredit the historical truth of the miracles reported by the Evangelists; the question of miracles was only the occasion for those debates which, largely because of Parker, shook the foundations of contemporary Unitarianism. Parker wanted to remove religion from the context of history altogether, and to imbed religion in the very structure of the human soul. It was history, according to Parker, which made difficult or impossible the presence of the real. The more historical information Parker gathered, the more he wanted to extract from the historical and transient what he began to call "the permanent elements of religion." It was a curious proceeding and highly American: to canvass the past exhaustively, in order to show that the individual soul in the New World had no organic relation to any scrap of it. Anticipating the historians and outdistancing them at their own game, Parker hastened to insist that the historical evidences of Christianity were dubious and finally irrelevant; Christianity was something other than a history; and he ended in the corollary conviction, which he accepted without ever quite confronting it, that neither religious experience nor religious effort required any help whatever from an organized tradition. This was his root principle, his position, and his doctrine: that religion was not something to be exercised in the center of a continuing historical life, but was an affair of the private soul, a matter of instantaneous, individual intuition—or "inspiration": one of Parker's favorite words.

In coming to his position, Parker drew, of course, upon the currently popular aids from abroad: for example, from the German idealism of Kant and Fichte which had so undermined the empirical psychology of John Locke. Edwards had used Locke to shore up a staggering Calvinism in the eighteenth century; Parker used Kant to dispose of all religious "outwardness," Calvinist or otherwise. His disciple and biographer, O. B. Frothingham, described the case well: "The authority of all outward instrumentalities, church, bible, creed, was tacitly repudiated before a single scripture was doubted, or a single miracle denied. The vessels of clergymen, rite, ceremony, church, were not scuttled until the spiritual freight they carried had been transferred to the spiritual nature, there to be secure from hidden reef or sudden tempest." Parker drew also upon the arguments by the school of David Strauss of Berlin (1808–74) that Jesus was not only a mere mortal and no God, but in all probability had never existed at all.

But those foreign aids were, for Parker as for most of his colleagues, precisely aids and no more: midwives of their ideas, not the source of them. The new theology, like the new ethical attitude, was the product of native pressures: the pressures of a joyous radicalism in all fields of thought and expression. Parker subjected the substance of religion to the radical critique: to see what remained of it, when the complex of historic legacies had been washed away—as others were purifying and reinspecting the moral personality. Parker found the condition of religion, before the act of purification, to be this:

> As old religions became superannuated and died out, they left to the rising faith [i.e., early Christianity] as to a residuary legatee, their forms, and their doctrines; or rather as the giant in the fable left his poisoned garment

to work the overthrow of his conqueror. . . . The stream of Christianity has caught a stain from every soil it has filtered through; so that now it is not the pure water from the well of life which is offered to our lips, but streams troubled and polluted by men with mire and dirt.

Those sentences—from Parker's stormily controversial sermon of May 19, 1841, "The Transient and the Permanent in Christianity"—are almost a pastiche of the favorite hopeful attitudes and imagery. The hopeful celebration elsewhere of "the clear conscience unsullied by the past" was echoed in Parker's clear new religion, unstained by history. For the mission of this hope-affirming Yankee Luther was to call his countrymen back to the source of the now sullied religious stream— filtering out of it those elements which over the centuries had muddied its depths: institutions, creeds, rites, customs, relationships, and forms of expression.

What was left? Parker planted himself, as Frothingham remarked, "on the ground that man has a spiritual nature endowed with *original* capacity to apprehend *primary* religious truth directly, without the mediation of sacrament, creed or Bible." Just what those primary or permanent truths consisted in, it is not easy to say; the Adamic vision was always more readily described by its opposition. Parker himself seemed to believe that language was the first spoliation of the primal simplicity, and it was better adapted to repudiate than to define. The permanent was, in any case, not a creed or even a proposition; it was perhaps an irreducible *awareness* of a being transcending the human being—related to it in an encompassing love, and so close and intimate with the individual soul that it was the soul's first, best object of awareness.

In the fall of 1841—only a few months after the sermon on "The Transient and the Permanent," and in the wake of the vicious attacks that sermon had aroused—Parker gave a series of lectures in Boston on "Matters Pertaining to Religion." The lectures were published in book form the following year. Their aim was to sink the whole of historical Christianity, Catholic and Protestant alike, beneath the weight of Parker's scholarly cross-examination. He assumed a position critical at once of "the Catholic party" and "the Protestant party." The whole parcel of traditional beliefs and practices, whether of the tough-spirited Calvinist or the genial Unitarian or the comprehensive Catholic variety, was undone, scrutinized, and tossed aside. Notions of sin and redemption were repudiated, and the institutional machinery erected to combat the sin and hustle the redemption was declared outdated and useless. The Trinity was exposed as an invention; Jesus identified as an attractive, if somewhat unstable, young man who had lived and died a good many years before; the Holy Ghost was never mentioned; and the Bible interpreted as a suggestive, but often contradictory and so hardly authoritative, collection of poems, fables, and gossip. Much more than half of the discourse was critical. What then remained—the tiny primitive nugget of belief, the stripped theology of what Parker called "the party that are neither Catholics nor Protestants"—came simply to this:

This party has an idea wider and deeper than that of Catholic or Protestant, namely that God still inspires men as much as ever; that he is imminent in spirit as in space. . . . This [doctrine] relies on no church, tradition, or scripture. . . . It relies on the divine presence in the nature of man. . . . It believes God is near the soul as matter to the sense. . . . It calls God father and mother, not king; Jesus, brother, not redeemer; heaven home, religion nature. It loves and trusts but does not fear.

Even there, in his desire to cut through to primary truth, Parker leans heavily on the negative.

Nineteen years more of reading, writing, and preaching would not bring Theodore Parker to elaborate very much upon that minimalist opinion. His career during those years was punctuated rather by his vigorous and admirable participation in the antislavery movement and in editorial and literary activities militantly devoted to the social condition of men and women in a genuine democracy. His slender theology could scarcely supply him with any answers to those great questions; but it could give him a radiant confidence in God and in man— and that confidence spurred him to intense social reformist efforts, erupting sometimes in a towering rage at all those who did not share it. Parker's religious doctrine was so small as to be nearly invisible; what was large about it was its boldness. For it was indeed bold, bold in the way of the entire party of Hope—breaking through the collected arguments of centuries to confront even God in fresh and personal terms. Where Emerson had saluted "the plain old Adam, the simple genuine self against the whole world," Parker saluted that Adam standing self-reliantly in the presence of transcendent being.

Parker continued to think of himself as a Unitarian, busy recalling the Unitarians to their true belief. "The Unitarians," he wrote, "have no recognised and public creed. It used to be their glory." It was, he urged, to be their glory once more; but his Unitarian colleagues did not thank him for saying so. After his sermon in May, 1841, he was abused as a scorner, a blasphemer, a hypocrite, a second-rater, and a sentimentalist; he was invited (but refused) to withdraw at once from the

Unitarian association. After his lectures the following autumn, the younger ministers took to dodging around corners when they saw him approaching; with every good reason, they trembled in the fear of guilt by association. And yet the Unitarians tended, if anything, to underestimate Parker's achievement, not to exaggerate it.

Ever since St. Paul, the spokesmen for Christianity had been preaching "the new man"—the individual who was born anew after the death of "the natural man," the individual who died into life. Christianity was a centuries-long admission that the majority of mankind was unable or unwilling to do so. Theodore Parker was the one to come up with the breath-taking suggestion that every individual was in spirit and in fact a perfectly new man, as new as Adam, each the first man, each the new unfallen. And this, Parker proposed, *without* the need for holy dying.

The challenge to the individual soul was nothing more than the exercise of that life already present to it. The perfect was instantly *present* to the soul, so long as that soul was itself unsullied by the past, or as soon as the "mire and dirt" of customs, practices, and doctrines—introduced by men across the ages—had been mentally washed away from the pure, primal revelation. The perfect lay ready to be known and enjoyed by any spirit capable of divesting itself of the muddying past.

III

Among those attending Parker's lectures in the fall of 1841 was a Unitarian minister named Orestes Brownson (1803–76). "At that time," Brownson recalled later, "[Parker] was one of my highly prized personal friends, a young man full of life and promise. There was no young man of my acquaintance for whom I had a higher regard, or from whom I hoped so much." Brownson came round to the lectures expecting to receive a further clarification of his own religious belief—with which, he assumed, Parker was largely in accord. The more he listened, the more uneasy he became.

> The lectures . . . contained nothing except a learned and eloquent statement of the doctrine which I had long defended, and which I have called the Religion of humanity. But, strange as it may seem, the moment I heard that doctrine from his lips, I felt a repugnance to it, and saw, or thought I saw, at a glance, that it was unphilosophical and anti-religious.

Parker's lectures, Brownson was to think, were what "forced my mind to take the direction it did": which was the direction of the traditional understanding of tradition; the direction, finally and after a great deal more meditation, of the church of Rome. For Theodore Parker himself, those lectures were a point of no return; for Orestes Brownson, they were a dramatic turning point.

Parker's approach to God depended upon "intuition" or "inspiration." The doctrine he unwittingly prodded Brownson into formulating turned rather on the notion of "communion." The difference between the two men is suggested by the difference between those key terms. They symbolized an ultimate difference in theologies, nourished by a profound difference in temperaments. Intuition and communion, two ways of touching the nature above nature, followed from two different judgments about the structure and the strength of the individual; and they involved two different appraisals of the value of the past. The conclusion Brownson reached respecting Protestantism, after many months of speculation in the light of Parker's discourses, was this: "The error of Protestantism was in that it broke with tradition, broke with the past, and cut itself off from the body of Christ, and therefore from the channel through which the Christian life is communicated."

It was a packed statement, linking together in one swift series of clauses the relation of man to the historic past and the relation of man to transcendent being. It was packed the more tightly because there went into it the long interior dialogue and the public and private experiences which had constituted Brownson's life to that moment (1844).

Brownson was a wanderer, in fact and in temperament. He prowled restlessly, during the first four decades of his life, from state to state (Vermont, New Hampshire, Michigan, New York, Massachusetts); from Protestant sect to Protestant sect (Presbyterian, Universalist, independent or "Humanitarian," Unitarian); from enterprise to enterprise (preaching, editing, social reform, literary criticism, political comment, theology). His Catholic biographers see him, not surprisingly, moving in a steady line to his true destination;[3] but, as Brownson himself might have said, a kind of nonhistorical evidence is needed for such an analysis. It might well be argued that he entered the Roman church (as he did on October 20, 1844) just because that church, for a New Englander of the age, was a trifle alien, a shade exotic. In a time when heresy was becoming the convention, there was a measure of startling originality in embracing the oldest, firmest orthodoxy of all. When Brownson's friend and colleague, Isaac Hecker, was contemplating conversion to Catholicism, it was Hecker whom his neighbors in Concord regarded as eccentric—definitely more so than Thoreau, in

3. E.g., Theodore Maynard, *Orestes Brownson* (New York, 1943), a learned, knowing, and ingratiating work.

whose house Hecker was then living; or Margaret Fuller; or Bronson Alcott.[4] Brownson's personal urgings were different from those of the mystical, poetic Isaac Hecker; they divided between them the legalistic and prophetic traditions of Catholicism; but Brownson seemed not much less peculiar to his many observers.

Like other wanderers and eccentrics, Brownson moved in and out of the center of many things. He had the universal curiosity of Parker and a comparable itch to make pronouncements about everything. The *Boston Quarterly Review*, which he founded and which he edited for four years (1838–42), was contributed to principally by himself;[5] and its successor, founded in 1844, was more fittingly called *Brownson's Quarterly Review*. He held forth with almost equal zest on politics, economics, literature, history, and theology, and any combination of these. And if his remarks upon immediate trends and newly published books (Cooper's *American Democrat*, for example, or Emerson's poems) were not always alight with perceptiveness, Brownson did have a sharp eye for the significant; in retrospect, it must be said that he talked about the important trends and the right books. Emerson said about him, somewhat impatiently, that Brownson never listened —either in conversation, or, what was more important according to Emerson, in solitude. We do indeed get the impression of a highly charged bear of a man, talking endlessly and often banging on the table, seizing in a rush of language upon any new idea or program which happened to arise, shifting his attention without pause to the subject arising next. His prose, which now fills twenty volumes, could have used a most merciless pruning; but Brownson was the kind of writer who never had the time to be brief. And if he failed to attend closely enough to Emerson's words or those of other interlocutors, it was partly because he had a very lively conversation on his hands already—a conversation with himself. Brownson wrestled and wrangled

4. Rev. Walter Elliott, *The Life of Father Hecker* (New York, 1898), pp. 88–89. Emerson, Hecker recalled many years later, "invited me to tea with him, and he kept leading up to the subject and I leading away from it. The next day he asked me to drive over with him to the Shakers, some fifteen miles. We stayed over night, and all the way there and back he was fishing for my reasons, with the plain purpose of dissuading me. Then Alcott and he arranged matters so that they cornered me in a sort of interview, and Alcott frankly developed the subject. I finally said, 'Mr. Alcott, I deny your inquisitorial right in this matter,' and so they let it drop. One day, however, I was walking along the road, and Emerson joined me. Presently, he said 'Mr. Hecker, I suppose it was the art, the architecture and so on in the Catholic Church which led you to her?' 'No,' said I; 'but it was what caused all that.' " Isaac Hecker (1819–88) attended both Brook Farm and Alcott's Fruitlands, in the course of his own wanderings.

5. Among other occasional contributers, there were George Bancroft, Margaret Fuller, George Ripley, Elizabeth Peabody, and Albert Brisbane.

with himself all his life; the give-and-take became perhaps more subdued and orderly after his conversion; but it erupted from time to
time even then, and on into his troubled but vigorous old age.

Brownson had a tireless affection for logical argument—an affection
at once outlandish and irritating for those temperaments (and they
were in the great intellectual majority) dedicated to intuition and
dreams, feeling and instinct. With Orestes Brownson, the logic excursion was a sort of austere brooding, a remorseless self-inquiry. Whether
his trust in logic hastened his decision about Rome, one cannot surely
determine. His brand of logic was of the sort indulged in far more by
the Romanists than by the romantics. And yet logic may not, perhaps, be the quickest path to the traditional theology for anyone who
begins quite outside that theology. The fact, anyhow, is this: that
Brownson came to his opinions about "communion"—and hence to
his opinion about the value of tradition, and hence, belatedly, to the
church of Rome, not out of emotional ecstasy, or because of a sentimental attachment to the art and the architecture, but because the
traditional doctrines were the ones that made the most sense to him.

Brownson pushed and reasoned his way toward his doctrine of communion during the year or so after attending Parker's lectures. He
offered a first brisk formulation of it in a letter to Dr. Channing, the
most eminent member of the Unitarian group to which Brownson
then belonged, and a man whom Brownson addressed as "my spiritual
father." By communion, Brownson wrote (in June, 1842), he meant
"the doctrine that man lives by communion with man, and through
the life derived from Jesus, with God." Two considerations which had
absorbed Brownson most for some years—the status of the past and
the question of community—began to be fused with that formulation.
And the fusion began under the force of Brownson's conviction that
only transcendent being—taken as interpenetrating natural being—
explained the living value of the past and the necessity of human
community.

As editor, critic, and commentator in his *Boston Quarterly Review*,
Brownson had been an alert trend-spotter and an able cataloguer of
the intellectual forces of the day. His sympathies were with the party
of Hope—or "movement party," as he liked to call it—but he was
never stampeded by that party's enthusiasm into abolishing all connection with the past. "We would think with the Radical, but often
act with the Conservative," he remarked, in a political address delivered in September, 1837. "If progress be a law of our race, as it unquestionably is, we must accept it in everything," he urged on another

occasion; but he normally included the admonition that "progress is always slow and slow let it be . . . we wish no haste, no violence in pulling down old institutions or in building up new ones." He was dourly amused by the thoughtful conservatism of Cooper's *American Democrat*, "a double batter," he wrote, "charged alike against those who believe too much in the past, and those who believe too much in the future." His scholastic temperament led him to make further distinctions between the contemporary parties, in terms of their attitudes to the past. Not only were there writers "in the twilight state . . . following with longing admiration the descending glory of the past," for whom "the present is weary and worn," and their opposites, those writers "in morning wakefulness" for whom "the present is bright . . . with hope." There were also certain idealists "in the midnight season of thought, lone and abstracted—watching the truths of eternity as they smile through far space on a darkened world"; and a fourth class, "in the noonday and sunny cheerfulness," full of contentment with "God's providence in the present time."

Brownson's sense of the profound value of continuity, nourished through several years of eclectic shifting ("I am myself an eclectic," he rashly announced in 1840), found its first serious expression in a long article of October, 1842, when he was part way toward Rome:

> The human race is subjected to a law of continuity which presides over all its development and growth. . . . The present was elaborated in, and evolved from the past. The future must be . . . the elaboration and evolution of the present. . . . According to this law, all radicalism, that is to say all destruction *of what was fundamental in that which has preceded*, or the creation of an order of life, religious, social or philosophical, that is new in its fundamental elements, is necessarily condemned.

Brownson wanted the present to be continuous with *what was fundamental* in the life of the past. By 1842, he was on the verge of identifying the foundation to his own satisfaction; but meanwhile he was also thinking about the nature of the human community, and about the purpose and value of social experience. He teased the Fourierites for their "assumption of that greatest of all absurdities, the perfection of nature." He discarded at once the first hopeful principle; but he approved of the Fourierite emphasis on social organization, and condemned the self-reliant and the sponsors of self-culture for their apparent belief that "mankind" was "a mere aggregate of individuals." Brownson was sure that mankind was—to adopt a modern slang phrase—really something; but what made it something, he could not as yet perceive.

As he tells the story in his personal memoir of 1857, *The Convert*, Brownson escaped from the closed circle of his own speculations by arriving at an insight about the theory of knowledge. With the help of Leroux, a French epistemologist, Brownson came to the conclusion that *thought* resulted from the co-operation of subject and object, of perceiver and thing perceived, and that it was not the exclusive product of either. This proposition, a former commonplace, ran counter to the two chief theories of the day: that of the empiricists, that the subject was passive before the impingement of the object upon it, and that of the idealists, that the object was formally the creation of the subject. Ethical, political, and even theological implications began to swarm in Brownson's mind as he further contemplated the notion of co-operation, working-together—or, as he took to calling it, communion. It seemed to him now that all individual spiritual growth depended on communion between the individual nature and the object which could enlarge and nourish it: the visible and intelligible world, the society of men, the continuing course of history.

If Brownson had been a novelist, he might at this moment have composed fiction not unlike the fiction of Hawthorne; for he had come as far as humanism could carry him, and he was equipped now to visualize experience dramatically as the interplay of personality with the complex historical social world. As it was, he argued his way onward toward identifying the ultimate object with which the human subject should commune; and his aspirations were momentarily appeased by the notion of humanity itself. Then he listened to Theodore Parker, and realized with disconcerting swiftness that both Parker and he had fallen into the contemporary trap of attributing religious or extra-human power to what was, after all, purely human. He saw that humanity could not, of itself, possess that larger-than-human dimension with which the human spirit needed to unite. And having seen so much, he saw also that humanity was, nonetheless, the channel to that larger-than-human dimension by means of the one human who was at the same time divine: indeed, by means of the organic historical process set abruptly in motion at the instant God entered into human history as Christ.

Pondering these fresh discoveries, Brownson put them at last in an order which, for him, made everything clear. The individual needed redemption but could be redeemed only by intense and enduring communion with God; but communion with God was possible for man only by means of the man-God, Christ. Communion with Christ was possible only by communion with continuing history, or "tradition"—

that is, historical Christianity ("forget historical Christianity," Emerson had long been warning). Brownson wrote in *The Convert:*

> We who live at this day do not communicate directly with Christ our Lord. We do it, and can do it, only through the medium of others. The Apostles and Disciples lived in personal intercourse with him, and therefore communed with him directly and immediately as their object. By this direct and immediate communion, his Divine-human life became infused into their life. Others, by communion with them, partake of the same life. The succeeding generation participated in it by communing with its predecessor. Thus by communion the life may be infused through all men living contemporaneously, and transmitted to the latest posterity.

In suggesting that tradition was an obstacle to the soul's relation with God and in breaking with tradition, Protestantism was unconsciously implying that the soul stood in no need of divine grace and was implicitly cutting itself off from the possibility of grace. For tradition was the very instrument of grace.

The error of Protestantism was in that it broke with tradition, broke with the past, and cut itself off from the body of Christ, and therefore from the channel through which the Christian life is communicated. Protestantism was a schism, a separation from the source and current of the Divine-human life which redeems and saves the world.

Only through the continuing vitality and the continuing invocation of traditional Christian customs and practices and creeds and ceremonies—all those things Theodore Parker had ceremoniously swept away—could God be made really present to the human soul. Quite contrary to Parker's belief that the past was an impediment to the soul's vision of perfection, Brownson now laid it down that the past and the perfect were inseparable, and that the perfect entered the soul only as the living tradition flowed steadily into the immediate present.

IV

A very comparable analysis of the character of genuine religious tradition had been made a few years earlier (1852), and in incomparably handsomer language, not by a theologian, but by a critic and poet —James Russell Lowell. Lowell's account of the mystery of the Real Presence as the very basis of tradition is doubly suggestive. It reminds us how close the discussion of these matters was in quite different fields of expression; and it shows that the subject of tradition was more suited, in the age of hope, to the language of the imagination than to the relatively crude and colorless terminology of an Orestes Brownson.

Lowell had gone to Europe in 1851. It was a symbolic gesture, a "signing-off" from the party of Hope, of which he had been an enthu-siastic member. The same young man who had remarked in 1845, and with all assurance, that "we deem that but a bastard greatness which must take root in the past, fearing to trust its seed to the dim future," was now proposing that "eyes were given us to look about us sometimes and not to be always looking forward"; he would shortly be unwilling to give up anything "that had roots to it, though it might suck up its food from graveyards." Lowell is a relatively uncommon instance of a move from hope to memory, reversing the more usual spiritual jour-ney of his age. By 1851, he had just begun his pilgrimage back; and, with traces of his former hopefulness still clinging to him, he was able to scrutinize what he found in Europe with an acute and critical as well as an appreciative eye.

He was impressed, first of all, by the extremes "of permanence, un-changeableness, repose," as against the New World, where everything seemed to be "shifting like quicksand." He wondered for a while whether some synthesis might not be possible, between the enduring and the changing. Reflecting thus on the double value of stability and vitality, Lowell came, at Rome, to one of the generation's most elo-quent statements of the character and behavior of a living tradition. A decade earlier, he had been impishly scornful of the nostalgic. "The educated taste" he had detected in the Boston galleries appeared to him merely a sterile failure to respond to anything but the uncom-promisingly classic. No new work was acceptable to the man of taste, Lowell thought, unless it reproduced to a detail "the charm of an old one." "Put the right foot of Apollo forward instead of the left and call it Philip of Pokanoket, and he is in ecstasies over a work at once so truly national and so classic." But now in Italy, as he watched the quite different way in which memory illuminated the present, he re-alized that tradition in America was as inflexible as a death-grip, an enslavement of the present by lifeless, isolated fragments of the past, and he understood that an authentic tradition was a comprehensive and life-giving affair.

Drawing his controlling figure from the ritual of the Mass and the doctrine of the Real Presence, Lowell explained tradition to his American readers thus:

Supposing that a man in pouring down a glass of claret could drink the South of France, that he could so disintegrate the wine by the force of imagina-tion as to taste in it all the clustered beauty and bloom of the grape, all the dance and song and sunburnt jollity of the vintage. Or suppose that in eating bread he could transubstantiate it with the tender blade of spring, the gleam-fitted corn-ocean of summer, the royal autumn with its golden beard, and the merry funerals of harvest. That is what the great poets do for us, we cannot tell how, with their fatally-chosen words, crowding the happy veins of language again with all the life and meaning and music that had been dribbling away from them since Adam. And this is what the Roman Church does for religion, feeding the soul not with the essential religious sentiment, not with a drop or two of the tincture of worship, but making us feel one by one all those original elements of which worship is composed; not bringing the end to us, but making us pass over and feel beneath our feet all the golden rounds of the ladder by which the climbing generations have reached that end; not handing us drily a dead and extinguished Q.E.D., but letting it rather declare itself by the glory with which it interfuses the incense-clouds of wonder and aspiration and beauty in which it is veiled. The secret of her power is typified in the mystery of the Real Presence.

The passage bogs down a little in the neoclassic conventions of style that Lowell was beginning to affect. But his own "force of imagination" had driven him to the heart of the experience and provided the language in which to expose it. The cumulative effect of the paragraph is to reveal religious experience (seen from the human side of it) as a gathering-together of those age-old energies of worship and belief which had gone into the celebration of the Eucharist for nineteen centuries. Lowell builds the religious experience out of the commonplace human experience of eating bread and drinking wine, and the more vivid experience of appreciative reading. In all cases, what he saw taking place was a vast individual enrichment through conscious participation in the full flow of history: the history of human actions, of language, of religious worship, as all that history is *recovered* in the individual imagination. That, Lowell suggests, is the meaning of tradition; to be related to a living tradition is to be touched and animated by those continuing energies.

V

The relationship dramatized by Lowell was exactly the relationship Brownson was seeking to formulate in theological terms. He might not have understood Lowell's later observation that the Roman church was the only poet among the churches, for he was temperamentally unequipped to follow Lowell's analogy between poetry and religion. Lowell's hint that the very words of an American poem tended to be isolated and lonely would have escaped him. But Brownson knew that individual men in America were isolated and lonely, and he felt that the hopeful theology of his friend Parker served only to make them more so. Parker, he wrote, would have "turn[ed] men in utter nakedness out into this bleak and wintry world, to rely on themselves alone and to support themselves as best they might from their own resources." Unlike Parker, Brownson did believe that the world was bleak and wintry and that a corrupted human nature had made it that way. The cure required a precise reversal of the Protestant achievement. It required the kind of enrichment Lowell described, by putting one's self in touch with the Real Presence through a willing involvement with the entire life of mankind, past and present.

What the cure required, in fact, was communion: a communion with human history which made possible the communion with God celebrated in the Eucharist. This was Brownson's major discovery; but it may be doubted that he would have come to it without the challenge of Parker's erect confidence in the individual man of the present hour. A recollection of that confidence may have been what saved Brownson, after his conversion, from lapsing into that dour and quasi-Calvinistic hopelessness so characteristic of Catholicism in America. Brownson absorbed into his religious vision something of the heretical jauntiness which his vision sought to moderate. Parker, it should be added, may have known as much; for having lent Brownson a part of his hopefulness, he sent after him his blessing. Observing the progress of his old friend, Parker remarked in 1843: "[Brownson] seems tending towards the Catholic Church. God bless him wherever he is! He has a hard head." It was the final word on the conversation from which both men had profited so greatly.

In arriving at his doctrine of communion, Brownson not only gravitated toward the Catholic church. He simultaneously became a member of what I have called the party of Irony. For communion was the concern which, more than any other, linked together the varied members of the third party in the dialogue of the day. The idea found expression in ways as different as Hawthorne's remark about opening "an intercourse with the world" and Dr. Holmes's image of ghostly assistance from a remote ancestor. But in all its forms, the preoccupation of the ironic mentality was communion with the common experience and common reality of the human race. Hopefulness and nostalgia had conspired to cut the American spirit off from those crucial resources, with pathetic and potentially tragic consequences. For the hopeful, the situation was symbolized in Whitman's wistful envy of the live oak which could thrive in Louisiana, though it stood "alone there without a friend near"; the symbol for the nostalgic was the impulse of Clifford Pyncheon, in *The House of the Seven Gables*, to throw himself from the window of the old mansion into the midst of the crowd below. Communion, in every instance, was an answer to both symbols by restoring the individual to a nourishing relation to community.

Each member of the third party had his own notion about the location and the character of the community he belonged to. For the elder Henry James, it was society taken as the embodiment of a "divine-natural" humanity. Horace Bushnell looked to those interlocking generations whose orderly march had created the pattern of educative forces that Bushnell identified as "tradition." For Hawthorne, there were the moral influences and artistic prototypes pressing down through the past, sources at once of repression and freedom. Melville came to terms with the world only after he had allied his genius to the disparate mythologies of Western literature. Experience, for Henry James the younger, was nothing else than the awareness of an achieved communion: man's apprehension of himself (as James put it) in his social being. Francis Parkman drew both strength and consolation from the historic experience of a more masculine age. And man's very chances for redemption rested, according to Orestes Brownson, upon his ability to commune with God by participating in the traditional life initiated by Christ and carried forward through time by the Christian church.

And yet each of these men sympathized with that sense of things which made communion difficult and even, as it seemed, altogether unnecessary. With the possible but not certain exception of Parkman, they all partook a little of the hopeful belief in the newness, the separateness, the self-sufficiency, the lack of moral involvement, and hence the innocence of the representative figure in the New World. They responded to the dangerous appeal of that figure. The party of Irony consisted of those men who wanted both to undermine and to bolster the image of the American as a new Adam. They urged their generation toward a communion—a renewal of contact—with moral reality and the traditional past, as the way to extend the range of contemporary life and letters. But they did so in the name of those same human and artistic possibilities that the hopeful were proclaiming; their mode of communion, therefore, was inevitably a kind of creative tussle with its object. For the perspective of their irony was not limited to the present; it extended to the past as well, and it threw its ambiguous light upon the sense of evil as upon the feeling of innocence. Their irony, in short, was in the great tradition: inclusive and charitable, never restrictive. Their aim was to enlarge. The shared purpose of the party of Irony was not to destroy the hopes of the hopeful, but to perfect them.

Epilogue
The Contemporary Situation

ADAM AS HERO IN THE AGE OF CONTAINMENT

A MERICAN thought and expression would not, in recent years, seem very hospitable to the moral and artistic sensibility of the nineteenth-century party of Hope. The hopeful attitudes are phenomena, indeed, about which we are today somewhat embarrassed: the culture's youthful indiscretions and extravagances. We have had to get beyond such simple-minded adolescent confidence, we suppose; we may even have got beyond the agonizing disillusion that unexamined confidence begets; and we sometimes congratulate ourselves austerely for having settled, like adults or Europeans, upon a course of prolonged but tolerable hopelessness. We call that state of hopelessness the human condition: something we study to realize in our literature and reflect in our behavior. The picture of man sketched by the dominant contemporary philosophies and ologies shows us a figure struggling to stand upright amid the most violent cross-currents: the American as Adam has been replaced by the American as Laocoön; the Emersonian figure—"the plain old Adam, the simple genuine self"— has been frowned quite out of existence.

The contemporary picture is not a dishonest one. It contains many remarkable and even irreversible psychological, sociological, and political insights. It seems to be the picture most clearly warranted by public and private experience in our time. But it remains curiously frozen in outline; it is anything but dialectical and contains within it no opposite possibilities on which to feed and fatten. In it irony has withered into mere mordant skepticism. Irony is fertile and alive; the chilling skepticism of the mid-twentieth century represents one of the modes of death. The new hopelessness is, paradoxically, as simple-minded as innocence; and it is opposed only by that parody of hope which consists in an appeal for "positive thinking"—a wilful return to innocence based upon a wilful ignorance, momentarily popular in the market place of culture but with no hold at all upon the known truth of experience.

The doctrine of positive thinking is a posture—that is, a substitute for morality. It need not be dignified by further consideration except to notice that its fraudulence, combined with its economic successes, has led to a still more extreme posturing of skepticism. That skepticism takes the form of a hostility to human nature as self-wounded and self-wounding beyond repair; something which began as a valuable corrective to the claims of innocence in America and which has declined into a cult of original sin. It expresses itself, too, in a distrust of experience. Ours is an age of containment; we huddle together and shore up defenses; both our literature and our public conduct suggest that exposure to experience is certain to be fatal. The hopeful and the ironic of a century ago were willing to risk it: Emerson because he could imagine nothing harmful in the path of the self-reliant; Hawthorne because of his passionate conviction that the fatalities of experience were indispensable for moral maturity. Instead of looking forward to new possibilities, we direct our tired attention to the burden of history, observing repeatedly that it is later than you think.

I do not suggest that, by pretending to a hopefulness we cannot possibly feel, we may add a number of cubits to our cultural stature. But I do suggest that recalling the moral and artistic adventurousness of a century ago may help release us a little from our current rigidity. There is, anyhow, some evidence to support such a hypothesis in recent American fiction. Most serious efforts at fiction in America have suffered, during the past few decades, from the two cardinal defects of the new hopelessness: from an antagonism to nature—for the very language of literature evaporates when it loses faith in and hence touch with natural objects; and from a distrust of experience—for fiction, as Lionel Trilling has said, imitates the will in action, and of late the will has become oddly disempowered and reluctant to initiate action. Yet there is, undoubtedly, an occasional vitality in American fiction. And wherever we find it, we encounter again traces of the hopeful or Adamic tradition, seen, as fiction must always see it, in a

Epilogue

comic or ironic perspective by novelists who have escaped what I have called the arrested development of innocence and the premature old age of an absorption with sin.

Scott Fitzgerald's *The Great Gatsby*, for example, demonstrates once more the dramatic appeal of the hero as a self-created innocent. Fitzgerald was right, despite Edith Wharton's stricture, not to give us any more of Gatsby's "background"; Mrs. Wharton argued that the tragedy was diminished because we know too little about Gatsby's origins, but the fact is that, as Jay Gatsby, Fitzgerald's hero had no background. He had repudiated his former self, with its ancestry, as represented by his former name of James Gatz. And in his new role he had (to use the phrase of Horace Bushnell) "just begun to be." That is what is acknowledged by the novel's narrator, Nick Carraway, when he says about Gatsby that he "sprang from his Platonic conception of himself." The legend of the second chance is thus poignantly re-enacted by Gatsby, as he carries forward his incorruptible dream beneath the surface of his guessed-at corruption. In *The Great Gatsby*, the Adamic anecdote retains a singular purity of outline; the young hero follows the traditional career from bright expectancy to the destruction which, in American literature, has been its perennial reward. But the image of the New World as a second, last chance for humanity—an image with which, in retrospect, the murdered Gatsby is associated—is subtly exploited by Fitzgerald as a mirror to reveal the true ugliness of society's hard malice and shallow sophistication.

That image is what remains inviolable in *The Great Gatsby*. In William Faulkner's *The Bear*, it is precisely what is transcended in an anger and a pity that give that *novella* its peculiar intensity. Faulkner's hero, Isaac McCaslin, knows about that hopeful legend and rehearses it for his cousin, Cass Edmonds, on his own twenty-first birthday. He knows, too, that the legend is false and that the New World began with its portion of historic, sinful inheritance. The knowledge protects him from the danger of innocence; but the memory of a lost hope sends him on a lifelong errand of private atonement for everything that had betrayed it. The notion of original innocence tantalizes Isaac's sensibility not less than the accepted fact of original sin. In *The Bear*, perhaps Faulkner's finest story, the hero's achievement of conscience and the author's achievement of drama both result from the application of imagination to old and familiar materials. Isaac is a Natty Bumppo re-created by the dark energies of a Hawthorne.

And in most of what I take to be the truest and most fully engaged American fiction after the second war, the newborn or self-breeding or orphaned hero is plunged again and again, for his own good and for ours, into the spurious, disruptive rituals of the actual world. We may mention especially *Invisible Man*, by Ralph Ellison; J. D. Salinger's *The Catcher in the Rye*; and *The Adventures of Augie March*, by Saul Bellow—novels in each of which the hero is willing, with marvelously inadequate equipment, to take on as much of the world as is available to him, without ever fully submitting to any of the world's determining categories. Ellison's hero is a nameless Negro, Salinger's an unstable adolescent, Bellow's an obliquely oriented Chicago Jew. But they share in their common aloneness that odd aura of moral priority over the waiting world which was a central ingredient in the Adamic fictional tradition. Each of them struggles tirelessly, sometimes unwittingly and often absurdly, to realize the full potentialities of the classic figure each represents: the Emersonian figure, "the simple genuine self against the whole world." Behind them stand their Adamic predecessors: Arthur Mervyn, Donatello, Redburn, Pierre, Billy Budd, Daisy Miller, Isabel Archer, Huck Finn, and all the others. Ellison is explicitly indebted to the circus vision of Melville and reproduces much of the Gothic scramblings of Charles Brockden Brown; Bellow is plainly recalling the slippery heroism of *Huckleberry Finn*. But these novelists are to be credited with an additional feat: that of engendering from within their work the hopeful and vulnerable sense of life that makes experience and so makes narrative action possible. It is their aim to test that sense of life by irony and drama; but they must create it from within, since they can scarcely find it any longer in the historic world about them.

These novelists do not, of course, write simply in order to keep alive some particular American tradition. Nor is it the tradition they are working in which accounts for their artistic accomplishment. But, taken together and along with a few others, the novels I mention do suggest the indestructible vitality of the Adamic vision of life—and what that vision can contribute to the alchemical process of the narrative art. They suggest that the vision and the process which transforms it can, after all, continue to present us with the means of grasping the special complexities, the buoyant assurance, and the encircling doubt of the still unfolding American scene.

Index

Index

Pascal, Blaise, 69
Peabody, Elizabeth, 185 n.
Phillips, Wendell, 179
Plato, 1, 24, 42, 67
Poe, Edgar Allan, 85, 102, 115
Praz, Mario, 94, 94 n.
Prescott, William, 8, 85, 160–61

Rabelais, François, 178
Racine, Jean, 78
Radcliffe, Mrs. Ann, 98
Ripley, George, 179, 185 n.
Ronsard, Pierre, 78

St. Augustine, 65, 163, 164
St. Bonaventura, 174
St. Paul, 22, 23, 31, 65, 183
St. Thomas Aquinas, 144
Salinger, J. D., 198
Savonarola, 178
Sealts, Merton M., Jr., 140 n.
Shakespeare, William, 48, 49, 55, 68, 78, 143
Simms, William Gilmore, 86 n.
Skidmore, Thomas, 16–17
Smith, Elihu Hubbard, 96
Smith, Henry Nash, 100 n., 110
Spirit of the Age, The, 45
Stendhal, 78
Strauss, David, 71, 180
Stuart, Moses, 29, 30
Swedenborg, Emanuel, 55, 56

Tappan, Mrs. Caroline, 54
Tate, Allen, 119, 120
Taylor, Edward, 64

Taylor, Nathaniel, 29, 30
Thompson, Lawrance, 129
Thoreau, Henry David, 7, 14, 20–27, 29, 37, 43, 45, 55, 56, 58, 82, 113, 119, 135, 136, 139, 142, 161, 168, 178, 184; *Walden*, 14–15, 20–27, 28, 50, 103
Tocqueville, Alexis de, 17–18, 43, 79, 88–89, 91, 105, 123, 159
Trilling, Lionel, 83, 84, 196
Twain, Mark, 86 n., 102

Van Doren, Mark, 113 n., 130
Virgil, 4, 5

Ware, Henry, 32
Warfel, Harry R., 95 n.
Warren, Robert Penn, 86 n.
Watson, E. L. G., 147
Webster, Noah, 5, 45, 72
Weinberg, A. K., 18 n.
Wells, Ronald V., 177 n.
Welty, Eudora, 86 n.
Wharton, Edith, 198
Whitman, Walt, 4, 7, 9, 20, 22, 28, 29, 33, 35, 41–53, 54, 57, 79, 86, 91, 161, 163, 192; *Democratic Vistas*, 24, 45, 52; *Leaves of Grass*, 4, 28, 41–53, 54, 57, 103
Wilkinson, Garth, 60
Williams, Roger, 165
Willis, N. P., 68
Winters, Yvor, 102
Wordsworth, William, 26
Wright, Fanny, 167

Yeats, William Butler, 78, 129

Zabel, Morton D., 128, 129

PHOENIX BOOKS
Literature and Language